Agile Technologies in Open Source Development

Barbara Russo
Free University of Bozen–Bolzano, Italy

Marco Scotto
Free University of Bozen–Bolzano, Italy

Alberto Sillitti
Free University of Bozen–Bolzano, Italy

Giancarlo Succi
Free University of Bozen–Bolzano, Italy

T0325216

 **INFORMATION SCIENCE REFERENCE**

Hershey · New York

Director of Editorial Content:	Kristin Klinger
Senior Managing Editor:	Jamie Snavely
Assistant Managing Editor:	Michael Brehm
Publishing Assistant:	Sean Woznicki
Typesetter:	Christopher Hrobak
Cover Design:	Lisa Tosheff
Printed at:	Yurchak Printing Inc.

Published in the United States of America by
Information Science Reference (an imprint of IGI Global)
701 E. Chocolate Avenue,
Hershey PA 17033
Tel: 717-533-8845
Fax: 717-533-8661
E-mail: cust@igi-global.com
Web site: http://www.igi-global.com/reference

Library of Congress Cataloging-in-Publication Data

Agile technologies in open source development / by Barbara Russo ... [et al.].
    p. cm.
 Includes bibliographical references and index.
 Summary: "The aim of this book is to analyze the relationship between agile
methods and open source, presenting the basic principles and practices and
providing evidence through a set of specific empirical investigations"--
Provided by publisher.
 ISBN 978-1-59904-681-5 (hardcover) -- ISBN 978-1-59904-683-9 (ebook) 1.
Agile software development. 2. Open source software. I. Russo, Barbara.
 QA76.76.D47A395 2009
 005.1--dc22

2008054195

British Cataloguing in Publication Data
A Cataloguing in Publication record for this book is available from the British Library.

Table of Contents

Section 2:
Agile Software Practices for Open Source Development

Section 3:
Empirical Evaluations

Section 4:
Industrial Adoption and Tools for Agile Development

Foreword

This book approaches two contemporary topics in the field of software engineering that have had more than a significant impact in the way the modern software is being developed. Agile movement raised the role of experience and people in the centre stage having a profound impact on large and small software organizations alike. Research and practice have shown that agile is penetrating practically in all industrial domains including the globally operating, hardware-bound software development.

Open source software development was considered to be outside of the scope of professional software development practice for long time. Companies perceived the voluntarily lead programming initiatives as something that could not be part of their strategic goal setting or daily practice. Today, a great majority of the companies utilize the open source solutions at many levels of the organization. The corporate strategies often include a plan where part of the software product has been opened for getting the benefits that are associated with the open source communities.

There are many similarities in agile and open source movements. They have taken the field by surprise and gained a significant momentum that bear long lasting impact on the practice of software development. Both were initiated by a small group of practitioners. They are based on a value structure, which is far from the traditional technology orientation of many other software engineering innovations. Finally, the two approaches value people, collaboration, and excellence as the primary drivers of software development.

This book shows you that open source and agile both deal with operational efficiency approaching it from different but mutually supporting angles. The authoring team has done a great job in highlighting the key differentiators and similarities of the two approaches. This book stands out from the others by presenting solid empirical evidence to support authors' argumentation. Practitioners will find many suggestions and guidance, and they can also see the rationale behind these ideas, which further raises the value of this book.

Pekka Abrahamsson
Professor
University of Helsinki

Pekka Abrahamsson, *PhD is a professor of computer science in University of Helsinki in Finland. He leads large European research projects on agile software development in large systems development settings. He has presented several key notes on agile software development in several international conferences He has published more than 65 refereed publications in international journals and conferences. His research interests are centered on agile software development, empirical software engineering and embedded systems development. He leads the IEEE 1648 working group on agile standardization and he was granted the Nokia Foundation Award in 2007. Dr. Abrahamsson is a member of both IEEE and ACM.*

Preface

This book presents agile methods (AMs) and open source development (OSD) from an unconventional point of view. Even if these two worlds seem very different, they present a relevant set of similarities and dependences that are identified and analyzed throughout the book.

The book is organized in four sections. The first one introduces and compares the agile and the open source (OS) movements analyzing their evolution, their main values and principles, and their organizational models. The second section focuses on some specific practices that are very relevant for both agile and OS movements (testing, code ownership, and design), and presents two success stories of integrating such worlds into a single and successful development process. The third section focuses on empirical studies. It introduces a framework for the collection and the comparison of empirical evidences and a set of empirical studies performed on agile and OS projects and teams. The chapters of this section focus on single aspects of the development process and present data collected in different kinds of experiments performed in different contexts. The last section aims at presenting topics relevant for industrial adoption, such as methodologies for selecting OS solutions to adopt in companies (agile and not) and presents a catalog of OS tools that are widely used in agile development. Since the large number of tools available may confuse practitioners and researchers interested in experimenting some of the techniques presented, the section aims at describing assessment methodologies and providing a reference set of tools from which people can start.

Part of this book has been based on the work done by the authors in the EU funded project QualiPSo and the FIRB project ArtDeco.

This book is organized as follows:

- Section 1 makes a comparison between AMs and open source software development (OSSD) investigating the founding principles.
- Section 2 focuses on a specific subset of practices through a deeper analysis based on empirical evidences.

- Section 3 presents a set of empirical evaluations performed in different settings to verify the effectiveness of specific practices.
- Section 4 investigates industrial adoption of OS and tools available for the agile development.

Section 1 includes the following chapters:

- **Chapter 1:** Historical Evolution of the Agile and Open Source Movements
  o The Win-Win Spiral Software Development Model
  o The XP Software Development Model
  o The Cathedral and the Bazaar
  o References
- **Chapter 2:** The Agile Manifesto and Open Source Software
  o Individuals Over Processes and Tools
  o Working Software Over Comprehensive Documentation
  o Customer Collaboration Over Contract Negotiation
  o Responding to Change Over Following a Plan
  o References
- **Chapter 3:** Values and Software Practices
  o Values in Agile and in Open Source
  o Principles in Agile and in Open Source
  o Software Practices in Agile and in Open Source Development
  o References
- **Chapter 4:** Models of Organization
  o Culture, People, Communication
  o Goals of Organization Models for AMs and XP
  o Organization
  o References
- **Chapter 5:** Coordination in Agile and Open Source
  o Interdependencies and Coordination Mechanisms
  o Coordination and New Software Development Approaches
  o References
- **Chapter 6:** Other Agile Methods
  o Crystal
  o DSDM
  o LSD
  o References

Section 2 includes the following chapters:

- **Chapter 7:** Testing
  - Introduction
  - Adoption of Test First in Open Source Development
  - Example: JUnit
  - References
- **Chapter 8:** Code Ownership
  - Introduction
  - Adoption of Code Ownership in Open Source Development
  - References
- **Chapter 9:** Design Approaches
  - Introduction
  - Adoption of Big Upfront Design in Open Source Development
  - References
- **Chapter 10:** Case Studies
  - The Eclipse Development Process
  - The Funambol Development Process
  - References

Section 3 includes the following chapters:

- **Chapter 11:** A Framework for Collecting Experiences
  - The Experience Framework
  - Data Collection
  - Data Analysis
  - Example of Application
  - References
- **Chapter 12:** Improving Agile Methods
  - Case Studies
  - References
- **Chapter 13:** Effort Estimation
  - Effort Estimation Models
  - Comparative Analysis
  - References
- **Chapter 14:** Discontinuous Use of Pair Programming
  - The Study
  - Results
  - References

Section 4 includes the following chapters:

Section I
Comparing Agile and Open Source Development

Introduction

Agile Methods (AMs) are very recent but many of their basic principles are rather old, inherited from the lean production pioneered in the '60s at Toyota for the production of cars. Moreover, many practices on which AMs are based have a long tradition in software development. For instance, unit testing has been used since the '60s. However, one of the major achievements of AMs is the integration of all these well established principles and practices with some others more recent such as pair programming.

The Open Source (OS) movement has a long tradition as well. However, it was born as a way of licensing software not as a development method. Moreover, people producing OS software use a wide range of different approaches to software development. Even if, it is not possible to define a single OS development method, there are some basic principles and approaches that have become common in several OS communities.

Surprisingly or not, there are many basic principles and development techniques that are similar in AMs and OS Software Development (OSSD). As an example further investigated in the first section of this book, the three of the four principles of the AMs are completely embraced by OSSD.

The analysis of commonalities and differences between AMs and OSSD is at the beginning but it is interesting to understand how some development approaches have evolved during the time and whether they produce concrete benefits in terms of software quality and customer satisfaction.

This book is a first attempt in the investigation of such relationship through of the analysis and the comparison of the basic principles and practices, the discussion of some empirical evaluations, and the presentation of promising assessment methodologies.

This book addresses three main audiences: managers, researchers, and students.

In this book, managers can find the basic principles and practices that are the base for AMs and OSSD, how they are related to each other, and how the organization of the work is affected. Moreover, the last section related to industrial adoption guides the reader into the main aspects to consider in using such technologies in a business environment.

Researchers can find not only a theoretical analysis of the phenomena of AMs and OS, but also the definition of an experimental framework for data collection and analysis and a set of empirical investigations.

This book can be used by software engineering students in BSc and MSc courses as a starting point to study how AMs and OSSD approaches the development process and how they are related to each other.

Besides the references listed in each chapter, here below the reader can find a small set of additional readings:

- **Section 1:** AMs and OSSD
  - Coplien, J. O., & Schmidt, D. (2004). *Organizational Patterns of Agile Software Development*. Prentice Hall.
  - Goth, G. (2007). Sprinting toward Open Source Development. *IEEE Software, 24(1)*.
  - Koch, S. (2004). Agile Principles and Open Source Software Development: A Theoretical and Empirical Discussion. In Eckstein, J., & Baumeister, H. (Eds.) *Extreme Programming and Agile Processes in Software Engineering* (pp. 85-93). Springer.
  - Mellor, S. (2005). Adapting agile approaches to your project needs. *IEEE Software, 22(3)*.
  - Stamelos, I. G., & Panagiotis, S. (Eds.). (2007). *Agile Software Development Quality Assurance*. IGI Global.
- **Section 2:** Analysis of Practices
  - Appleton, B., Berczuk, S., & Cowham, R. (2005). Branching and Merging: An agile perspective. CM Journal. Retrieved November 11, 2008 from: http://www.cmcrossroads.com/content/view/6657/264/

- o Cockburn, A., & Williams, L. (2001). The Costs and Benefits of Pair Programming. In Succi, G., & Marchesi, M. (Eds.) Extreme Programming Examined (pp. 223-248). Addison-Wesley Professional.
- o Davis, R. (2005). Agile requirements. Methods & Tools, 13(3).
- o Poole, C. J. (2004). Distributed product development using extreme programming. In Eckstein, J., & Baumeister, H. (Eds.) Extreme Programming and Agile Processes in Software Engineering (pp. 60-67). Springer.
- o Turnu, I., Melis, M., Cau, A., Marchesi, M., & Setzu, A. (2004). Introducing TDD on a free libre open source software project: a simulation experiment. 2004 Workshop on Quantitative Techniques For Software Agile Process.
- **Section 3:** Empirical Evaluations
- o Cordeiro, L., Mar, C., Valentin, E., Cruz, F., Patrick, D., Barreto, R., & Lucena, V. (2008). An agile development methodology applied to embedded control software under stringent hardware constraints. SIGSOFT Software Engineering Notes, 33(1).
- o Hazzan, O., & Dubinsky, Y. (2006). Can diversity in global software development be enhanced by agile software development? 2006 International Workshop on Global Software Development For the Practitioner. Shanghai, China.
- o Racheva, Z., & Daneva, M. (2008). Using measurements to support real-option thinking in agile software development. 2008 International Workshop on Scrutinizing Agile Practices Or Shoot-Out At the Agile Corral, Leipzig, Germany.
- o Rumpe, B., & Schroder, A. (2002). Quantitative Survey on Extreme Programming Project, 3rd International Conference on eXtreme Programming and Agile Processes in Software Engineering (XP 2002).
- o Turnu, I., Melis, M., Cau, A., Setzu, A., Concas, G., & Mannaro, K. (2006). Modeling and simulation of open source development using an agile practice. Journal of System Architecture, 52(11).
- **Section 4:** Industrial Adoption
- o Cohn, M., & Ford, D. (2003). Introducing an Agile Process to an Organization. IEEE Computer, 36(6).
- o Hansson, C., Dittrich, Y., Gustafsson, B., & Zarnak, S. (2006). How agile are industrial software development practices? Journal of Systems and Software, 79(9).
- o Hodgetts, P., & Phillips, D. (2001). Extreme Adoption Experiences of a B2B Start-up. Retrieved November 11, 2008 from: http://www.agilelogic. com/files/eXtremeAdoptioneXperiencesofaB2BStartUp.pdf
- o Martin, K., & Hoffman, B. (2007). An Open Source Approach to Developing Software in a Small Organization. IEEE Software, 24(1).

Chapter 1
Historical Evolution of the Agile and Open Source Movements

1.1 AGILE METHODS

Agile Methods (AMs) were born in the mid 1990s as part of a reaction against "heavyweight methods" (also called plan-driven methodologies) like the waterfall model. Heavyweight processes were seen as bureaucratic, slow, and inconsistent with the business needs. Initially, AMs were called *lightweight methods*; in 2001, prominent members of the raising community met in Utah and decided to adopt the name *Agile Methods*. Later, some of these people formed the Agile Alliance, a non profit organization that promotes Agile development. Early AMs, established before 2000, include Scrum (1986), Crystal Clear, Extreme Programming, Adaptive Software Development, Feature-Driven Development, and DSDM. Even if Extreme Programming (XP) was not the first Agile Method, it established their popularity. XP was created in 1996 by Kent Beck as a way to rescue the Chrysler Comprehensive Compensation (C3) project. The aim of this project was to replace several payroll application of Chrysler Corporation with a single system.

DOI: 10.4018/978-1-59904-681-5.ch001

1.2 THE WIN-WIN SPIRAL SOFTWARE DEVELOPMENT MODEL

The Win-Win spiral software development model (Boehm & Bose, 1994) is based on the ground-braking work of Barry Boehm, the first software engineering researcher to formalize an agile process. It is based on two pieces of research elaborated by Barry Boehm:

- The Win-Win approach to requirement negotiation (Boehm *et al.*, 1994)
- The spiral software development model (Boehm, 1988)

1.2.1 The Win-Win Approach to Requirement Negotiation

Requirement negotiation is a very critical part of the software development process; it deals with the elicitation of the desires of customer and with the negotiation of what needs to be developed. Often, during such negotiation critical situations emerge, where the desires of the customers clash with what the developers think it is important and feasible to do. In such circumstances, the risk is high for the project to go nuts or, even worse, for the developer to say "yeah!" to the customer or to the manager, just to keep his or her position while looking for another job. The former is risky because, at the end, the software developers needs a customer, otherwise money will not come. The latter is terrible, as for sure the functionality will not be delivered to the customer. Moreover, more money will be wasted. "Customers are always right." Well, this is what old-fashioned marketing books tell us. This is true in the sense that the customer pays the bill. Therefore, s/he has the right to get value for his or her money. However, for the customer to be always right, two provisions are necessary:

- The developer understands fully what the customer wants, and acts accordingly.
- The customer understands fully what the developer can provide him or her in the time framework and with the money given, and acts accordingly.

If such provisions are not met and we still proceed, we are in a loose-loose situation:

- The developer looses her or his jobs and gets a bad reputation.
- The customer wastes her or his time, and, sometimes, even his or her money and reputation.

Now, there are two possibilities. First, the positions of the developer and the customer cannot be accommodated together. In such circumstances, it is better to acknowledge that there is no sense in proceeding with any agreement. Second, the positions can be accommodated. In such case, we would like to find a way to identify such point of accommodation with mutual benefit, the win-win point. The win-win approach to requirement negotiations is a process that aims at ensuring that the two provisions are satisfied whenever possible, leading to a win condition for the customer, who gets the job done, and a win condition for the developer, who is paid and builds up a good reputation.

The key idea is to try to make the process as transparent as possible, so that if a win-win condition exists, it can be found and implemented. This is accomplished using various kinds of tools. We describe the process; we define steps to make it as objective as possible; we eliminate cultural barriers; and we put together customer and developer. Among the tools to use, there are diagrams detailing the negotiation process, like the ones available at http://sunset.usc.edu/research/WINWIN/EasyWinWin.

In such diagrams, for instance, it is evidenced that there the process of defining an agreement between a labor provider, the customer, the funds provider, and the customer. The customer has issues s/he wants to solve. There are several alternatives on how to address the issue. Our goal is to find that alternative that not only addresses the issue to solve, but that can be carrier out with satisfaction by the developer. Such alternative, if it exists, is for us the win-win condition. It satisfies both the customer and the developer. An agreement is a set of such alternatives. Well… isn't here something missing? Where is the manager? After all, the customer does not talk directly with the development *usually*, s/he talks to a marketing person, who then refers the issues for development to a manager.

Here there is yet another aspect of the wickedness of software development. The manager is indeed important. However, a satisfactory negotiation does require the presence of also the developer, or a person very much knowledgeable of what is going on, otherwise the risk is high, not to be able to build a solid relationship.

1.2.2 The Spiral Development Model

The incremental software development model has the advantage of focusing on small increments, making easier for developers to understand what happens at the different stages and so on. One of the major limitations of this model lied on its inability to involve the customer in the planning of the iterations. On one side, the presence of the customer is beneficial as it helps the team to be in sync with his or her desires. On the other side, the presence of the customer may become detrimental in incremental model. The customer may not understand why effort is placed for a long time on issues whose relevance s/he is not able to capture. The main idea of Barry Boehm has been to propose alternative. Try to slice the increments to develop not in terms of the inner functionality, but by the functions deployed to the customer. The model is called spiral, as:

- At each "increment"… well "iteration," or "ring of the spiral" we get a more complete version of the system to develop and
- At each increment we repeat everything, including the interactions with the customer.

The key issue is that the ring is a portion of the system that does something useful for the customer. Each ring should not require the building of the entire infrastructure; otherwise, it would be just a waterfall development! Each ring, though, should contain functionalities that are useful to the end customer. Such functionalities may need a portion of the overall infrastructure. Altogether, it is not easy to identify the rings of the spiral. It requires a deep understanding of the system to build and an extensive interaction with the customer, so that a "reasonable" ring can be produced. To simplify the process we could use the win-win approach that we discussed earlier. This is what is called the win-win spiral method (Figure 1).

It is important to remember that the spiral software development model is a "model," that is, is not a process itself. Rather, different processes can be built on its basis. In Figure 1, there is the description of a sample process built on the spiral model. Again, this is an implementation of the general win-win spiral model. The model can be implemented very differently in various contexts.

The sample model entails the following eight steps:

1. Identification of the stakeholders of the ring to develop. This involves the customers, or the portion of them that relates to what to do next.
2. Determination of the win-win condition: here customers, developers, and, if needed, managers evaluate if a win-win condition exists and, if so, they develop it.
3. Analysis of what to build on the basis of the identified win-win condition – in the picture we omit the way out that occurs if the win-win condition does not exist. Here we need to reconcile what to build with what has already been built. Clearly, we want to develop an analysis performed on the top of what is already there and we do not want to restart everything from scratch.
4. Design of what to build on the basis of the identified win-win condition. Also in the case, we want to extend the previously built design. Definitely, redoing everything from scratch is not to be considered.

Figure 1. Structure of the win-win spiral development model

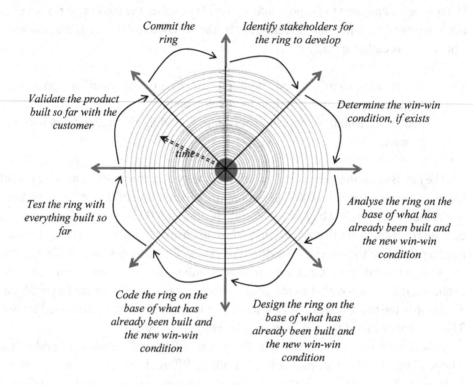

5. Coding of what to build on the basis of the identified win-win condition. Here it is extremely important to extend the previous functionalities and not restart. Redoing everything is not an option now.
6. Test of the new ring alone and within the entire system developed so far.
7. Evaluation with the customer of the new version of the system built so far.
8. Commitment of the work done so far.

This sample model evidences once more the critical issue of building the system ring by ring. The first ring, the "nucleus," is especially critical. The nucleus requires: a) a good general understanding of what to develop and b) the ability to build a system that does not commit "too much" the future developers in terms of architectural and design lock-ins. Note that in the spiral model the customer is involved in each ring.

Each ring in the spiral can then be organized in a V-shaped manner, quite like the incremental model. Likewise, an object oriented approach appears an ideal match for the spiral model, for the same reasons listed in the incremental model plus the easier understandability on the side of the customer of part of the object oriented models, such as the Use Case model. Frameworks can be applied in designing the nucleus, if they can be deployed pretty fast and they are perceived as a valuable asset by the customer. Otherwise, they can still be applied, but they need to be built a piece at a time in each ring, together with the provision of functionality to the customer. This poses an additional burden on the developers, as it may delay the overall development and create dissatisfaction on the customer side. Within XP, this problem is addressed by refactoring. We will discuss this aspect shortly hereafter.

1.2.3 Evaluation of the Win-Win Spiral Model

The win-win spiral method is probably the first application of an agile model to software engineering. It includes several aspects of what later on are called AMs (Boehm, 2002; Boehm & Turner, 2003):

- Direct connection between the customer and the developer, in the search of a win-win condition;
- Absence of a big "architectural" phase upfront and requirement to keep the system flexible for changes;
- Customer-driven selection of the features to develop in each increment
- Possibility to stop the development at any time, still providing something valuable to the customer
- Adaptive control of the development: at each ring there can be a significant shift in the overall direction of the project based on the outcome of the ring and on the feedback of the user.

The model is less rigid than the incremental model and requires an even lower upfront investment, as there is not architecture to build per se. The development in rings has beneficial aspects both at the technical level and dealing with the customer. At the technical level, it allows lower initial commitments to specific hardware and software that may cause undesired irreversibility. Dealing with the customer, it supports evolving and changing requirements, with rapid feedback on what is going on.

The spiral model requires developers to have a wide range of capabilities, not only at the technical level, but also dealing with the customer. As such, it is well suited to the profiles of most of today software development organizations.

The flow of communication between phases is simplified by the small sizes of the rings: it is possible to perceive in a fairly short amount of time if there is an overall understanding of the system to develop at the customer level, the analysis level, the design level, and the coding level. Object oriented methodologies fit pretty well the structure of spiral development models. When they are used, the flow of information becomes more seamless.

The small sizes of the ring also help to reduce the occurrences and the relevance of panic situations. Moreover, such small sizes and the higher integration between phases ensure that panic situations do not create inconsistencies throughout the different phases of development.

Altogether, the spiral development model looks like a panacea. But nothing comes for free. There are two major caveats to consider when thinking using it.

The first is that the coordination complexity is much higher than in the model we have discussed before. Such coordination complexity cannot be managed using (only) standard, plan-based techniques like Gantt charts, todo lists, and so on.

Moreover, the spiral model is quite theoretical, with a limited body of knowledge on its applications. Before the advent of the so-called "agile movement" only a handful instances of it have been described. The advent of AMs has provided possible solutions to the problem of coordination and a lot of example of the instantiation of "spiral-like" structures.

1.3 THE XP SOFTWARE DEVELOPMENT MODEL

Extreme Programming (XP) is not a pure process model. XP was originally conceived as a description of a well defined, successful process, the one of the C3 team (Jeffries, 1999). After four years of unsuccessful effort to build the Chrysler Payroll System, the large team in charge of it was laid off. Kent Beck, then a Smalltalk guru, was hired. With a handful of colleagues he implemented and followed a process that lead to the successful delivery of the system in less than two years. The success of the C3 project has resulted in the diffusion of XP beyond its original scope. People have tried to replicate the C3 experience by adapting to their context the XP approach. Altogether, we can say that XP is a "model by similarity," while most of the models we have seen so far are "models by generality". Being a model by analogy explains lots of the successes and the issues related to XP. We will explain them later on, in the section related to the evaluation of the XP process. There are three important drivers in the XP approach:

- Focus on the value and on what generates the value
- Generation of the value with a constantly-paced flow of activities, driven by the desire of the customer
- Aim at the highest possible absence of defect, without any trade-off decision

The entire XP extravaganza focuses on these three aspects, which can be then related to lean management. In this book we will not discuss lean management.

There are lots of interesting works on this new field of management sciences. The interested reader can refer to the work of Womack and Jones (1996) and Poppendieck and Poppendieck (2003) for the implementation of lean management in software development. Being born as the support for a specific project rather than in an "aseptic" research environment, the language of the first description XP by Kent Beck is committed itself to produce value. The first description was valuable if it was able **(a)** to support the first users of XP – the developers of the C3 project, in the use of XP itself and **(b)** to persuade such users of its goodness. Given the success of it, subsequent descriptions of XP have maintained the same, very suggestive and metaphorical style. We notice this not only in the XP manifesto (Beck, 1999), but also the subsequent works (Highsmith, 2002; Beck & Fowler, 2000; Fowler *et al.*, 1999), Wake's (2002), etc. Here below we summarize XP using the commonly used XP jargon. XP has four founding values:

- **Communication:** developers communicate among themselves and with customers a lot.
- **Simplicity:** the simplest solution is always preferred; no time is devoted to seek "beautiful" solution, with no real, tangible, evident value for the customer.
- **Feedback:** feedback is always sought from fellow developers, from customers and from all sort of testing tools, to ensure to be on the right track.
- **Courage:** developers are not scared of making modifications to their code, to let customers discuss and re-discuss over and over what they have done, to negotiate with the customers the amount of functionality to deliver; customers are not afraid that developers waste their money.

The relationship between the three drivers and the four founding values is not a simple one-to-one relationship. Rather, there is a bit of a few values in each of the drivers and vice versa. Here below there is a short description of the match (Figure 2).

The *focus on the value and on what generate value* is evident in the **simplicity**: only those features that of interest for the customers are generated. Such focus is also present on the **communication** with, and **feedback** from the customers: the customers define the priorities of what to develop. The *generation of value with a constantly paced flow of activities, based on the desire of the customers*, is apparent in the **feedback**, where the developers ask the customers their priorities and in the **courage**, where developers negotiate with the customers the amount of functionalities to deliver, without any fear from the customer side that developers "do not work enough". The *aim at the highest possible absence of defect* requires **simplicity** of design, to avoid inserting defects, **feedback** from tools and customers, to elimi-

Figure 2. Drivers and values

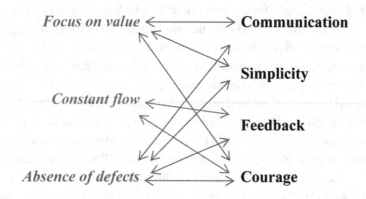

nate existing errors and detect non conformance with the wishes of the customers. Moreover, **communication** among developers and **courage** to test the code under the most severe circumstances help very effectively to eliminate defects. The XP extravaganza then says that the four founding values are implemented via a set of 12 XP practices (according to the first edition of the Beck's book[1]). It further claims that such practices are so much interconnected that it is very difficult to implement only a portion of them:

- Planning game
- Short releases
- Metaphor
- Simple design
- Testing
- Refactoring
- Pair programming
- Collective code ownership
- Continuous integration
- 40 hours working week
- On-site customer
- Coding standards

It is important to remember that these practices have been conceived in the framework of the C3 project. This is the spring of XP. We refer the reader to the Beck (1999) for clarification of each practice. As for the relationships between drivers and values, the relationships between values and practices are many-to-many (Figure 2) (Table 1). It is difficult to just try to alter the balance achieved by Kent Beck in

Table 1. Drivers and values of the XP practices

	Drivers			Values			
	Focus on value	Constant flow	No defects	Communication	Simplicity	Feedback	Courage
Planning game	√	√		√		√	√
Short rel.	√	√		√		√	
Metaphor	√			√		√	
Simple des.	√		√		√		
Testing		√			√	√	√
Refactoring		√	√		√		√
Pair progr.			√	√	√	√	
Collective code own.	√		√	√		√	√
Cont.integr.	√	√	√			√	√
40hrs week		√			√		√
On-site customer	√			√		√	
Coding std.	√		√		√	√	

orchestrating different activities to match the overall goal of the methodology.

Such intricate mix has leaded a few developers to accept each of the XP practices as a sort of magical device that solves all sorts of problems of software development. This is indeed completely false. Moreover, this is the exact opposite of the intention of the founder, who has repeatedly claimed that the practices need to be adjusted to each individual situation and that even the value set has to fit each individual circumstances.

1.4 OPEN SOURCE SOFTWARE DEVELOPMENT

At the beginning, there was only free software. Later on, proprietary software was born and it quickly dominated the market, to the point that it is today considered as the only possible model by many people. Only recently, the industry started to consider free software and OSS as an option.

In late 1970s, two different groups established the roots of the Open Source software movement. On the US East coast, Richard Stallman, a former software developer at the MIT AI lab, launched the GNU Project and founded the Free Software Foundation (FSF). The aim of the GNU project was to build a free operating system.

Stallman started by coding some development tools (GCC[2], Emacs[3]). He also created the GNU General Public License (GPL), a legal tool with the aim to guarantee that software produced by GNU will remain free and promote free software.

On the other side of the US coast, the Computer Science Research Group (CSRG) of the University of California at Berkeley improved the Unix system and developed many applications which quickly became "BSD Unix". For many time, this software was not redistributed outside the community of holders of a Unix AT&T license. But in the late 1980s, it was finally distributed under the "BSD license'", one of the first Open Source license. Unfortunately, users of Unix BSD also needed an AT&T Unix license since some parts of the kernel and some utilities, which were needed to have a usable system were still proprietary software.

During the 90s, the landscape of software development was changing. In Finland, Linus Torvalds, a student of computer science, unhappy with Minix[4], developed the first versions of the Linux kernel. Soon, many people were contributing to the kernel by adding more and more features to create GNU/Linux, a real operating system. At present, Linux and the Apache web server dominate the market of web site (http://www.netcraft.com/).

1.4.1 The Cathedral and the Bazaar

The Cathedral and the Bazaar[5] is an essay by Eric S. Raymond on software development methods, based on his observations of the Linux kernel[6] development process and his personal experience on managing Fetchmail[7], an Open Source project. His work is considered the manifesto of the Open Source Initiative. Raymond presents two contrasting free software development models:

- In the *cathedral model*, source code is available with each software release, but the access to code developed between releases is restricted to an exclusive group of software developers, i.e. GNU Emacs, GCC. The Cathedral model is the typical development model for proprietary software, with the additional restriction that source code is not released.
- On the contrary, in the *bazaar model* the code is developed over the Internet in view of the public. Linus Torvalds, leader of the Linux kernel project, is the inventor of this process.

Raymond's thesis is that *"given enough eyeballs, all bugs are shallow"*: the more available the source code is for public testing, the more rapidly all kind of bugs will be discovered. On the other hand, Raymond claims that projects developed with the Cathedral model require a huge amount of time and energy for hunting bugs, since the working version of the code is available to only few developers.

Figure 3. Open source community development process (adapted from Scacchi (2002))

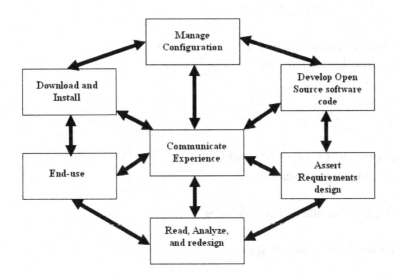

1.4.2 The Development Model

OS products are distributed along with their source code and under an OS license that allows to study, change, and improve their design. In OSS, requirements are rarely gathered before the start of the project, instead they are based on early releases of the software product. Scacchi (2002) proposes a model that includes seven phases: 1) Download and Install; 2) End-use; 3) Communicate Experience; 4) Analyze and Redesign; 5) Assert Requirements-Redesign; 6) Develop OSS code; 7) Manage Configuration (Figure 3).

Now we describe each phase of the project.

1.4.2.1 Download and Install

This phase includes the following steps:

1. Check Open Source software web sites (e.g., SourceForge, FreshMeat, etc.) for news and/or latest release information
2. Download packaged OSS (e.g., RPM files) containing source code and/or executable files
3. Unpack and install source code

1.4.2.2 End-Use

The typical flow of this phase includes:

1. Review any application documentation or web pages.
2. Use downloaded executable image

Optional:

1. Perform local source code build
2. Perform local integration test

1.4.2.3 Communicate Experience

The main activities of this phase are:

1. Browse Open Source software project web site, discussion forum, or other on-line resources.
2. If observe bugs, then do bug report.
3. If observer performance bottlenecks, external innovation opportunities, or localization shortfalls, then do enhancement, or code restructuring request.

1.4.2.4 Analyze and Redesign

This phase includes the following steps:

1. Select application, process, or web site to redesign
2. Analyze and model (components, connectors, interfaces, I/O resources, configuration, and versions.
3. Identify applicable redesign heuristics
4. Develop redesign transformation plan
5. Execute plan

1.4.2.5 Assert Requirements-Design

The main activities of this phase are:

1. Assert software requirements or design update using communication tools/ artifacts.

2. Read and make sense of updates, determine accountability.
3. Browse and extend software discourse web.
4. Harden discourse web via navigational cross-linkage.
5. Provide global access to software web.

1.4.2.6 Develop OS code

This phase includes the following steps:

1. Check-out and download source code from project repository/Web site
2. Edit source code file(s)
3. Compile local source code into executable image
4. Debug as needed
5. Perform unit test on executable image
6. Submit source code to configuration management

1.4.2.7 Manage Configuration

The main activities of this phase comprise:

1. Compose/integrate source code files (e.g., via make files).
2. Build/make executable composed image.
3. Regression test executable image.

Optional:

- Submit source code for review
- Review and approve/reject submitted source
    4. Check-in source code into source code repository
    5. Create remote installation package (e.g., RPM) for release
    6. Create and build multi-platform executable images for release
    7. Create release "news" information
    8. Post news and release on project web site
    9. Track and record source/image downloads

1.4.3 Starting an OS Project

An OS project can start, mainly, in four ways:

1. An individual, who feels the need for a project, announces the intent to develop the project in public. The individual may receive offers of help from others. The group may then proceed to work on the code.
2. A developer working on a limited but working codebase, releases it to the public as the first version of an OS program. The developer continues to work on improving it, and possibly is joined by other developers.
3. The source code of a mature project is released to the public, after being developed as proprietary software or in-house software (e.g., Netscape).
4. A well-established OS project can be forked by an interested outside party. Several developers can then start a new project, whose source code then diverges from the original.

1.4.4 OS Development Tools

OS developers use different kind of tools to support the development process. The most important tools can be grouped in the following categories.Testing Tools and Integration.

OS developers use tools to automate testing during system integration since OS projects are frequently integrated. For example, CruiseControl (Table 2) runs a continuous build process and inform users about the parts of the source code that have issues. In particular, it polls, in the background, a version control repository looking for changes. When a change does occur, the tool executes a predefined build script through Ant, for example.

Bug Tracking

Bug tracking is an important aspect of the management of OS projects. Bug tracking activities include: keeping a record of all reported bugs, whether the bug has been fixed or not, which version of the software does the bug belong, and whether the bug submitter has agreed that the bug has been fixed. The most popular bug tracking system in the OS environment is Bugzilla (http://www.bugzilla.org) (Table 3).

Table 2. CruiseControl

Feature	Description
Developer	CruiseControl development team, originally created by employees of ThoughtWorks
Operating System	Cross-platform
License	BSD-style license
Website	http://cruisecontrol.sourceforge.net

Collaboration and Communication

OS communities need tools to aid in organizing communication between project participants since they are dispersed. This is done through OS portals (Freshmeat, Savannah, Sourceforge), mailing lists (GNU mailman), and instant messaging tools (IRC, ICQ, etc.).

1.5 COMPARISON OF OS AND AGILE DEVELOPMENT

Warsta and Abrahamsson (2003) consider OS a paradigm that lies between agile and plan-driven methods, though it presents more commonalities with AMs. The most important differences are in the proximity and size of the development teams, the customers' representation during the development of the project, and with the primary objective of the development work. The results of the analysis shows the

Table 3. Bugzilla features

Feature	Description
Advanced Search	Two forms of search: 1) a basic Google-like that is simple for new users and searches the full text of a bug; 2) A very advanced search system where users can create any kind of search, including time-based searches (such as "show me bugs where the priority has changed in the last 3 days") and other very-specific queries.
Email notifications	Users can get an email about any change made in Bugzilla, and which notifications users receive is fully controlled by the personal user preferences.
Bug Lists in Multiple Formats	When users search for bugs, they can get the results in many different formats than just the basic HTML layout. Bug lists are available in Atom, if the user wants to subscribe to a search like it was a feed. They are also available in iCalendar format, by using the time-tracking features of Bugzilla it is possible to see where the bugs in the calendar. There are even more formats available, such as a long, printable report format that contains all the details of every bug, a CSV format for importing into spreadsheets, and various XML formats.
Reports and Charts	Bugzilla has a very advanced reporting system. Results can be seen as tables, bar graphs, or pie chart.
Time Tracking	Bugzilla allows estimating how many hours a bug will take to fix, and then keep track of the hours spent working on it. It is also possible to set a deadline that a bug must be complete by.
Request System	The Request System is a method of asking other users to do something with a particular bug or attachment. That other user can then grant the request, or deny it, and Bugzilla keeps track of their answer. It is useful for various purposes; whether it is needed to ask for code review, request information from a specific user, or get a sign-off from a manager, the system is extremely flexible.
Patch Viewer	This tool provides a nice, colorful view of any patch attached to a bug. It is integrated with LXR[8], CVS, and Bonsai to provide even more information about a patch. In particular, it makes code review much easier.

Table 4. Comparison between agile, plan-driven methods, and open source software development (Warsta and Abrahamsson, 2003)

Home-ground area	Agile methods	Open Source software	Plan-driven methods
Developers	Agile, knowledgeable, collocated, and collaborative	Geographically distributed, collaborative, knowledgeable and agile teams	Plan-oriented, adequate skills; access to external knowledge
Customers	Dedicated, knowledgeable, collocated, collaborative, representative, and empowered	Dedicated, knowledgeable, collaborative, and empowered	Access to knowledgeable, collaborative, representative, and empowered customers
Requirements	Largely emergent; rapid change	Largely emergent; rapid change, commonly owned, continually evolving – "never" finalized	Knowable early; largely stable
Architecture	Designed for current Requirements	Open, designed for current requirements	Designed for current and foreseeable requirements
Refactoring	Inexpensive	Inexpensive	Expensive
Size	Smaller teams and Products	Larger dispersed teams and smaller products	Larger teams and products
Primary objective	Rapid value	Challenging problem	High assurance

OS approach is close to a typical AM, with the distinction that OS developers are geographically distributed. In OSSD, the customer often is also a co-developer, which is not the case in agile software development.

Table 4 shows the comparison of agile, Open Source, and plan-driven processes using Boehm's analytical lenses [Boehm, 2002].

1.6 REFERENCES

Beck, K. (1999). *Extreme programming explained: Embrace change*. Addison-Wesley Professional.

Beck, K. (2004). *Extreme programming explained: Embrace change, second ed.* Addison-Wesley Professional.

Beck, K., & Fowler, M. (2000). *Planning extreme programming*. Addison-Wesley Professional.

Boehm, B. (1988). A spiral model of software development and enhancement. *IEEE Computer, 21*(5), 61–72.

Boehm, B. (2002). Get ready for agile methods, with care. *IEEE Computer, 35*(1), 64–69.

Boehm, B., & Bose, P. (1994). A collaborative spiral software process model based on theory W. *3ʳᵈ International Conference on the Software Process (ICSP94)*. New York: IEEE Press.

Boehm, B., Bose, P., Horowitz, E., & Lee, M. J. (1994). Software requirements as negotiated win conditions. *1ˢᵗ International Conference on Requirements Engineering (ICRE94)*. Colorado Springs, CO: IEEE Computer Society Press.

Boehm, B., & Turner, R. (2003). *Balancing agility and discipline: A guide for the perplexed*. Addison-Wesley Professional.

Fowler, M., Beck, K., Brant, J., Opdyke, W., & Roberts, D. (1999) *Refactoring: Improving the design of existing code*. Addison-Wesley Professional.

Highsmith, J. (2002). *Agile software development ecosystems*. Addison-Wesley Professional.

Jeffries, R. (1999). *We'll try*. Retrieved on November 11, 2008 from http://www. xprogramming.com/xpmag/well_try.htm

Poppendieck, M., & Poppendieck, T. (2003). *Lean software development: An agile toolkit*. Addison-Wesley Professional.

Scacchi, W. (2002) *Open source software development processes. Version 2.5.* Retrieved on November 11, 2008 from http://www.ics.uci.edu/~wscacchi/Software-Process/Open-Software-Process-Models/Open-Source-Software-Development-Processes.ppt

Wake, W. C. (2002) *Extreme programming explored*. Addison-Wesley Professional.

Warsta, J., & Abrahamsson, P. (2003). Is open source software development essentially and agile method? *3ʳᵈ Workshop on Open Source Software Engineering*, Portland, OR.

Womack, J. P., & Jones, D. T. (1996). *Lean thinking: Banish waste and create wealth in your corporation*. Simon & Schuster.

ENDNOTES

[1]   In the second edition (Beck, 2004), the number of practices listed is much higher and they are not already well accepted by the agile community.

[2]   http://gcc.gnu.org/ (accessed on November 11, 2008)

[3]   http://www.gnu.org/software/emacs/ (accessed on November 11, 2008)

[4]   Minix is an operating system designed to be useful for learning about the implementation of operating systems.

[5]   http://catb.org/~esr/writings/cathedral-bazaar/cathedral-bazaar/ (accessed on November 11, 2008)

[6]   http://www.kernel.org/ (accessed on November 11, 2008)

[7]   http://sourceforge.net/projects/fetchmail (accessed on November 11, 2008)

[8]   http://sourceforge.net/projects/lxr (accessed on November 11, 2008)

Chapter 2
The Agile Manifesto and Open Source Software

2.1 INTRODUCTION

The four main statements shared by all AMs are listed in the so-called Agile Manifesto[1]:

1. Individuals and interactions over processes and tools
2. Working software over comprehensive documentation
3. Customer collaboration over contract negotiation
4. Responding to change over following a plan

In this section, we review these statements to determine the extent to which they apply to OSS.

2.1.1 Individuals Over Processes and Tools

The development process in OS communities definitely puts more emphasis on individual and interaction rather than on processes and tools. The interactions in OS communities, though, tend to be mainly based on emails; the pride and the in-

DOI: 10.4018/978-1-59904-681-5.ch002

dividuality of the developer, though, become predominant, while in AMs there is a strong push toward establishing team spirit among developers.

2.1.2 Working Software Over Comprehensive Documentation

Both AMs and OSD view the working code as the major supplier of documentation. In OS communities the most common forms of user documentation are screenshots and users forums (Twidale & Nichols, 2005), which both come from the direct use of the systems, and the most common source of technical documentation are class hierarchies directly extracted from the code, bug-tracking databases, outputs from diffs between versions, etc.

2.1.3 Customer Collaboration Over Contract Negotiation

In OSS, customers and developers often coincide. This was especially true in the early era of OSS, when it was clearly said, for instance, that Unix was a system developed by developers and for developers. In such cases, the systems are clearly customer driven. There are now situations where the customers are clearly separated from developers. New systems such as Subversion, ArgoUML, etc., have a clear customer base, separated from the developers. Still, looking at how the releases occur, the functionalities are added, and the problems are solved it appears that the system is developed with a clear focus on customer collaboration. Moreover, in Europe it is becoming more popular the request that systems developed with public funds are releases with OSS licenses of various kinds.

2.1.4 Responding to Change Over Following a Plan

Following the discussion above on "Customer collaboration over contract negotiation", the evolution of an OS project typically is customer driven. It appears that OS systems do not have a "Big Design Upfront"; they are pulled rather than pushed and their evolution depends on real needs from the customers. However, most of such analysis is based on situations where customers and developers coincide. It would be interested to see how this situation would evolve in the newer scenarios where there are customers separated from developers. Altogether, it is evident that OS adopts most of the values fostered by supporters of AMs. Such evidence calls for subsequent analysis to determine the extent and the depth of such adoption. Moreover, AMs and OSD classes of software development methods, which include a wide number of specific methods. Therefore, it is important to consider specific instances of them to determine how the interactions between AMs and OSD really occurs in practice, beyond considerations that, left alone, ends up being quite useless.

2.2 Principles of Agile Software Development

This paragraph lists the agile development principles taken from the Agile Manifesto and show how these principles apply to OSSD (Goldman & Gabriel, 2005):

1. *Our highest priority is to satisfy the customer through early and continuous delivery of valuable software*
   OS does not talk about the customer, but in general, OS projects do nightly builds and releases frequently, mostly for the purpose of testing and gather feedback from the community of users.
2. *Welcome changing requirements, even late in development. Agile processes harness change for the customer's competitive advantage*
   OS projects resist major changes as time goes on, but there is always the possibility of forking a project if such changes strike enough developers as worthwhile.
3. *Deliver working software frequently, from a couple of weeks to a couple of months, with a preference to the shorter time scale*
   OS delivers working code every night, usually, and an OS motto is "release early, release often".
4. *Business people and developers must work together daily throughout the project.*
   OS projects do not have a concept of a business person with whom they work, but users who participate in the project serve the same role.
5. *Build projects around motivated individuals. Give them the environment and support they need, and trust them to get the job done*
   All OS projects do this, almost by definition. If there is no motivation to work on a project, a developer will not participate. OS projects are purely voluntary, which means that motivation is guaranteed. OS projects use a set of agreed-on tools for version control, compilation, debugging, bug and issue tracking, and discussion.
6. *The most efficient and effective method of conveying information to and within a development team is face-to-face conversation*
   In this case, OS differs from most from AMs. OS projects value written communication over face-to-face communication. On the other hand, OS projects can be widely distributed, and do not require collocation.
7. *Working software is the primary measure of progress*
   This is in perfect agreement with OSD.
8. *Agile processes promote sustainable development. The sponsors, developers, and users should be able to maintain a constant pace indefinitely.*

Although this uses vocabulary that OS developers would not use, the spirit of the principle is embraced by OSD.

9. *Continuous attention to technical excellence and good design enhances agility.*
    OSD is predicated on technical excellence and good design.

10. *Simplicity, the art of maximizing the amount of work not done, is essential.*
    OS developers would agree that simplicity is essential, but OS projects also do not have to worry quite as much about scarcity as agile projects do. There are rarely contractually committed people on OS projects – certainly not the purely voluntary ones – so the amount of work to be done depends on the beliefs of the individual developers.

11. *The best architectures, requirements, and designs emerge from self-organizing teams.*
    Possibly OS developers would not state things this way, but the nature of OS projects depends on this being true.

12. *At regular intervals, the team reflects on how to become more effective, and then tunes and adjusts its behavior accordingly"*
    This is probably not done much in OS projects, although as OS projects mature, they tend to develop a richer set of governance mechanisms. For example, Apache started with a very simple governance structure similar to that of Linux and now there is the Apache Software Foundation with management, directors, and officers. This represents a sort of reflection, and almost all community projects evolve their mechanisms over time.

In short, both the agile and open-source methodologies embrace a number of principles, which share the ideas of trying to build software suited especially to a class of users, interacting with those users during the design and implementation phases, blending design and implementation, working in groups, respecting technical excellence, doing the job with motivated people, and generally engaging in continuous design.

2.3 VTK EXAMPLE

The Visualization Toolkit (VTK)[2] is an example of OS project that embraces OS and Agile values (Twidale & Nichols, 2005). VTK is a software system for 3D computer graphics, image processing, and visualization. Some parts of it are subject to patents held by General Electric and a smaller company called Kitware.

The kit is substantial, encompassing over 600 C++ classes and around half a million lines of code. There are over 2,000 people on the VTK mailing list. General Electric considers VTK as a commercial advantage:

"We don't sell VTK, we sell what we do with VTK." General Electric has a number of internal and external customers of the toolkit, it is used in a variety of projects General Electric is involved with. Kitware provides professional services associated with VTK.

As an OS project, VTK is a bit unusual, and this is the result of some of its principals being involved with General Electric, which is the prime supporter of a design and implementation methodology called six sigma. Six sigma refers to a statistic that states that a manufactured artifact is 99.99966% defect-free, and it also refers to a process in which factors important to the customers' perception of quality are identified and systematically addressed during a design and implementation cycle whose steps are Define, Measure, Analyze, Improve, Control (DMAIC). OS involves the possibility of diverse innovations and also provides opportunities for interacting with customers in a direct way, which is appealing to an organization focused on customers, but there is also the possibility of erratic results when there is not a strong, explicit emphasis on quality that can be enforced. Therefore, OS went only part of the way to satisfying General Electric goals for quality.

Moreover, the original VTK implementation team was small and dispersed within General Electric, and its members were admittedly not software engineers. The open-source component added to this the need to find a way to handle quality. The solution was to adopt some of the practices of XP, in particular Test Driven Development (TDD), in which tests are written at the same time as, or before, the code is designed and written. Writing tests first has the effect of providing a sort of formal specification, as well as a set of tests to be used for regression and integration testing. XP calls for frequent releases, and VTK combines this with the OS practice of "release early, release often" to do nightly, fully tested builds.

The VTK developers implemented a system in which submitted code is tested overnight using a large corpus of regression tests, image regression tests (comparing program output to a gold standard), statistical performance comparisons, style checks, compilation, error log analyses, and memory leak and bounds-check analyses; the software's documentation is automatically produced; and the result is a quality dashboard that is displayed every day on the website. The tests are run on around 50 different builds on a variety of platforms across the Internet, and distributions are made for all the platforms.

The reasons for this approach, as stated by the original team, are as follows:

- To shorten the software engineering life cycle of design/implement/test to a granularity of 1 day.
- To make software that always works.
- To find and fix defects in hours not weeks by bringing quality assurance inside the development cycle and by breaking the cycle of letting users find bugs.
- To automate everything.
- To make all developers responsible for testing (developers are expected to fix their bugs immediately).

Among the values expressed by the original development team are the following:

- Test early and often; this is critical to high-quality software.
- Retain measurements to assess progress and measure productivity.
- Present results in concise informative ways.
- Know and show the status of the system at any time.

2.4 CONCLUSION

Twidale and Nichols (2005) claim that the primary source of similarity between OSD and AMs is their shared emphasis on continuous Some OS projects, especially hybrid projects, use more formal processes and produce more formal artifacts such as specifications, but even these projects accept the idea that the design should change as the requirements are better understood.

2.5 REFERENCES

Goldman, R., & Gabriel, R. P. (2005). *Innovation happens elsewhere: Open source as business strategy*. Morgan Kaufmann.

Twidale, M. B., & Nichols, D. M. (2005). Exploring usability discussions in open source software. *38th Annual Hawaii International Conference on System Sciences (HICSS'05)*. IEEE Computer Society Press.

ENDNOTES

[1]   http://agilemanifesto.org/ (accessed on November 11, 2008)
[2]   http://www.vtk.org/index.php (accessed on November 11, 2008)

Chapter 3
Values and Principles Practices in Agile and Open Source Development

3.1 INTRODUCTION

Values are ideals that that a group of people embrace. They can be positive or negative, for example empowerment or control. These values are implicit in the personality or culture of a company. Values are often emotive; they represent driving forces behind people. The word principle stems from the Latin for leader or emperor, however in this context we mean it as a general law or essence, for instance principles of modern physics.

Values and principles are related to practices, which are sets of repeatable actions you perform, e.g., practice developing software by driving with tests.

A practice works in a given context due to an underlying principle. For example, the practice of continuous integration is backed by the principle of reducing bottlenecks to enable flow in software development. Practices produce effects that support one or more values. If a software company values the ability to meet their customer needs, then a practice such as Test Driven Development (TDD) (Beck, 2002) will support that value as it keeps the cost of change low over time. In early 2001, a group of industry experts met to outline the values and principles that would allow software teams to develop quickly and respond to change. They called themselves the Agile Alliance. Over two days they worked to create a statement of values. The

DOI: 10.4018/978-1-59904-681-5.ch003

result was the manifesto of the Agile Alliance[1]. The document provides a philo-sophical foundation for effective software development. In the next paragraphs of this chapter, we review values and principles of the Agile Manifesto to determine the extent to which they apply to OSD.

3.2 VALUES IN AGILE AND IN OPEN SOURCE DEVELOPMENT

AMs are centered in four major values. Here we briefly introduce them. A comprehen-sive discussion is in the two editions of Beck's book (Beck, 1999; Beck, 2004):

1. **Communication:** Developers need to exchange information and ideas on the project among each other, to the managers, and to the customer in a honest, trusted and easy way. Information must flow seamless and fast.
2. **Simplicity:** Simple solutions have to be chosen wherever possible. This does not mean to be wrong or to take simplistic approaches. Beck often uses the aphorism "simple but not too simple".
3. **Feedback:** At all levels people should get very fast feedback on what they do. Customers, managers, and developers have to achieve a common understanding of the goal of the project, and also about the current status of the project, what customers really need first and what are their priorities, and what developers can do and in what time. This is clearly strongly connected with communications. There should be immediate feedback also from the work people are doing, that is, from the code being produced – this entails frequent tests, integrations, versions, and releases.
4. **Courage:** Every stakeholder involved in the project should have the courage (and the right) to present her/his position on the project. Everyone should have the courage to be open and to let everyone inspect and also modify his/her work. Changes should not be viewed with terror and developers should have the courage to find better solutions and to modify the code whenever needed and feasible.

Agile Modeling (Ambler, 2002) adds a further value: humility. This value states that every one has equal value on a project.

3.2.1 Communication

These values are present in various ways in Raymond's description of OSD (Raymond, 2000). We will now analyze them one by one and evidence the points of contact. The very same concept of OS is about sharing ideas via the source code, which becomes a propeller for communication (page 10). So, with no doubt communication is a major value in the work of Raymond. The role of communications is reinforced by Raymond throughout his essay. He clearly states the paramount importance to listening to customers (page 17) "But if you are writing for the world, you need to listen to your customers – this does not change just because they are not paying you in money." Then, it is evidenced that to lead an OS project good communication and people skills are very important (page 19): he carries as examples Linus Torvalds and himself, allegedly, two people capable at motivating and communicating.

3.2.2 Simplicity

Simplicity in the system is highly regarded in the OS community. In general, Raymond mentions the "constructive laziness", which helps in finding existing solutions that can be adapted to new situations. Beck's concept of simplicity is clearly reflected in rule number 13 of Raymond; it is an excerpt from Antoine de Saint'Exupéry (page 15): "Perfection (in design) is achieved not when there is nothing more to add, but rather when there is nothing more to take away."

3.2.3 Feedback

Working in a distributed community, Raymond acknowledges the value of a fast feedback at all levels:

- Between distributed developers, potentially working on the same fix, see for instance the comment on page 9;
- Between developers and customers – rule number 11 is a clear example: "The next best thing to having good ideas is to recognize good ideas from your users. Sometimes the latter is better."

   Feedback is achieved especially running and testing the code, this is why early and frequent releases are instrumental – rule 7 says "Release early, release often. And listen to your customers. Needless to say most of the comments made about feedback could apply as well to communication. This is not awkward. Beck acknowledges explicitly that the two concepts overlap.

3.2.4 Courage

The value of courage is less present in the presentation of Raymond. He hints at courage when he presents the initial difficult in getting the work exposed to (page 8) "thousands of eager co-developers pounding at every single new release."

3.3 PRINCIPLES IN AGILE AND IN OPEN SOURCE

As noted by Fowler (2003), hidden inside the first version of Beck's book there are 15 principles, divided into 5 fundamental principles and 10 other principles. The fundamental principles are:

1. **Rapid feedback:** Going back to the value of feedback, such feedback should occur as early as possible, to have the highest impact in the project and limiting to the highest extent the possible disruptions.
2. **Assume simplicity:** As mentioned, simplicity is a major value. Therefore, simplicity should be assumed everywhere in development.
3. **Incremental change:** Change (mostly resulting from feedback) should not be done all at once. Rather, should be a permanent and incremental project, aimed at creating an evolving system.
4. **Embracing change:** Change should be handled with courage and not avoided. The system as a whole, and the code, should be organized to facilitate change to the largest possible extent.
5. **Quality work:** Quality should be the paramount concern. Lack of quality generates rework and waste that should be avoided to the large degree.

Other principles of XP are:

1. **Teach learning:** Requirement elicitation is an overall learning process. Therefore, learning is of paramount importance in the system.
2. **Small initial investment:** The upfront work should be kept as minimum as possible, as subsequent changes may destroy it.
3. **Play to win:** All the development should be guided by the clear consciousness that what we do is effectively doable.
4. **Concrete experiments:** The ideas should be validated not though lengthy and theoretical discussions but via concrete experimentations on the code base.
5. **Open, honest communication:** The communication should be kept simple and easy. The customer should not hide his/her priorities nor the developers and the managers should hide the current status of the work.
6. **Work with people's instincts – not against them:** The role of the managers is to get the best out of developers, so their natural inclinations should be exploited. A strong team spirit should be exploited. Moreover, in the interactions between managers, developers, and customers, the fears, anxieties, discomforts should not be ignored but properly handled.

7. **Accepted responsibility:** All the people in the project should voluntary take their own responsibilities, customers, managers, and developers. Such responsibilities should then be assigned with complete trust.
8. **Local adaptation:** The methodology should be wisely adapted to the needs of each development context.
9. **Travel light:** In XP projects it is important to keep the lowest amount of documents possible, clearly without compromising the integrity of the project.
10. **Honest measurement:** The project should be tracked with objective and understandable measures. The measures should be collected in a lean way not to alter the nature of XP.

3.3.1 Review of the Fundamental Principles

In this section, we review the application in the OSD of the fundamental principles: rapid feedback, assume simplicity, incremental change, embracing change, quality work.

We have already discussed the issue of **feedback** and **simplicity**.

Regarding the **incremental changes**, Raymond acknowledges upfront it as one of its guiding principles since his early Unix experience (page 2): "I had been preaching the Unix gospel of small tools, rapid prototyping and evolutionary programming for years."

As for **embracing changes** proposed by others, we have already mentioned Raymond's opinion on listening to customers even if they do not "pay you in money." Raymond goes further and in rule number 12 he states the pivotal role of embracing the change: "Often, the most striking and innovative solutions come from realizing that your concept of the problem was wrong."

Raymond goes farther than Beck on this subject. The both agree that prototypes (spikes in Beck jargon) can be instrumental to achieve a better understanding of a complex application domain. Raymond also claims that the system being developed can help identifying new ideas for new developments – rule 14: "Any tool should be useful in the expected way, but a truly great tool lends itself to uses you never expected." Needless to say, when drafting rule 14 Raymond is not concerned in ensuring the customer that he will not waste customer's resources.

Regarding **quality** work, in Raymond's there is not an explicit reference to the paramount role of quality as it is in Beck's. However, throughout the essay there is a constant evidence of the pride that OS developers put in their code, a pride that comes only from deploying quality work.

3.3.2 Review of the Other Principles

Now we turn our attention to the other principles: teach learning; small initial investment; play to win; concrete experiments; open, honest communication; work with people's instincts – not against them; accepted responsibility; local adaptation; travel light; honest measurement.

Raymond emphasizes the role of listening and learning from other's comments. However, there is not an explicit mention on **teaching learning**.

There is also little concern of not having **small initial investment** and **travel light**. The reason is that OS projects are lead more by developers, less likely to spend ages in the "analysis paralysis" or in producing useless documentation and more concerned on delivering useful code. Rather, the attention of Raymond is on evidencing that a little bit of upfront work is required (page 18) "When you start building a community, what you need to be able to present is a plausible promise. Your program does not have to work particularly well. It can be crude, buggy, incomplete, and poorly documented. What it must not fail to do is (a) run, and (b) convince potential co-developers that it can be evolved into something really neat in the foreseeable future."

Playing to win and **concrete experiments** are an integral part of any self-motivated effort, so it does not require any further explanation.

Discussing values, we have already evidences the role given by Raymond to an **open, honest communication**.

Being developer-centric, Open Source also advocates **working with people's instincts – not against them** and relies on **accepted responsibility**. The very first two rules of Raymond are "Every good work of software starts by scratching a developer's personal itch," and "Good programmers know what to write. Great ones know what to rewrite (and reuse)." Also rule 4 appears quite applicable: "If you have the right attitude, interesting problems will find you."

While there is no formal measurement in place in Raymond's essay, there is an emphasis on releasing often, thus making clear the status of the project and the bugs still presents. This resembles **honest measurement**.

3.4 SOFTWARE PRACTICES IN AGILE AND IN OPEN SOURCE DEVELOPMENT

For example, Extreme Programming has 12 practices (in the first edition of the Beck's book). As suggested by Ron Jeffries *et al.* (2001), they can be divided into four categories:

Fine scale feedback

1. **Test first:** Test should be written together with the customer and before the actual code; they should also cover all the most relevant aspects of the system. In this way, they serve as a way to ensure requirements are met and as a form of formal specification of the behavior of the system.

2. **Planning game:** Planning should be done together by developer, managers, and the customer. Together, these three stakeholders write user stories of the system; then the customer sets the priorities, the manager allocates resources, and the developers communicate what is likely to be feasible to do. The communication on plan should be kept honest and open.

3. **Customer on-site:** The customer and the developers should be easily accessible and, if possible, co-located. In this way the customer would be ensured that the developers are working along their plan and the developers could receive fast feedback from the customer.

4. **Pair programming:** Programmers should always work in pair, where one stays at the keyboard and write the code, while the other proposes ideas and verifies the code being written.

Continuous process rather than batch

5. **Continuous integration:** The code should be integrated frequently, to ensure that all the pieces fit seamlessness together.

6. **Refactoring:** The code should be constantly revisited and made simpler and more understandable, with a clear constraint that (a) such simplifications should be done test first, (b) the simplifications should be checked in only when passing all the existing and new tests, and (c) the simplifications should be done in pair.

7. **Small releases:** The development of the system should proceed in small increment with frequent releases.

Shared understanding

8. **Simple design:** The design should be kept simple and developed incrementally.

9. **System metaphor:** The overall project team should be a jargon shared among developers, customers and managers, so that developers could better understand the problem domain and customers could better appreciate developers' solutions. Such jargon could be built around an overall analogy of the system being built.

10. **Collective code ownership:** Everyone in the team should have complete accessibility to any piece of code developed by anyone else in the team, and should be able to modify in and check in a new version of it, provided that (a) proceeds test first, (b) checks in only a new version passing all the existing and new tests, and works in pair.
11. **Coding standard:** The code should be written in a style agreed upon by all the people in the team, to promote sharing and easy understanding. What standard to use is not so important provided it is reasonable and it is accepted by everyone. But it is important to have one.

Programmer welfare

12. **Forty hours week:** The project should proceed at a sustainable pace, along the lines of the constant flow advocated by lean management. Therefore, major efforts might be tolerable for a week or two per term, but overall the effort distribution should be flat and not exceed what is normally bearable: 40 hours per week.

We use these categories in the further discussion. Clearly, now there will be some repetitions with what we have previously said.

The practices of fine scale feedback are not particularly adopted in OSD – **test first**, **planning game**, **customer on site**, **pair programming**. They appear particularly difficult to implement in their literal form in an OS community, where everyone provides his/her own contribution.

There are a few remarkable analogies, though.

There is an emphasis on test, especially automated tests. Raymond cites as a criteria of success of Emacs/Lisp the virtuous cycle (page 7) "release/test/improve."

Rule 6 advocates trying to convert users as co-developers: "Treating your users as co-developers is your least-hassle route to rapid code improvement and effective debugging." Moreover, dealing with the users/co-developers, Raymond notes that "ideas and prototypes were often rewritten three or four times before reaching a stable, final form."

A peculiar role is played by beta-testers. Beta-testers play a mixed role: they are both co-developers and customers. According to Raymond, it is very important to pay a lot of consideration to such beta-tester – rule 10: "If you treat your beta-testers as if they're your most valuable resource, they will respond by becoming your most valuable resource."

Moreover, the idea of a large test base is present in rule 8 dealing with beta-testers: "Given a large enough beta-tester and co-developer base, almost every problem will be characterized quickly and the fix obvious to someone."

This is not having the customer on site or running the planning game; however, it is quite similar.

Dealing with distributed teams, where usually there is only one programmer per physical site, pair programming is quite impossible.

3.4.1 Practices of Continuous Process

Continuous integration, **refactoring**, and **small releases** are almost entirely adopted in OSD.

The concepts of releases and integrations are mixed in the work of Raymond. He promotes very frequent releases. Rule 7 says "Release early. Release often. And listen to your customers." And down on page 7 he supports the idea of releasing once per day.

Rule 3 advocates constant refactoring: "Plan to throw one away; you will anyhow." We have discussed in the previous section the role of constant rewriting of ideas and prototypes. All of this is quite along the lines of Rule 13 (already mentioned) on perfection via simplicity.

3.4.2 Practices of Shared Understanding

Shared understanding is also of paramount importance for OSD. **Simple design** has already been discussed.

Raymond does not mention the **system metaphor** in any format. However, he asserts the importance to try to use plain English whenever feasible – rule 16 says: "When your language is nowhere near Turing-complete, syntactic sugar can be your friend."

Source code awareness is advocated throughout the essay and is evidences in page 10: "Thus, source-code awareness by both parties greatly enhances both good communication and the synergy between what beta-tester reports and what the core developer(s) know." This lends toward **collective code ownership**, especially when Raymond mentions that Torvalds has been "open to the point of promiscuity" (page 3).

However, this does not means that everyone can modify any portion of the project, as the project manager (or however one wants to call it) has still the right of selecting what to insert. There is evolutionary, self-selection mechanism for creating a team of core developers who contribute to the projects, and this clearly imposes implicitly coding standards. To this end, it is remarkable rule 5 that even discusses what to do when someone is not any more interested in guiding an OS project: "When you lose interest in a program, your last duty to it is to hand it off to a competent successor."

Coding standards are not explicitly mentioned by Raymond, even if, in practice, they are present.

3.4.3 Practices of Programmer Welfare

Being largely self-motivated, the issue of programming welfare is not of primary interest for Raymond. Still on page 27 he claims that "A happy programmer is one who is neither underutilized not weight down with ill-formulated goals and stressful process friction. *Enjoyment predicts efficiency*." This is not quite the concept of the **forty hours week**, but it is quite similar.

3.5 PUTTING THE ANALYSIS TOGETHER

Altogether, we note that there is a pretty high level of overlap between the values adopted by XP and that of OSD according to Raymond. Communication, feedback and simplicity are fully endorsed. Courage is also implicitly assumed to carry out an OS project.

Going to the principles, there is still a good level of agreement in the fundamental principles, apart from quality that in Raymond's work is assumed, rather than advocated.

For the "other principles" of XP, the only differences come from the different point of view: Raymond deals with mostly volunteers, while Beck mostly with employees. Concepts such as traveling light, limited upfront design, etc., do not concern particularly Raymond that, on the other hand, is more interested that the open source developers do at least a little bit of design upfront.

As to the practices, clearly the situation is quite different. Practices related to process, shared understanding and programmer welfare are somewhat similar in the two cases. Practices related to fine-scale feedback are not so widely present in the description of Raymond.

As a final note, we would like to evidence that both Beck's and Raymond's experience comes from an early use of very easy to use, expressive, and powerful programming languages: Smalltalk and Lisp respectively. An analysis of the role of programming languages in AMs and in OSSD could be an interesting subject for a further study.

3.6 REFERENCES

Ambler, S. (2002). *Agile modeling: Effective practices for extreme programming and the unified process*. Wiley.

Beck, K. (1999). *Extreme programming explained: Embrace change*. Addison-Wesley Professional.

Beck, K. (2002). *Test driven development: By example*. Addison-Wesley Professional.

Beck, K. (2004). *Extreme programming explained: Embrace change, second ed.* Addison-Wesley Professional.

Fowler, M. (2003). *Principles of XP*. Retrieved on November 11, 2008 from http://www.martinfowler.com/bliki/PrinciplesOfXP.html

Jeffries, R., Anderson, A., & Hendrickson, C. (2001). *Extreme programming installed*. Addison-Wesley Professional.

Raymond, E. S. (2000). *The cathedral and the bazaar*. Retrieved on November 11, 2008 from http://www.catb.org/~esr/writings/cathedral-bazaar/cathedral-bazaar/

ENDNOTE

[1] http://agilemanifesto.org/ (accessed on November 11, 2008)

Chapter 4
Models of Organization

4.1 INTRODUCTION

The essence of XP, but in general of AMs, is making the customer a part of the team who works very closely with the developers, ideally communicating on a daily basis. However, this is not always feasible: this is due to a number of different reasons, some connected with difficulties of the customer, but others may exist, for instance, situations where the development team is offshore. In this document, we will illustrate the organizational models of XP, also throughout a number of techniques used to obtain at least a part of the benefits of close interactions in case where they are impossible.

In fact, the momentum to the development of a project deriving from an ongoing communication flow is the key point of AMs and XP, in order to have a prompt integration of the deliverables into the customer's production environment.

The reason to implement XP or AM projects with the proper organization model is to obtain the maximum outcome from the chosen methodology:

* **Lower risks.** By implementing XP (or any AM) properly, it is possible to truly control the development spend by getting daily estimations of how far the allocated budget will take the project in terms of implementing the desired

DOI: 10.4018/978-1-59904-681-5.ch004

functionality. In short, what is possible to obtain is a "fixed price, variable scope" situation, with very close control over how every dollar is spent.

- **Scope prioritization and early release of the core functionality.**
- **Possibility to throw in changes as the project goes (as many as possible).** It is the projects with highly fluid requirements that especially benefit from XP. The cost of change relative to project phase is linear here rather than exponential as in conventional projects. This is where such XP practices as "no design in advance" and "keep it simple" really add value.
- **Projects can be started with a minimal set of requirements.** Ideally a new project should have user stories, story tests and mockups, but this is not a must. Clients can kick off an XP project without the long preliminary phase of requirements preparation, because it is possible for the client, thank to the improved communication facilities, to define its requirements iteratively.

4.2 THE AGILE MANIFESTO

Indications coming from the Agile Manifesto state the concepts of the organizational models in the Agile Methodologies:

- Organizations must live with the decisions developers make
- Organizations need to have an environment that facilitates rapid communication between team members

These sentences have two great implications in the usual structure of organizations:

- Developers can make decisions for the whole project, and the whole team should just accept them
- Any organization willing to embrace AMs or XP should provide facilities and adapt its environment, and not only in material way, to allow and ease communications between team members: as the team is composed by people from heterogeneous departments (business and technical), this is a great boost for horizontal communications inside a company.

4.3 CULTURE, PEOPLE, COMMUNICATION

As stated by Cohen *et al.* (2004), an organization can be assessed by examining three key dimensions: culture, people, and communication. In relation to these areas a number of key success factors have been identified:

- The culture of the organization must be supportive of negotiation
- People must be trusted
- Fewer but more competent people
- Organizations must live with the decisions developers make
- Organizations need to have an environment that facilitates rapid communication between team members

Most agile methods are more suitable for projects with small teams, with fewer than 20 to 40 people. Large scale agile software development remains an active research area (Eckstein, 2004; Ambler, 2006). Based on empirical evidence, the case can be made that very large projects (more than 200-1000 software engineers) are the natural terrain for agile methods. The case does not depend on running these projects as confederations of small teams.

4.4 GOALS OF THE ORGANIZATION MODELS FOR AMS AND XP

Review of the required adaptations to the organization models for AMs and XP, starting from C3 project described by Beck (1999).

4.4.1 Scheduling

XP specifically prescribes two levels of scheduling, which make up the Planning Game. These levels, called Commitment Schedule and Iteration Plan, are based on developers' own estimates for the production of the necessary software. The joint Commitment Schedule process results in a comprehensive estimate of what will be produced, and when. The joint Iteration Plan schedules a short interval, and results of each iteration feed back into the Commitment Schedule to refine the schedule. C3 progress is in no way characterized by a series of crises.

The C3 team specifically prohibits heroics, and works almost no overtime. Instead, the team treats a desire for heroics as an indication that there is something wrong with the process. They dig in and determine what is going wrong, and fix the process.

While the C3 team members are quite competent, they are generally not exceptional. The team's Pair Programming practice brings two good minds to bear on each problem: this is generally better than bringing one excellent mind to bear.

The team manager offers no exceptional support. Rather, he serves only to track progress, and to interface to management, with all technical decisions and assignments being done jointly by the team and by a volunteer process.

A second XP project, with a new team, has not yet been attempted at Chrysler, so we cannot yet speak to how well the success will be replicated. Our thoughtful opinion, however, is that it is our process, not us as individuals, that is making C3 work so well.

4.4.2 Training and Monitoring

XP clearly specifies a number of practices. These are well-defined, and are documented. The team has been trained at the beginning of the project, has a full-time coach, and trains new members in the team practices. Practices are generally measured and enforced by the shared responsibility of the team. Pair Programming and an open process ensure that all developers know what is happening all over the system. In the rare instances where a developer may violate one of the team's practices, the offending developer will be advised, reprimanded, or, in rare cases, allowed to work on some other project.

The practices are improvable, and in fact are improved as we go along. In XP, there are Four Variables that are tracked: Resources, Scope, Quality, and Time. These variables let us determine whether we are meeting the schedule, with the desired quality, as we go along. We report these variables uniformly, from ourselves all the way to the top of the organization.

4.4.3 Definition of Organizational Processes

XP rules encompass the readiness criteria (e.g., completion of User Stories, presence of key resources), inputs (User Stories), standards and procedures (the many "Extreme Programming Rules"), verification mechanisms (Unit Tests and Functional Tests), outputs (the software plus anything else defined in the User Stories), and completion criteria (user-acceptable scores on the Functional Tests), defined for CMM level 3 (Chrissis *et al.*, 2003).

Using the Four Variables, XP provides management with simple and clear insight into actual project performance.

4.4.4 Management

XP requires that quality goals for products be set via the Functional Tests. We require Unit Tests to be at 100% all the times, so that's not very interesting as a statistic. We measure our Load Factor, which relates elapsed time to developers' estimates of difficulty. We have not set quantitative goals for this figure, but we do use changes in Load Factor as a cue to look into the process and see where we can improve.

When the schedule is tracking and test scores are good, it is not always necessary to track other quantitative values. Some candidates to consider would be: number of unit tests vs. number of system classes; rate of change of test creation; number of system classes; class/method/code lines ratios, and so on.

Looking at XP through CMM eyes, especially if XP were being done throughout an entire large organization, it is possible to expect that more measurement might be needed than the required in a single project. An interesting question in those circumstances is how much to invest in measurement "in case we need it". The XP advice would be to measure only things that have low cost, and start measuring when you see the need. We would advise recording additional (low-cost) measures but (literally) not looking at them unless and until there is a perceived use for the figures. Otherwise you're just wasting time that could be used writing more software – which is, after all, the point.

4.4.5 Optimization

At the Optimizing Level [..]. software teams analyze defects to determine their causes. They evaluate software processes to prevent known types of defects from recurring and [they] disseminate lessons learned throughout the organization. (Chrissis et al., 2003)

XP practice is to meet every defect by implementing tests that display the defect, then fixing the software so that the tests run. Other tests are to be built in the same or related areas, to catch similar or related problems.

It is fair to say that the C3 team, being human, sometimes falls a bit short in terms of creating tests for things that are outside our current scope. This is an area that needs continual attention from the Extreme Coach, and it may need shoring up in some other way as well.

XP teams prefer to implement software to check for and detect errors, whether in the base software or in process, rather than to set up involved procedures which leave open the possibility of human error or laziness. Thus, an XP team will write software to make sure that changes are not stepped on by subsequent developers, rather than set up a more involved release procedure.

4.5 ORGANIZATION

There is a template of an ideal organizational structure to run multiple XP projects. This role definition starts from generalizing a set of data collected in a number of studies (Ambler, 2006; Ceschi *et al.*, 2005; Chrissis *et al.*, 2003; Eckstein, 2004; Sillitti *et al.*, 2005).

4.5.1 Business Project Manager (BPM) and Business Analyst (BA)

- Carry out business analysis and prepare prioritized user stories and story tests.
- Allocate the project budget (BPM).
- Answer business questions and update the documentation.
- Provide early feedback for completed stories. Verify implemented stories.
- Open, prioritize, and track change requests and defects.
- Participate in release planning sessions, planning games, and daily Scrums.

The business team should drive the story creation and prioritization. Stories and subsequent change requests are consolidated and channeled to the development team through the BPM. The business team's main task is to be responsive to the development team, answering questions early and often, thus enabling the development team to move quickly through the implementation of stories. As the development team delivers its daily builds, the business analysts also continuously verify that the functionality implemented by the developers is really what the business wanted.

4.5.2 Technical Integration Lead (TIL) Responsibilities

- Keep the balance between the development team and the customer (moderator role).
- Cannot be BPM or BA!
- Supervise the team staffing process.
- Track progress of the entire project.
- Make sure that all resources (environment, documentation, back-end access) are arranged and made available to the development team.
- Get external resources (e.g., a stress testing team), as necessary.
- Make sure that all questions are answered in timely manner and that the documentation is updated accordingly.
- Arrange and participate in release planning sessions, planning games, and daily Scrums.

The TIL deals strictly with the technical and organizational side of the project, leaving the issues related to the business logic to the BAs and the BPM. This is to ensure that the BPM is focused on getting the requirements right 100% of the time and does not have to be distracted from communicating with the development team for non-essential, administrative tasks.

4.5.3 Enabler Responsibilities

- Participate in the project feasibility study preceding the project.
- Review user stories and creates technical stories.
- Provide proper interfaces and stubs to back-end systems.
- Review the source code daily and checks compliance with architecture standards and coding guidelines.
- Check product metrics (unit test coverage, automatic unit test coverage, cyclomatic complexity).
- Help the development team by answering difficult technical questions and suggesting better solutions.
- Participate in release planning sessions, planning games, and daily Scrums.

The enabler acts as the first filter on the customer side. He receives the daily build from the StarSoft team and deploys it in the client's integration environment (which emulates the production environment), since the offshore team is not allowed direct access to the client's highly sensitive environments. He also performs code reviews to make sure the team follows coding and architectural guidelines. In short, the enabler's responsibility is to ensure the code's consistency and to make sure the business analysts can proceed to test the system's functionality. More often than not, a separate Technical Data Analyst (TDA) is working alongside the enabler and takes care of the database side of things.

4.5.4 TDA Responsibilities (When Present as a Separate Role)

- Create technical stories relating to databases.
- Provide the necessary schemas and data of back-end databases.
- Review DDL, DML, and query scripts.
- Perform load and stress testing, if necessary.
- Help the development team by answering the difficult technical questions and suggesting alternative solutions.

Due to the global nature of the client's organization, the BMP, TIL, Enabler and the development team can be in different countries for the same project. This is to adapt at maximum level the organization to any client request.

4.5.5 Project Manager's Responsibilities

- Put the team together from the available resource pool, based on the requirements of the project at hand. Serve as the central communication point to the client.
- Sort out everything that can potentially decrease the team's velocity.
- Arrange and participate in release planning sessions, planning games, and daily Scrums. Write and circulate minutes.
- Participate in estimations; track status.
- Gather questions and forward them to the client, receive answers, and discuss them with the team.
- Arrange standup meetings, and make sure that everyone has his/her daily tasks assigned and that the tasks are clear.

The project manager shall staff the development team and act as the central communication conduit to the customer. On a daily basis, he or she shall run the morning standup meeting to kick off the daily "mini project." Right after that, the PM proceeds to collect the questions from his team, answering the easier ones and consolidating the rest into the daily email to the client's analyst team.

In the middle of the day, the project manager holds the daily Scrum telephone call with the customer. Generally speaking, it is important to propagate this communication between developers and the customer through the PM: if each team member communicated with the customer directly, the customer could be flooded by duplicate questions or by questions that can be easily answered by the PM. However, team members might also take part in the Scrum. For example, in the case of a complex technical problem, Tech Lead shall speak directly to the Enabler on the customer side. Immediately after the Scrum, the PM holds the second stand-up meeting for the day, passing back the answers he received during the Scrum call.

4.6 KEY POINTS FOR ORGANIZATIONS

- **Face to face communication is important.** Over time, data gathered in some studies (Ceschi *et al.*, 2005; Sillitti *at al.*, 2005) have shown that some companies moved to holding planning games on the phone rather than face to face, for economic reasons: it can be expensive to send a team of three to five managers from Ireland or the UK to Russia for up to four days. Although phone planning games are cheaper, those companies still report that it is advisable to hold at least the first planning game face-to-face with the client. It is less likely that questions will be asked during telephone planning games than in face-to-face meetings, which can result in more errors, more bug fixing down the line, and ultimately more expensive projects. Another reason why face-to-face meetings are so important (at least once per client) is because the personal connection made at the first meeting makes subsequent communication much more effective. So in the long run, face-to-face planning games may still make economic sense.

- **Separation of roles.** Having the Enabler, TIL, and BPM/BA as separate roles really helps with the focus and the efficiency of communication. This requires a certain degree of dedication from the client. Generally speaking, since usually there is no direct access to the client's integration and production environments, the adoption of an enabler is a must to ensure the proper deployment of the daily (or interactions) releases. The separation of the TIL and BPM roles is really helpful in focusing people's energies on the right things.

- **The importance of tools.** Tools provide the much needed daily visibility into the project for the management on the client side, enabling them to truly harness the power of XP. This is especially critical if the development team is located offshore.

4.7 REFERENCES

Ambler, S. (2006). Supersize me. *Dr. Dobb's Journal*. Retrieved on November 11, 2008, from http://www.ddj.com/architect/184415491

Beck, K. (1999). *Extreme programming explained: Embrace change*. Addison-Wesley Professional.

Ceschi, M., Sillitti, A., Succi, G., & De Panfilis, S. (2005). Project management in plan-based and agile companies. *IEEE Software*, *22*(3), 21–27. doi:10.1109/MS.2005.75

Chrissis, M. B., Konrad, M., & Shrum, S. (2003). *CMMI: Guidelines for process integration and product improvement*. Addison-Wesley Professional.

Cohen, D., Lindvall, M., & Costa, P. (2004). An introduction to agile methods. In M. Zelkowitz (Ed.), *Advances in computers* (pp. 1-66). New York: Elsevier Science.

Eckstein, J. (2004). *Agile software development in the large: Diving into the deep.* Dorset House Publishing.

Sillitti, A., Ceschi, M., Russo, B., & Succi, G. (2005). Managing uncertainty in requirements: A survey in documentation-driven and agile companies. *11th IEEE International Symposium on Software Metrics (METRICS 2005).*

Chapter 5
Coordination in Agile and Open Source

5.1 INTRODUCTION

Although the situation in the software industry is improved in the last years, the percentage of software project cancelled 18%, or challenged (late, over budget, and with less than the required features) 53% is still high[1]. Researchers and practitioners are looking for the magic solution or the *silver bullet* that will allow software companies to overcome the *software crisis* (Brooks, 1987). New development approaches like AMs and OSD models are some of the solutions identified (Feller & Fitzgerald, 2002; Abrahamsson *et al.*, 2003).

One critical problem in software development consist of coordinating interdependent processes involving many interacting stakeholders with different interests, points of view, and expectations (Toffolon & Dakhli, 2000).

Two inherent characteristics of software make coordination a critical issue and a primary cause of the software crisis. These characteristics are (Kraut & Streeter, 1995; Marchesi *et al.*, 2002):

1. **Complexity:** software systems are often very large and far beyond the ability of any individual or small group to create or even to understand in detail. Several, different groups work toward a common goal, share information, and

DOI: 10.4018/978-1-59904-681-5.ch005

need to coordinate their activities. A lot of interdependent decisions have to be made in the presence of incomplete information and high uncertainty.

2.   **Uncertainty:** software development is permeated by uncertainty. Environmental factors like technological innovations and market changes introduce uncertainty into software projects. The intangibility of software makes it difficult to review progress, thus introducing uncertainty into software project management. The flexibility of software and the volatile environment that software projects face makes change a main source of uncertainty. Changing and incomplete requirements increase uncertainty in software development. Finally, software is uncertain because the different subgroups involved in its development often have different beliefs about what it should do and how it should do it.

Coordination becomes much more difficult as project complexity and uncertainty increase (Kraut & Streeter, 1995).

This chapter focuses on how to coordinate software development when there is a high level of complexity and uncertainty. Companies adopting new development approaches like AMs and OSD models are investigated. In fact, AMs are suitable for developing software in dynamic and uncertain environment, while OSD models develop software in particularly complex conditions.

Using the framework provided by organization and game theory, we are going to identify the main kind of dependencies and coordination mechanisms both in OSD models and AMs.

5.2 WHAT IS COORDINATION?

5.2.1 Organization Theory

A common way to deal with complex problems consists of splitting the problem in smaller sub-parts easier to manage. The Fordist approach in product manufacturing is an example of this method (Ohno, 1988). According to the Fordist approach, division and specialization of labor permit to achieve perfection in the tasks and economies of scales (Womack *et al.*, 1991). In particular, complexity can be tamed through:

•   Clear identification of different activities to do
•   Specialization of competences

Clear division of tasks and separation of labor reduces complexity but can increase the integration need of the organization. Specialization causes *interdependency* among production units, and interdependency requires *coordination*.

Therefore, in a production process, it is important to manage and coordinate the interdependences among different units (Lawrence & Lorsch, 1967).

Nevertheless, there could be two different situations of interdependency. Only one results in coordination problems (Camerer & Knez, 1996).

The first situation is when there is a conflict between the individual goals and the common goals. For example, when more subjects have to share the same limited resources but there are not incentives to cooperate.

The second situation occurs when different decision makers have a common goal, but they can choose among different alternatives to achieve such goal. Different decision makers may choose different alternatives because of the lack of information about the choices of the others. In these situations, even though the goals are aligned, the lack of mutual expectations among actors results in *strategic uncertainty* and thus in *coordination problems* (Camerer & Knez, 1996).

5.2.2 Game Theory

Game theory is an extension of decision theory to situations involving strategic interaction (Weber, 2001).

Coordination problems have received a lot of attention from game-theorists. According to game theory, the essential aspect of coordination is the presence of *multiple equilibria* (Cooper, 1999).

To analyze these kinds of problems, game-theorists use a game called *pure coordination game* (Figure 1). This game represents the most basic form of the coordination problem, and it presents a situation of *strategic uncertainty*.

A game theoretic-representation of a situation has the following basic elements (Weber, 2001):

Figure 1. Pure coordination game

Player 2

		A	B
	A	1,1	0,0
Player 1	B	0,0	1,1

1. A set of decision makers or players
2. A set of actions available to each of the players
3. A mapping from all combinations of actions into outcomes
4. Preferences for each player over each of the outcomes
5. The information and beliefs held by players at any point in the game

In this game, there are two players and each has two actions (in this case they are labeled *A* and *B*). Each player values positively only the outcomes in which both players make the same choice. This game has two pure-strategy equilibriums: (A, A) and (B, B). Players do not care which equilibrium is reached, but only that their actions coincide. The only problem is figuring out which of two equally valued equilibriums will result.

The coordination problem arises because of the presence of two equilibriums and uncertainty about which one should be played. The game therefore captures the aspect of a problem that makes it a coordination problem: *strategic uncertainty*. Strategic uncertainty results from uncertainty about what actions others will take.

5.3 INTERDEPENDENCIES AND COORDINATION MECHANISMS

According to the framework proposed by Malone and Crowston (1994), coordination can be defined as "the act of managing interdependencies between activities performed to achieve a goal". They analyze group action in terms of actors performing interdependent activities to achieve goals. These activities may also require or create resources of various types.

This definition gives a prominent role to interdependence. In fact, if there is no interdependence, there is no need to coordinate activities (Malone & Crowston, 1990).

In order to address the *coordination problem* it is necessary to follow two main steps (Malone & Crowston, 1994):

1. Identify the main kinds of dependencies that can exist among production units, activities, or actors
2. Identify the coordination mechanisms that can be used to manage these dependencies

There are a wide variety of potential dependencies and the following list is by no means intended to be exhaustive. Different authors, mainly from the organizational research area, provided different conceptions of dependencies and alternative categorizations of the existing dependencies.

On the basis of the dependencies identified, organizational researchers have proposed several coordination mechanisms. For example, Thompson (1967) described three patterns of dependency (pooled, sequential, reciprocal) with corresponding coordination mechanisms (standardization, plans, mutual adjustment).

Mintzberg (1979) presented a similar set of coordination mechanisms: mutual adjustment, direct supervision and four kind of standardization.

Malone and Crowston (1994) identify several common dependencies (shared resources, producer-consumer, simultaneity constraints, etc.) with the related coordination mechanisms (resource allocation, standardization, and synchronization).

Game theorists similarly have a list of coordination mechanisms useful for addressing strategic uncertainty. Among these are making certain actions salient or focal points, using precedent to coordinated activity, statements by people in authority positions, communication between players, and repeated interaction (Weber, 2001).

It is possible to find a parallel between the types of coordination mechanisms provided by organizational researchers and game theorists. For example, both standardization and salience facilitate coordination creating tacitly expectations of the correct action to be performed (Weber, 2001).

Finally, it is important to notice that there are many different coordination mechanisms that could be used to address the same kind of dependence. For instance, to address a shared resource dependency it is possible to use both plans and authority.

5.3.1 Interdependences

Crowston (1994) suggested a structural taxonomy of dependencies and associated coordination mechanisms based on all the possible relationships between *tasks* and *resources*. For simplicity, he considered *tasks* both the goals to be achieved and the activities to be performed. With the term *resources* he included everything used or affected by activities, both material things and effort/time of actors.

According to this framework, there are three main kinds of dependencies between tasks and resources (Crowston 1994; Crowston 2005):

1.   Task-resource dependencies
2.   Task-task dependencies
3.   Resource-resource dependencies

5.3.1.1 Task-Resource Dependencies

This dependency occurs when a task requires some resource to be performed. If there is only one appropriate resource known, then that resource must be the one used. However, in many situations there are many possibly appropriate resources, creating the problem of resource assignment. A general resources allocation process encompasses the following five steps:

- Identification of the resource required by the task
- Identification of the resources available
- Choice of a particular resource
- Assignment of the resource to the task

One very important special case of resource allocation is task assignment, that is, allocating the scarce time of actors (resource) to the tasks they will perform (Malone & Crowston, 1994).

Different coordination mechanisms can be used for resource assignment, for instance, hierarchy or market (Crowston, 1994).

5.3.1.2 Task-Task Dependencies

According to Crowston (1994) the only way two tasks can be dependent is via some kind of common resources. Consequently, there are three major kinds of dependencies among tasks:

1. Shared resource
2. Producer-consumer
3. Common output

Shared Resource
The first kind of dependency arises whenever multiple tasks/processes share some limited resources (Malone & Crowston, 1994).

Thompson called this dependency *pooled interdependence* and described it as a weak or indirect interdependence that arises only in the global functioning of the organization as a whole (Thompson, 1967).

To understand the potential constraints of this dependency it is necessary to introduce the notions of reusability and shareabilty (Crowston, 1994).

Reusability describes a situation in which many tasks can use the resource over time. Not all the resources are reusable; some of them such as raw materials and time can only be used once. Because of this, these kinds of resources are non-shareable.

Shareablity describes a situation in which many tasks can use the same resource. If the common resource is shareable, there is no conflict for two actors to use it. On the contrary, if the resource is not shareable, then the two tasks cannot be performed simultaneously and a coordination mechanism is necessary (prioritization, plans, etc.).

Nevertheless, in some situations in which there is no conflicting use of a resource, and more tasks require at the same time the same resource, a *simultaneity constraint* can emerge. A suitable coordination mechanism for this dependency can be the adoption of a synchronization process (Malone & Crowston, 1994).

Producer-Consumer

A producer-consumer or sequential dependency arises when a task creates a resource (output) that another task requires as an input (Thompson, 1967).

In this case there is a precedence or prerequisite dependency between the two tasks, requiring that the tasks be performed in the correct order and the flow of the resource between the two be managed (Crowston, 1994).

Precedence dependencies often imply additional constraints on how tasks are performed, such as (Malone & Crowston, 1994; Weber, 2001):

- Usability constraints: the first task has to produce something that should be usable by the second task that receives it.
- Transfer constraints: the output produced by the first task must be transferred to the second task when needed.

To address prerequisite dependency a notification or planning process can be used. Usability constraints can be managed by standardization, participatory design, customer involvement and negotiation, or by testing (Crowston, 1994).

Managing transfer constraints may involve physical transportation or in the case of intangible assets such as information, the suitable coordination mechanism is communication (Malone & Crowston, 1994). Managing transfer dependency sometimes involves storing things. Thus, inventories represent buffers between tasks that permit to control the timing of the different tasks.

A particular category of sequential dependency is the *reciprocal dependency*. Malone and Crowston defined reciprocal dependence as "where each task requires inputs from the other" (Malone & Crowston, 1994). According to Thompson reciprocal dependence occurs when the outputs of each task become inputs for other tasks creating a bilateral dependency (Thompson, 1967).

Reciprocal dependence has several of the features of sequential dependence. Its unique aspect is the fact that actors can affect outcomes reciprocally and repeatedly. Their role may not be competed once they have acted (Weber, 2001). Due to its continuity, reciprocal dependency can be primarily managed through mutual adjustment (Thompson, 1967).

Common Output
The third kind of dependency, common output, occurs when two tasks contribute to create the same resource or output (Crowston, 2005). This dependency can have either positive or negative effects. In fact, if both tasks do exactly and unintentionally the same thing, it may result in a problem of duplication or waste of resources.

Nevertheless, two tasks can affect different aspects of a common resource. This is the case of more actors that collaborate in order to achieve a common goal.

This kind of dependency is quite complex because it requires coordination of the resources and time of the different actors. Moreover, there is a problem of interoperability among the different parts produced by the different actors.

The coordination mechanism can involve two stages, that is, goal selection and goal decomposition (Malone & Crowston, 1994)

5.3.1.3 Resource-Resource Dependencies

It is possible for different resources to be interdependent, for example, by being connected together in some kind of assembly (Crowston, 1994).

In this case, changes to a resource could affect the state of another resources and it is not always easy to identify the relationships among resources.

A critical step to manage these dependencies is to identify all the potential relationships among resources. Afterward, it is necessary to adopt a coordination mechanism such as standardization of the interfaces or a rapid information sharing process.

5.3.2 Coordination Mechanisms

Coordination problems arise because there are interdependencies among activities (Malone & Crowston, 1990). Consequently, there are two possible and main ways to deal with coordination problems:

1. Managing interdependencies
2. Reducing interdependencies

5.3.2.1 Managing Interdependencies

The above dependencies can be managed by a variety of coordination mechanisms. Projects with different characteristics rely on different coordination techniques (Kraut & Streeter, 1995).

The main characteristics that should be evaluated in order to choose an appropriate coordination mechanism are:

- Project uncertainty/complexity
- Project goals (quality, customer satisfaction, efficiency
- Project phase

Coordination mechanisms can be *informal* or *formal*. The *informal* coordination techniques are more suitable when uncertainty is greater, the projects is particularly complex, or it is in the requirements analysis phase, and the goal is to deliver an effective project. Informal techniques are communication-oriented and highly interactive; they can be divided in two main types:

1. Remote, technology mediated, such as emails, chat, etc.
2. Direct, face-to-face such as informal meetings, ad-hoc communication, etc.

The *formal* coordination techniques are more suitable when uncertainty is lower, the projects is not complex, or it is during the implementation/ testing phases, and the goal is to deliver an efficient project (Kraut & Streeter, 1995).

Formal techniques are more control-oriented and less interactive. Formal coordination techniques mainly involve written communication such as plans, reports, and formal standards.

Both game theory and organization theory provide formal and informal techniques to manage coordination problems. The main coordination mechanisms are the following:

Focal Points, Precedents, Standardization
When it is difficult or impossible to communicate one way of solving coordination problems is by providing everyone with some focal point for each person's expectation. Focal points are equilibriums that for different reasons become expected solutions to coordination problems.

Such equilibriums or norms can emerge in a spontaneous way, for example as result of past interactions (precedents), or they can be *recommended* or *imposed* by an authority. An example of this second case is standardization.

Organization standards can be considered as focal points as they create coordination by tacitly indication the correct action to be performed (Weber, 2001).

Coordination by standardization can be accomplished by establishing rules or procedures that govern the performance of each activity. These predetermined rules enhance the predictability and regularity of the actions in a given process (Mintzberg, 1979).

This coordination mechanism is a common way of managing sequential and reciprocal dependency and work best in repeated and stable environments (Malone & Crowston, 1994).

Plans, Authority

Coordination by plans involves addressing a particular interdependence problem by developing schedules and formal rules for action.

Coordination by plan often requires an organizational authority (Thompson, 1967). In fact, an authority position is responsible for implementing the correct plan, or set of actions (Weber, 2001).

An authority can also solve a coordination problem simply recommending or imposing a particular action. Another important role of the authority is that of creating a common knowledge among project participants. This common knowledge stimulates mutual expectations and reduces strategic uncertainty.

Mutual Adjustment, Repeated Interactions, Communication

Repeated interactions result in information and common knowledge that allows different actors to mutually adjust their expectations and actions (Thompson, 1967).

Communication is a powerful coordination mechanism. It creates common knowledge and shared expectations thus enabling mutual adjustment. These coordination mechanisms are useful in changing environments where the same informal or formal rules cannot be applied repeatedly across situations (Weber, 2001).

5.3.2.2 Reducing Interdependencies

Studies in R&D provide alternative solutions to coordination problems (Grinter *et al.*, 1999; Herbsleb & Grinter, 1999). These solutions address the coordination problem focusing on its primary source, that is, the existing interdependencies among activities. These approaches focus on designing the organization and assigning the work so as to reduce the amount of interdependence and communication among activities. There are three main solutions:

1. **Functional areas model**: in the *functional area* model, expertise for a specific functional area involved in development of the product is located at a single site.

2. **Product structure model**: decisions about a product structure would determine who would need to coordinate their work with whom. The architecture of the system influence the communications required among project members (Grinter *et al.*, 1999). In particular, tasks associated with a particular component are generally highly interrelated, so co-locating everyone performing those tasks should facilitate needed communication. On the other hand, tasks associated with different components, are likely to be much more loosely coupled and require less communication and coordination. This model provides the basis for designing modular products.

3. **Process steps model**: the activities for a given process step are co-located. In fact, the coupling of tasks within a process step is likely to be much tighter than the coupling between process steps.

To deal with strategic uncertainty it is possible both to reduce the interdependencies and to manage them with the existing coordination mechanisms. These two strategies can be used in parallel.

5.4 COORDINATION AND NEW SOFTWARE DEVELOPMENT APPROACHES

One of the most challenging aspects in software development is achieving a tight coordination among the various groups involved in the development process (Curtis *et al.*, 1988). Complexity and uncertainty make coordination a major but inevitable problem in software development.

The next sections will present the main dependencies and coordination mechanisms in two particularly complex and uncertain domains: OS and AMs.

5.4.1 Open Source Software Development

Large software development projects tend to be highly complex. Consequently, they need to be tightly coordinated. In the recent years, increasing numbers of large software development projects are conducted on a global scale that disperses processes to different locations (Carmel & Agarwal, 2001).

The driving force behind this tendency toward globalization of software projects is largely economic. In particular, the two strategic reasons for distributed software development are cost advantage and labor availability (Carmel, 1999).

Due to globalization of large software projects, achieving a tight coordination among the various groups involved in the development process is even more complex. Consequently, new and different coordination mechanisms have to be identified and applied.

The extreme of distributed development is OSD. With its globally distributed developer force and extremely rapid code evolution, open source is the extreme in *virtual software projects*, and exemplifies many of the advantages and challenges of distributed software development.

OSS is software for which the source code is distributed or accessible via the Internet without charge or limitations on modifications and future distribution by third parties. This definition highlights two main characteristics of the software open source that are (Feller & Fitzgerald, 2002):

- **Free redistribution:** There should be no restriction from selling or giving away the software, and no royalties or other fees for such sale.
- **Availability of the source code:** The program must include source code, and must allow distribution in source code as well as compiled form. One of the key technological strengths of OSS is the ability for users to evaluate and modify the underlying source code.

The OSSD process can be briefly characterized as consisting of distributed, parallel development supported by rapid release cycles and communication methods, and collaboration among highly talented and motivated developers and users (Feller & Fitzgerald, 2002).

Some of the characteristics highlighted in this definition are particularly important for the purpose of this chapter:

- *Parallel development* is a key characteristic of the OSD process. Parallel development refers to the practice of individual developers working on one aspect of a large system at the same time that other individuals work on another aspect of the same system. However this is not always the case. In fact, in OSS projects can happen that individual developers work in parallel on the same aspect of the same system. In the first case development speed is improved while in the second case product quality is improved.
- OSD processes involve large communities of *globally distributed developers* that interact and collaborate primarily using a wide variety of Internet technologies. This global nature of OSS communities improves the overall quality of OSS. It guaranties truly independent peer reviews and prompt feedback.
- Other key aspects of the OSD processes, critical to the success of the projects, are the *high level of skills* in the core developers and their *high motivation*.
- In OSD, due to the prompt feedback/communication and to the parallel development process, the process is organized in *rapid, incremental releases*.

- Typically, in OS projects there are two tiers of developers participating in the effort: a core group that is relatively small, and a much larger pool of contributors. The core developers are actively and frequently involved in the development of the product. Often, the core developers as initial project founders are responsible of the requirement definition, analysis, and design phases. Contributors submit occasionally to the system, as they have time, interest, or ideas.

Findings from different studies (Curtis *et al.*, 1988; Kraut & Streeter, 1995; Herbsleb & Grinter, 1999) show that informal coordination mechanisms, such as unplanned and ad-hoc communication, are extremely important in supporting collaboration and coordinating activities. This is particularly true in complex environments as distributed software development. Therefore, one of the central problems of OSD is generated by the fact that distance profoundly reduces the amount of such informal mechanisms (Grinter *et al.*, 1999). Some of the barriers which led to coordination breakdowns in OS projects are (Herbsleb & Grinter, 1999):

- Lack of unplanned contact
- Knowing who to contact about what
- Cost of initiating contact
- Ability to communicate effectively
- Lack of trust or willingness to communicate

To understand how OSD overcomes the barriers to coordination that are imposed by distance, it is necessary to identify the main kind of potential dependencies in open source projects and the most used coordination mechanisms.

5.4.1.1 Task-Resource Dependencies

In OSD the time of the different actors or contributors involved in the project is a limited and consumable resource that has to be assigned to the different tasks of the development process. This task-resource dependency requires a coordination mechanism called task allocation.

In a proprietary process the choice is made based on specialization and division of labor. Typically, the project manager assigns developers to the process tasks on the basis of the skills required by the task and the specialization of the person. This approach requires a fair amount of work and experience for the assigner, but it easier to coordinate (Crowston, 1994).

OSD does not rely on explicit assignment but instead relies on developers to assign themselves to tasks on the basis of their experiences and interests. Task allocation occurs through voluntary assignment. This approach makes the assignment process similar to the market approach where a description of each task is sent to all available agents. Each evaluates the task and if interested in working on it, submits a bid. The task is then assigned to the best bidder (Crowston, 1994).

In OSD the description of the tasks is available in terms of requirements specification and design of the application. Each contributor evaluates the tasks and chooses autonomously whether to work on a task if interested. In contrast to the market mechanism, contributors do not submit a bid for the task. In fact, studies affirm that OS programmers usually tend to perform the tasks without declaring the commitment for them. In particular, they perform the tasks without a formal assignment mechanism (Yamauchi *et al.*, 2000). Their contributions are subsequently reviewed and evaluated by the core developers (Cubranic & Booth, 1999) or by the community (Yamauchi *et al.*, 2000; Feller & Fitzgerald, 2002).

5.4.1.2 Task-Task Dependencies

Shared-Resources

This dependency arises when multiple tasks require the same limited resource. In OSD contributors provide their own computing resources, bring their own software development tools with them, and do not have to share the same workplace. Nevertheless, there is an important limited resource that needs to be shared among contributors: information.

Contributors to an OS project need to share information about (Gutwin *et al.*, 2004):

- Who is on the project
- Where in the code they are working
- What they are doing
- What their plans are

Since developers rarely meet face-to-face, the informal communication channels do not work in a distributed development context, it is necessary to find substitutive communication mechanisms. In game theory terms, the contributors need to share information that creates a common knowledge, thus enabling the coordination of their efforts. In OS projects there is not an authority that creates common knowledge.

Gutwin *et al.* (2004) named this common knowledge *group awareness information* and described different mechanisms that allow distributed developers to maintain awareness of one another.

The primary mechanisms for sharing information in OS project are informal and technology mediated communication tools: mailing lists and chats web sites (Yamauchi *et al.*, 2000; Gutwin *et al.*, 2004).

The mailing list is the primary communication channel for an OS project. It is used to gather and provide a reasonable awareness of who is on the project and what their activities are. Furthermore, by *overhearing* conversations on the list it permits a considerable implicit information sharing (Gutwin *et al.*, 2004)

Chat conversations provide a general awareness of the project. The real-time and informal nature of the channel provides an opportunity for the *unplanned contacts*. These contacts are particularly important in order to keep the project coordinated (Herbsleb & Grinter, 1999).

The success of the above mechanisms for sharing information and creating a common knowledge depend strongly on the incentives to cooperate of the contributors. In fact, in order to maintain group awareness, contributors have to spend some extra effort reading the lists, writing good-quality responses, and helping others. In OS projects, there are many incentives to cooperate. For example, the sense of belonging to a community, or the reputation factor (Gutwin *et al.*, 2004; Feller & Fitzgerald, 2002).

Developers use web sites to share information. As instance, such information includes architecture, access policies, bugs, etc.

OS developers can contribute adding new code or fixing bugs to the existing code. In both cases the code itself becomes a resource that has to be shared (Crowston, 1994).

For example, if there are two problems on the same module, then both fixing tasks need the same code, thus creating a shared resource dependency. Moreover, if more developers are interested in changing the same module (to add or modify functionalities), the code is the initial resource for their tasks and has to be shared.

In the proprietary development process, this dependency is managed by assigning modules of code to individual programmers (individual code ownership) (Crowston, 1994)

In OSD, there is no code ownership because of the basic open source principle of free availability of the source code. Thus, it is necessary to coordinate the use of the code that becomes a limited but shareable resource.

To manage this dependency most open source projects use configuration tools like CVS[2] or Subversion[3] (Feller & Fitzgerald, 2002).

CVS and Subversion are Version Control Systems (VCS) that allow remote access to the source code and enable multiple developers to work on the same version of the source code simultaneously. They centralize the source code so that developers can always refer to the latest code. This centralization gives consistency and is crucial to merge the work of dispersed individuals in a context of parallel development without formal division of work (Yamauchi *et al.*, 2000).

VCS allow developers to work both on different components of the same system and also on the same components in parallel of the same system.

Producer-Consumer

The producer-consumer or prerequisite dependency arises when a task creates an output that another task requires as an input (Thompson, 1967).

A key characteristic of OS processes is parallel development. Because of the modularity of the code (Feller & Fitzgerald, 2002), a large number of developers can work simultaneously rather than wait on each other. The various members of OS projects usually work on highly cohesive tasks within loosely coupled modules. Consequently, there is not sequential tasks dependency among modules that has to be managed. The only coordination mechanism among modules is standardization of the modules interfaces.

Nevertheless, among tasks within a single module there is a sort of prerequisite dependency requiring that the tasks be performed in a sequential order (Crowston, 1994). These tasks results in the following life cycle of the implementation phase (Feller & Fitzgerald, 2002).

1. **Code:** The contributors submit the code to general OS community
2. **Review:** The community gives truly independent feedback as suggestions and contributions
3. **Pre-commit test:** Contributors test the code carefully mainly delegating testing to the user community
4. **Development release:** The module is incorporated in the development release
5. **Parallel debugging:** A global parallel debugging is performed by the community or by new contributors
6. **Production release:** Contributions became part of the production release

To coordinate these tasks the notification process used in OS projects is mainly based on informal, technology mediated communication tools: mailing lists and chats.

The above prerequisite dependencies imply additional constraints: usability and transfer constraints (Malone & Crowston, 1994). The output of each task must be usable as input for the other task and must be transferred.

In OSD, the main mechanisms for managing usability constraints are testing and user involvement. The releases of the code are used to manage the transfer constraint (Crowston, 1994).

Common Output

This dependency occurs when two tasks contribute to the same output (Crowston, 2005).

OS is a collectivist phenomenon; more individuals join their efforts in order to achieve a common goal (Feller & Fitzgerald, 2002). Core developers and contributors collaborate to develop or enhance the same application; their goals are aligned but there is a lack of information about the mutual choices.

Due to the parallel development process and the modular nature of most open source products, it may happen that more developers choose to work on the same component. In this case there is a risk of duplication or waste of effort. In most OS projects, this kind of parallelism and duplication is not viewed negatively. In fact, in situation where developers contribute to the same components product quality is improved (Feller & Fitzgerald, 2002).

In OS projects, to manage this dependency, all developers need to have the same *tail-light to follow*. In fact, having well-understood requirements and well-established design patterns is fundamental in order to allows a multiple developers to contribute independently (Feller & Fitzgerald, 2002).

Furthermore, in the OS community there are some cultural and social norms that govern implicitly the behaviors of the developers and take the place of formal project management (Feller & Fitzgerald, 2002). These norms avoid dangerous behaviors like *forking* and create mutual expectations regarding the actions of the contributors thus reducing the coordination need.

5.4.1.3 Resource-Resource Dependency

This dependency occurs when multiple resources are interdependent and changes to a resource could affect the state of other resources.

In software development there could be this kind of dependency between modules. A module depends on another if the first makes use of services provided by the second (Crowston, 1994). Interactions between the different parts of software are not always easy to identify or avoid, and it is necessary to find a solution for this coordination problem.

To manage these dependencies, OSD tends to use highly modular architectures for their products. Modules must be loosely coupled but also highly cohesive and address a single well-defined purpose. To achieve this goal, modules interfaces have to be defined upfront.

This solution allows developers to work in parallel thus affecting positively the development speed. Furthermore, the loosely coupled modules can be modified and implemented independently reducing the need of communication among developers (Feller & Fitzgerald, 2002).

The adopting of modular architectures can also be noticed considering the strong tendency towards object-oriented programming languages in OS projects (Feller & Fitzgerald, 2002).

In some cases, it is necessary to coordinate changes on different modules. This requires a rapid information sharing process. OS projects adopt mainly the informal, technology mediated, communication tools like mailing lists and text chat.

5.4.2 Agile Methods: The XP case

Coordination is not only a problem for large and distributed software development projects. Coordination can be difficult to achieve even if the development teams are co-located and the project does not involve many actors.

In particular, in highly dynamic and turbulent contexts the level of uncertainty is higher and it is very difficult to coordinate successfully. The situation evolves over time, information emerges during the project, and the communication need is higher. To develop software in this kind of environments, it is necessary to be adaptive rather than predictive. The development team has to change its direction quickly on the basis of incomplete knowledge. In these highly uncertain environments it is necessary to adopt a flexible development approach and thus a flexible coordination strategy.

AMs are a set of development techniques designed to address modern challenges of changing and uncertain environments.

AMs highlight the importance of *Agility*. Agility is the ability to both create and respond to change in order to profit in a turbulent business environment. Consequently, agile organizations have an ability to react, to respond quickly and effectively to both anticipated and unanticipated changes in the business environment.

AMs emphasize the human factor in the development process and the importance of direct, face-to-face communications among key stakeholders, the value of simplicity, perceived as an elimination of waste, and continuous process improvement, as the transposition to the Software Industry of Total Quality Management (Poppendieck & Poppendieck, 2003; Beck, 1999).

The XP four values are implemented via a set of 12 practices. Hereafter only the practices that will be useful for our discussion will be briefly described:

- **Pair programming:** All code to be included in a production release is created by two people working together at a single computer.
- **Collective code ownership:** It encourages everyone to contribute new ideas to all segments of the project. Anyone can change any part of the code at any time.

- **Continuous integration:** Developers should be integrating and releasing code into the code repository every few hours, whenever possible. Continuous integration avoids diverging or fragmented development efforts.
- **Coding standards:** Coding rules exist and are followed by the programmers. Coding standards keep the code consistent and easy for the entire team to read and refactor. Communication through the code should be emphasized.
- **Testing:** Software development is test-driven. Unit tests are implemented before the code and are run continuously. Customers write the functional tests, this permit to increase the trust of the customer in the system.
- **Metaphor:** This practice gives a coherent and consistent vision of the system both to the customer and to the developers.
- **Refactoring:** It keeps the system simple avoiding unnecessary complexity. This practice consists in removing redundancy, eliminating unused functionality, and revitalizing obsolete designs.

In the following sections the main dependencies and coordination mechanisms will be presented.

5.4.2.1 Task-Resource

In Agile approaches, due to the importance of rapidity, the time of the developers is the most important and limited resource. This resource has to be allocated to the different tasks of the development process. In XP the task-resource dependency is managed with the following task allocation process.

The XP development process starts with the developers, manager, and customer collaborating in order to write the user stories. A user story is a chunk of functionality that is of value to the customer. Customers prioritize the user stories.

The development team, brainstorm the things that must be done to accomplish a user story; each of these is an engineering task. Tasks are scheduled by asking developers to sign up for the tasks they want, then asking them to estimate their tasks (Fowler *et al.*, 1999).

By signing up, a programmer accepts the responsibility for working on those tasks during the iteration. Programmers can sign up for things they have a desire to do, which keeps them motivated. Developers are so varied that there is almost always someone who likes doing anything. For unpopular tasks, there could an informal or formal sharing process. In the second case team members may choose to do a rotation to take turns doing unpopular work (Fowler *et al.*, 1999).

In agile teams, as in the OS community, there is not an authority assigning tasks on the basis of the people specialization. XP adopts cross-functional teams with team members that are more generalists that specialists. XP teams draw together individuals performing all the roles and rotations from one role to another are common. Consequently, every member of the team plays different roles at different times during the project, and has to be skilled enough to play all the roles effectively (Chau *et al.*, 2003).

The difference between the voluntary task allocation process of the agile and the OS approach is in the fact that developers have to declare their commitment for the tasks chosen. Each member of the team knows who is performing what. This information or common knowledge is critical to coordinate the development process.

5.4.2.2 Task-Task Dependencies

Shared-Resource

In fast-moving environments, in which information is often scarce and uncertain, decisions need to be made quickly and well. In order to make rapid decisions, individuals require knowledge and mechanisms to share knowledge. Consequently, knowledge becomes a critical resource that has to be shared among team members. In XP, this shared-resource dependency is managed as follows.

More traditional software development approaches, like the Waterfall model, facilitate knowledge sharing primarily through documentation. Accordingly, documentation transfer is the mechanism used to coordinate knowledge sharing.

In contrast, agile methods suggest that most of the written documentation can be replaced by informal, face-to-face communications among team members with a stronger emphasis on tacit knowledge rather than explicit knowledge (Chau *et al.*, 2003).

The limited sizes of the co-located development teams allow developers to communicate frequently and directly. These informal communication mechanisms compensate for the reduction in documentation and allow developers to keep coordinate during the project (Curtis et al., 1988; Kraut& Streeter, 1995, Herbsleb & Grinter, 1999).

The key of knowledge sharing here are the interactions among members of the teams, which happen voluntarily, and not by an order from the managers.

In XP there are several specific practices that facilitate knowledge sharing. For example, pair programming encourages the sharing of tacit knowledge such as system knowledge, coding convention, design practices, and tool usage tricks. Furthermore, pair rotation improves communication, mutual trust, and informal training (Chau *et al.*, 2003).

Another practice that facilitates creation and distribution of common knowledge are the stand-up meetings. During these daily meetings, each developer presents his/her work done since the last meeting. Such presentations allow team members to know who has worked/is working on which part of the system. Thus, they know whom to contact when they need to work on parts of the system that are unfamiliar (Chau *et al.*, 2003).

To reduce the knowledge transfer time, XP uses coding standards. The standards are made public for the entire team thus avoiding time-consuming debates of coding styles. Furthermore, agile methods and in particular XP suggest that explicit knowledge including user stories, designs, and models should be visible and collectively owned (Chau *et al.*, 2003).

In XP the collective code ownership practice create a shared-resource dependency where the resource to share is the code.

This practice is different from the traditional individual code ownership where each module of the system has a single owner who performs all tasks that modify that code. It is also different from the no code ownership of the OSD approach where the code is freely available to all contributors and nobody owns any particular piece of code (Crowston, 2005).

In XP every member of the development team owns the code and can change any piece of code in the system at any time (Beck, 1999). Everybody takes responsibility for the whole of the system.

This dependency can be managed through two XP practices continuous integration and testing. Continuous integration avoids diverging or fragmented development efforts while testing ensure that all the changes in the code do not contain errors and can be accepted (Beck, 1999).

Producer-Consumer

XP adopts an incremental and iterative development process with short and frequent releases. The releases are made of more iteration of two/three weeks. During an iteration the analysis, design, testing, and code tasks are performed by pairs of programmers (Beck, 1999).

Among these tasks there is a particular category of prerequisite dependency: reciprocal dependency. In fact, the outputs of each task become inputs for other tasks through the mechanism of feedback. In other words, there is not a unilateral dependency between tasks as for the sequential dependency. The tasks are reciprocally dependent and the actors performing the tasks can affect outcomes repeatedly (Weber, 2001).

For example, the result of the design task becomes input for the coding task thus affecting it. Then, as programmers code, a better design solution can be found. In this case, the coding task produces something affecting the design task (feedback).

Reciprocal dependencies result in a process of mutual adjustment. Actors perform their tasks using the input received and adjust the output of their tasks on the basis of the feedback received.

5.5 REFERENCES

Abrahamsson, P., Salo, O., Ronkainen, J., & Warsta, J. (2003). *Agile software development methods: Review and Analysis* (p. 478). Espoo, Finland: Technical Research Centre of Finland, VTT Publications.

Beck, K. (1999). *Extreme programming explained: Embrace change*. Addison-Wesley Professional.

Brooks, F. (1987). No silver bullet: Essence and accidents of software engineering. *IEEE Computer, 20*(4), 10–19.

Camerer, C. F., & Knez, M. (1996). Coordination in organizations: A game-theoretic perspective. In Z. Shapira (Ed.), *Organizational decision making*. New York: Cambridge University Press.

Carmel, E. (1999). *Global software teams: Collaborating across borders and time-zones*. Prentice Hall.

Carmel, E., & Agarwal, R. (2001). Tactical approaches for alleviating distance in global software development. *IEEE Software, 18*(2), 22-29. doi:10.1109/52.914734

Chau, T., Maurer, F., & Melnik, G. (2003). Knowledge sharing: Agile methods vs. tayloristic methods. *12ᵗʰ International Workshop on Enabling Technologies: Infrastructure for Collaborative Enterprises*.

Cooper, R. W. (1999). *Coordination game: Complementarities and macroeconomics*. Cambridge University Press.

Crowston, K. (1994). *A taxonomy of organizational dependencies and coordination mechanisms*. Retrieved on November 11, 2008, from http://ccs.mit.edu/papers/CCSWP174.html

Crowston, K. (2005). The bug fixing process in proprietary and free/libre open source software: A coordination theory analysis. In V. Grover & M. L. Markus (Eds.), *Business process transformation*. Armonk, NY: M. E. Sharpe Inc.

Cubranic, D., & Booth, K. S. (1999). Coordinating open-source software development. *8ᵗʰ Workshop on Enabling Technologies (WETICE '99)*.

Curtis, W., Krasner, H., & Iscoe, N. (1988). A field study of the software design process for large systems. *Communications of the ACM, 31*(11), 1268-1287. doi:10.1145/50087.50089

Feller, J., & Fitzgerald, B. (2002). *Understanding open source software development*. Addison-Wesley.

Fowler, M., Beck, K., Brant, J., Opdyke, W., & Roberts, D. (1999) *Refactoring: Improving the design of existing code*. Addison-Wesley Professional.

Grinter, R. E., Herbsleb, J. D., & Perry, D. E. (1999). The geography of coordination: Dealing with distance in R&D work. *ACM SIGGROUP Conference on Supporting Group Work.*

Gutwin, C., Penner, R., & Schneider, K. (2004). Group awareness in distributed software development. *2004 ACM Conference on Computer Supported Cooperative Work.*

Herbsleb, J. D., & Grinter, R. E. (1999). Splitting the organization and integrating the code: Conway's law revisited. *International Conference on Software Engineering (ICSE'99).*

Kraut, R., & Streeter, L. (1995). Coordination in software development. *Communications of the ACM, 38*(3), 69-81. doi:10.1145/203330.203345

Lawrence, P. R., & Lorsch, J. W. (1967). *Organization and environment: Managing differentiation and integration*. Harvard Business School Press.

Malone, T. W., & Crowston, K. (1990). What is coordination theory and how can it help design cooperative work systems. *1990 ACM Conference on Computer-Supported Cooperative Work.*

Malone, T. W., & Crowston, K. (1994). The interdisciplinary theory of coordination. *ACM Computing Surveys, 26*(1), 87–119. doi:10.1145/174666.174668

Marchesi, M., Succi, G., Wells, D., & Williams, L. (2002). *Extreme programming perspectives*. Addison-Wesley.

Mintzberg, H. (1979). *The structuring of organization*. Englewood Cliffs, NJ: Prentice-Hall.

Ohno, T. (1988). *Toyota production system: Beyond large-scale production*. Productivity Press.

Poppendieck, M., & Poppendieck, T. (2003). *Lean software development: An agile toolkit*. Addison-Wesley Professional.

Thompson, J. D. (1967). *Organizations in action: Social science bases of administrative theory*. New York: McGraw-Hill.

Toffolon, C., & Dakhli, S. (2000). A framework for studying the coordination process in software engineering. *2000 ACM Symposium on Applied Computing.*

Weber, R. (2001). *Organizational coordination: A game-theoretic view*. Retrieved on November 11, 2008, from http://www.andrew.cmu.edu/user/rweber/Files/org-coord.pdf

Womack, J. P., Jones, D., & Roos, D. (1991). *The machine that changed the world: The story of lean production*. Harper Perennial.

Yamauchi, Y., Yokozawa, M., Shinohara, T., & Ishida, T. (2000). Collaboration with lean media: How open-source software succeeds. *Computer Supported Cooperative Work Conference (CSCW'00)*.

ENDNOTES

[1]   The Standish Group International (2001). *Extreme Chaos*.
[2]   http://www.nongnu.org/cvs/ (accessed on November 11, 2008)
[3]   http://subversion.tigris.org/ (accessed on November 11, 2008)

Chapter 6
Other Agile Methods

6.1 INTRODUCTION

The most well known AMs are Extreme Programming (XP) (Beck, 1999) and SCRUM (Schwaber & Beedle, 2001) but there are several more (Abrahamsson *et al.*, 2002):

- Crystal (Cockburn, 2004)
- Dynamic System Development Method (DSDM) (Stapleton, 1997)
- Lean Software Development (LSD) (Poppendieck & Poppendieck, 2003)
- Feature Driven Development (FDD) (Palmer & Felsing, 2002)
- Agile Modeling (AM) (Ambler, 2002)
- …

In this chapter we briefly summarize some of them highlighting their specific features.

DOI: 10.4018/978-1-59904-681-5.ch006

Table 1. Crystal subgroups

Methodology	Team (n° people)
Crystal Clear	2-6
Crystal Yellow	6-20
Crystal Orange	20-40
Crystal Red	40-80

6.2 CRYSTAL

In the early '90s, the IBM Consulting Group hired Alistair Cockburn to build a methodology for object-oriented development.

Cockburn investigated a large number of software projects and asked to each team to identify the main reasons for their own success. Cockburn has defined Crystal (Cockburn, 2004) as a family of AMs, because he believed that different kinds of projects require different development methodologies.

All the Crystal methodologies are based on the following paradigm: "strong on communication, light on work products". Compare to XP (Beck, 1999), the Crystal family shows many differences: XP is based on a well defined set of development rules, on the contrary, Crystal does not include such rigid constraints but gives a lot of freedom to the development team. Hence, this methodology allows a greater individuality inside the team and a more relaxed work habits. Crystal is easier to adopt for a team, but XP produces better results and guarantees a higher productivity.

6.2.1 Crystal Family and its Subgroups

There are several subgroups in the Crystal methodology. These groups, identified with a color, are defined by the number of the developers in the team (Table 1).

Table 2 shows project qualities in relation to the size of the development team. On the vertical axis it shows the number of people (from 1 till 1000). The basic idea is that the more people are working on a single project the greater will be the need of coordination among team members. The vertical axis shows the potential damage caused by the hidden defects of the system. In the graph, every square identifies a set of projects that could use the same combination of coordination and politics.

The label of every cell shows the maximum damage and the importance of common coordination in these projects; for example, D40 refers to projects with 20-40 people and a potential loss of the available money.

The different levels show that projects have different priorities; some of them stress the productivity, others the legal responsibility or the costs.

Table 2. Characteristics of different projects

Life (L)	L6	L20	L40	L100	L200	L500	L1000
Essential money (E)	E6	E20	E40	E100	E200	E500	E1000
Discretionary money (D)	D6	D20	D40	D100	D200	D500	D1000
Comfort	C6	C20	C40	C100	C200	C500	C1000
	1-6	-20	-40	-100	-200	-500	-1000

Figure 1 shows three quantities: the weight of the methodology to use, the size of the problem to solve, and the size of the team.

At the beginning, a small size team can focus on a specific kind of problems. Adding some elements to this methodology it is actually possible to improve the quality of the work and cope with larger problems. The continuous addition of others elements to the methodology, generates an increment of the bureaucratic load, therefore it is necessary to spend more effort to find out the appropriate methodology for a specific kind of problem. For this reason, the size of the problem has to be reduced.

For larger teams the curve is similar, but it does not present a so abrupt decline. These kinds of teams require more coordination elements for working in an optimal way and they consist of more people that are able to solve the larger problems.

As time goes by and the size of the methodology grows, also larger teams begin to be less productive; therefore, solving larger problems successfully becomes more difficult.

To find out whether small or large teams are better, it is necessary to consider two different subgroups: Crystal Orange and Crystal Clear.

Figure 1. Methodology and size of the problem

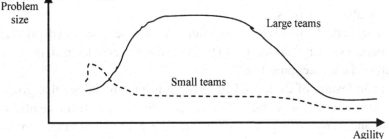

6.2.2 Crystal Orange

The Crystal Orange methodology designed for teams of 20-40 people; this approach is used for projects with a maximum length of a year, the time-to-market is important, and it is necessary to control both the development time and costs.

Since the number of team members is high, an important feature of this methodology is the constant effort in improving the information flow among the different members.

Crystal Orange is a methodology used by at most 40 people, working in the same building. Given the high number of team members, the failure of a project could cause a considerable loss of capitals. This is due both to the missing delivery and sale of a product with such a size and to the expenses sustained, including the wages of all the team members; in the case of smaller teams, these costs are clearly lower.

This kind of methodology requires a very different structure and coordination of the team, compared to a project with a few members.

The personnel is organized in teams and every one of these carries out a well defined role: system planning, project monitoring, architecture, technology, infrastructures and external tests. This methodology requires the usage of automatic regression tests in order to verify the presence of all the required functionalities and guarantee that the quality of the delivered software is tested every three months. Furthermore, Crystal Orange requires the direct involvement of the users and the supervision of two of them during every release. It is necessary to perform these operations every time developers add new code. In the usage of this methodology it is obligatory to follow these standard even if, sometimes, the usage of other methodologies, such as XP and Scrum (Schwaber & Beedle, 2001), is allowed.

Every product is developed until it is comprehensible for all the colleagues and until it has achieved a level of precision and stability allowing a peer review. Finally, every developer can freely decide the technique to use for obtaining a running product, and meeting the date of the delivery.

6.2.3 Crystal Clear

Crystal Clear is a methodology for teams with 2-6 members working in the same room or in adjacent offices.

With a team made of only six components it is not necessary to divide the group in subgroups, as in Crystal Orange. In this way it is easier to keep all the colleagues informed of the project progress.

The main feature of Crystal Clear is that it is a methodology that gives a high level of freedom to the developers. This is due to the fact that team members are not numerous and, consequently, it is possible to have a direct and fast communication among developers and more feedback.

The features of Crystal Clear are almost similar to those of Crystal Orange; the main difference is the possibility, for the former, to obtain a better product due to a small team.

In Crystal Clear, some team members are *thinkers* and others are *typers*. They use two very different approaches for solving problems. The *thinkers* think to a way for solving the problem, write down annotations on a board or on a sheet of paper, when they think to have reached a solution, they start to write the code.

The *typers*, on the contrary, are able to find out the more suitable solution to a problem, only when they are writing code.

In Crystal Clear, the time spent to write the user manual is a task with a high tolerance level, while, for example, the regression tests, the interactions among users and the releases, are all tasks with a lower level of tolerance because these are considered more important.

The size of the team is not very constrained; the members could vary from 2 to 6. In every team it is necessary to have a person with a good level of experience; that is a person that knows exactly how to move in the project.

Developers can choose the development technique to use; in fact, the important thing is not the used sequence, but the accomplishment of the expected results.

The primary objective of this methodology is the discovery of the best technique, that is, the technique that allows both to modify the product without problems and to deliver a working version of it in the least time possible.

6.2.4 Advantages from the Adoption of Crystal

The primary strengths of the Crystal family methodologies are:

- To identify the elements of success of a project.
- To allow team members to choose how to do their job.

Furthermore, this methodology is substantially based on a specific and new concept of software development: "Software development is a cooperative game, in which every participant helps the others in order to reach the aim of the game, that is the software" (Cockburn, 2004).

6.3 DSDM

DSDM (Dynamic System Development Method) is a new AM for the development of software products. During the early '90s, a company called Magic Software coined the term *Rapid Application Development* (RAD).

RAD was different from the traditional methodologies such as the waterfall approach and it was born for being used in an evolutionary economic environment.

Because RAD was not a well defined process, different users gave it dissimilar interpretation.

The DSDM consortium was born in the 1993, it had the aim to develop and to promote an unique framework, RAD. In the same time were created three main workgroups to supervise the various activities:

- **The technical workgroup** that had to create the DSDM framework and to decide in detail the contents of the framework.
- **The workgroup for the politics and the procedures** that had to make the decisions regarding the process and to write the book on the rules of the consortium.
- **The promotional workgroup** that had to lead the marketing plan

In order to obtain rapid results the technical workgroup established the task groups regarding the development and the management of the tools, of the techniques, of the personnel, of the quality and of the software implementation.

Originally DSDM was focused around the RAD process and the IT; currently it is utilized as a framework for finding timely solutions able to satisfy the business needs.

6.3.1 Features of DSDM

The traditional approaches focus on the requirements satisfaction and on the compliance of the product code with the prior deliverables, even if the requirements are often inaccurate and the market demand can change during the project.

Moreover, the time and the resources are both factors that vary over and over again during the development process.

On the contrary, in the DSDM methodology, the time and the resources are frozen at the outset of the project and the requirement that have to be satisfied can change.

This flexibility has a considerable impact on the development and control process and also on the whole system.

DSDM methodology is based on a fundamental hypothesis that is, nothing can be produced in a perfect way the first time, but 80% of the system can be produced in the 20% of the total project time.

One of the basic principles of DSDM is that the software implemented should add value to the company and should satisfy the business.

DSDM can be used together with other frameworks and development approaches, such as RUP (Rational Unified Process) and XP.

6.3.2 The DSDM Life Cycle

DSDM is more a framework than a methodology. The process entails five phases:

- *Feasibility study*
- *Business study*
- *Functional model iteration*
- *Design and build iteration*
- *Implementation*

These five stages occur before the pre-project and after the post-project phases.

The pre-project, the feasibility phase and the business study are performed in a sequential order. These stages set the general rules for the subsequent development cycle that is iterative and incremental and in spite of this it must be completed before carrying out any other task on a given project.

After having solved the problems regarding the business, the project team disjoins itself and starts the post-project phase, during which are accomplished activities such as the check of the actual operability of the project and of the obtainment of the expected benefits.

6.3.2.1 Pre-Project

The pre-project phase makes sure that only the most interesting projects will be considered. After having decided this, it is possible to proceed with the feasibility study.

6.3.2.2 Feasibility Study

It is important in the feasibility study to evaluate if the DSDM is the correct approach for the type of project that has to be realized.

Furthermore, in this phase it is necessary to assess the costs and the technical feasibility in delivering a product that corresponds to the business requests.

DSDM have to be utilized for the development of rapid solutions, therefore the feasibility study stage must be as short as possible.

6.3.2.3 Business Study

As the name suggests, this phase focus on the business analysis. Given the short time required by DSDM, the business study is a very collaborative activity and it has to be performed by work teams made up of competent personnel.

The results obtained, are used for creating the *Business Area Definition* that will define the business process and the classes of the users interested in the introduction of the system.

6.3.2.4 Functional Model Iteration

This activity is necessary to improve the basic aspects of the system. Both the functional model iteration and the design and build iteration are made up of cycles with four main activities that are:

- To identify what must be produced;
- To establish how and when produce it;
- To produce the product;
- To verify that the software has been correctly produced.

6.3.2.5 Design and Build Iteration

The *design and build iteration* phase occurs only when the system designed has reached such a level that can be delivered to the users. In this stage the best product obtained is the *tested system*.

6.3.2.6 Implementation

The transfer from the development environment to the operational environment is accomplished during the implementation phase. This stage as well involves the training of the users that have not taken part to the team of the project.

6.3.2.7 Post-Project

It is the post-project phase that makes really operative the product. The iterative and incremental nature of DSDM indicates that also the maintenance stage can be viewed as a continuous development phase.

6.3.3 Advantages Deriving by the Adoption of DSDM

DSDM utilizes an iterative process based on the users' involvement throughout the life cycle of the project. The advantages deriving from the usage of this methodology are:

- The users are very satisfied since they can take part of the software development process;
- The risk to produce a not working system is remarkably reduced;
- The final system is more oriented to the satisfaction of the actual users needs;
- The time-to-market is significantly improved.

The key point of DSDM methodology is the communication among project components; this factor increase the quality of the product obtained. In addition, DSDM delineates the necessary documentation for every type of project.

As a rule, the majority of the documentation produced, refers to the transfer of the ideas between developers and users.

DSDM methodology does not consider necessary a lot of documentation thus this approach reduces the amount of it till the minimum level.

6.4 LSD

In order to set the groundwork, we should consider the definition of *lean* and *lean thinking*. According to the National Institute of Standards and Technology Manufacturing Extension Partnership's Lean Network, *lean* is: "A systematic approach to identifying and eliminating waste through continuous improvement, flowing the product at the pull of the customer in pursuit of perfection" (Kilpatrick, 2003).

The *lean thinking* was born in Japan in the late '40s with a small company named Toyota that had to deal with a problem in the car production area. The cars had to be cheap but they could not use the mass production system because of the small number of cars required by the Japanese market.

To solve this problem, Taiichi Ohno, the father of the Toyota Production System, created a very new way to think about manufacturing, logistics, and product development (Ohno, 1988).

The basic principle of Ohno's philosophy was to eliminate waste: anything that does not create value for the customer. The goal of Ohno was to both make and deliver a product immediately after a customer placed an order, without the need of inventories, warehouses, and forecasts.

The efficiency and effectiveness of this new approach create a massive transition from the mass production to the lean manufacturing in the last two decades.

Lean Software Development (LSD) enhances the theoretical foundations of agile software development by applying well-known and accepted lean principles to software development. LSD is more strategically focused than other AMs and is not a management or development methodology per se, but it offers principles that are applicable in any environment to improve software development.

6.4.1 Principles of Lean Software Development

The seven principles of Lean Thinking can be translated in the following seven Software Development principles. These general principles are guidelines for devising appropriate practices for specific domains. When translated properly, they can change radically the basis of competition of a firm.

6.4.1.1 Eliminate Waste

Anything that does not add value to a product, from the customer perspective, is waste. In order to eliminate every possible waste, firms have to identify what the customer wants, then develop it, and deliver it almost immediately.

The first step to remove waste is to see it. Good starting points include those activities that do not contribute directly to the value of the final product: everything different from analysis and coding. Creating a value stream map and outlining the process details to satisfy a customer request, helps to identify the sources of the waste.

The seven main wastes of software development are the following (Poppendieck & Poppendieck, 2003):

1. *Partially done work*. Partially done software development can carry huge financial risks because it ties up investments that have yet to yield results. The strategy is to reduce it.
2. *Extra processes*. Paperwork has a lot of drawbacks: it consumes resources, slows down response time, hides quality problems, gets lost, degrades, and become obsolete. When paperwork is required, it is better to keep it short, high-level and always verify if there is a more efficient and effective way to share information.
3. *Extra features*. Every line of code in the system has to be tracked, compiled, integrated, and tested every time the code is touched and it has to be maintained for the whole life of the system. Furthermore, every line of code increases the complexity and is a potential point of failure. The solution is to implement only the features that are needed at the moment.
4. *Task switching*. Assigning people to multiple projects and multiple teams is a source of waste because of the switching time and the continuous interruptions. Thus, the fastest way to complete two projects that use the same resources is to make them one at a time.

5.   *Waiting*. Delays are common in most projects; they are waste because prevent the customer from the savings or improvements generated by the system.
6.   *Motion*. Development is an activity that requires concentration, so every movement is waste because it takes time to reestablish focus on his work. For this reason, agile practices recommend to a team to work in a single, open room.
7.   *Defects*. The amount of waste caused by defects depends on the defect impact and on the time they go undetected. The way to reduce the impact of defects is to find them as soon as they occur. Thus, the way to reduce the waste due to defects is to test and integrate immediately and release the product as soon as possible.

6.4.1.2 Amplify Learning

Development is a typical learning process involving trial and error that is carried out in order to discover the best product for satisfying the customers.

The knowledge coming from the feedback loops is critical to any process with inherent variation. The goal is not to eliminate changes but to adapt to variation through feedback.

Developers use frequent iterations in order to identify the differences between what the product does and what the customer wants. This knowledge is useful to make adjustments accordingly. Typically, a lean organization focuses on increasing feedback and learning. The main way to do this is through short iterations that produce working software able to be tested by the customer.

6.4.1.3 Decide as Late as Possible

In domains characterized by high uncertainty, it is useful to delay commitment and to use an option-based approach. The lean concept is to defer irreversible and uncertain decisions until they can be made based on known events, rather than forecasts.

Delaying decisions allows making better and more reliable decisions. This practice is particularly valuable in evolving markets.

A key strategy for delaying commitments is to include the support for changes into the system. This support is related strictly to the design and development activities.

The sequential development forces designers to make low-level binding decisions before experiencing the consequences of the high-level decisions. In this way, many costly mistakes are possible and it is very expensive to repair them.

Iterative development is the better approach when the understanding of the problem is evolving or there is a high level of uncertainty in the domain.

Concurrent development means to start the implementation from the features with the highest value as soon as a high-level conceptual design is ready, even while detailed requirements have to be investigated. This is an exploratory approach allowing the development team to learn by trying a bunch of options before to be locked in a specific direction.

In addition, iterative development is the best way to deal with changing requirements. When change is inevitable, concurrent development reduces delivery time and the overall cost while improving the performance of the final product.

In an iterative development process, the *crucial* decisions at the beginning of the development process have to be minimized. In this way, the cost of the changes has a low-cost escalation factor. Concurrent design defers decisions as late as possible. This approach has four effects (Poppendieck & Poppendieck, 2003):

1. Reduces the number of high-stake constraints.
2. Gives a breadth-first approach to high-stakes decisions, making it more likely that they will be made correctly.
3. Defers the bulk of the decisions, significantly reducing the need for change.
4. Dramatically decreases the cost escalation factor for most changes.

According to this approach, developers can start to implement the system even if partial requirements are available. Every iteration provides essential feedback that allows the final application to emerge.

The important thing is not to delay a commitment over the *last responsible moment* that is the time at which failing to make a decision eliminates an important alternative. Here are some tactics for making decisions at the last responsible moment (Poppendieck & Poppendieck, 2003):

- Organize for direct, worker-to-worker collaboration
- Share partially complete design information
- Develop a sense of how to absorb changes:
  ○ Use modules, interfaces, parameters, abstractions
  ○ Avoid sequential programming
  ○ Beware of custom tool building
  ○ Avoid repetition
  ○ Separate concern
  ○ Encapsulate variation
  ○ Defer implementation of future capabilities
  ○ Avoid extra features
- Develop a sense of what is critical in the domain
- Develop a sense of when decisions must be made
- Develop a quick response capability

6.4.1.4 Deliver as Fast as Possible

Rapid development has many advantages. First, without speed it is not possible to let the customers take an options-based approach, letting them to delay decisions as long as possible in order to make decisions based on the best possible information. In fact, once a customer decides what he wants, the goal of the development team is to implement it as fast as possible.

With rapid development cycles (design, implement, feedback, improve), it is simple and immediate to obtain reliable and valuable feedback. Consequently, the shorter these cycles are, the more can be learned.

Furthermore, rapid delivery means fewer customers' changes. In fact, the easiest way to keep customers from changing their minds is to give them what they ask for so fast that they do not have the time to change their mind.

6.4.1.5 Empower the Team

In a lean organization, everything moves at high speed and the decisions have to be taken very fast. For this reason, it is very important to involve developers in technical decisions and let them the responsibility.

In fact, the people on the front line have enough knowledge and experience to make better technical decisions than anyone else in the higher levels of the organization hierarchy.

Furthermore, because decisions are made late and execution is fast, a central authority cannot orchestrate the activities. Thus, lean practices use pull techniques to schedule work and contain local signaling mechanisms so workers can let each other know what needs to be done. In lean software development, the pull mechanism is an agreement to deliver increasingly refined versions of working software at regular intervals. Local signaling occurs through visible charts, daily meetings, frequent integration, and comprehensive testing (Poppendieck & Poppendieck, 2003).

In order to empower a development team, it is fundamental to have highly motivated people.

In a context where the team is empowered to make its own decision, the project manager has to carry out these main activities:

- Identify waste
- Sketch the value stream map and tackle the biggest bottlenecks
- Coordinate iteration planning meeting and daily status meetings
- Help the team get the resources it needs to meet commitments
- Coordinate multiple teams
- Provide a motivation environment and keep skeptics away

6.4.1.6 Build Integrity In

There are two kinds of integrity: perceived and conceptual. Software with perceived integrity delights the customers because it is exactly what they want and what they ask for. The way to achieve perceived integrity is to have continuous and detailed information flow from users to developers.

Conceptual integrity means that all the pieces of a software system work together to achieve a smooth, well functioning entity. This kind of integrity is achieved through continuous and detailed information flow among the several technical people working on a system.

There is a further level of integrity: products have to maintain their usefulness over the time. Thus, they have to evolve gradually as adapting to the future. Software with integrity has a coherent architecture, scores high on usability and fitness for purpose, and is maintainable, adaptable and extensible.

Research has shown that integrity comes more from wise leadership, relevant expertise, effective communication, and healthy disciple, than from processes and measurements.

6.4.1.7 See the Whole

The development of every complex system requires a deep expertise in many different areas. One of the most difficult problems with product development is that often an expert of a specific area has a tendency to maximize the performance of a specific subsystem rather than focusing on overall system performance. Quite often, the common goal suffers if people are focused too much in their own areas.

Lean thinking suggests that optimizing single subsystems almost always leads to sub-optimized overall systems. The best way to deal with sub-optimization and promote collaboration is to make people responsible for their own behavior, not just for what they control. This means measuring performance *one lever higher* than one would expect.

6.4.2 Advantages Deriving by the Adoption of LSD

Software companies that want to outperform their competitors and get successful results should consider the lean approach to software development. Lean software development can be summarized as follows. Instead of adding process complexity, the focus is on simplifying processes. Enhanced customer relationship improves the understanding of what produces value. Performance breakthroughs can be created by identifying and removing waste from the value streams. Development teams should be responsible for making improvements and they have to be rewarded as the whole project progress. The entire company can be reorganized to help teams to create and optimize value streams based on two kinds of learning: what customers will need next and how to deliver it in a better way.

Focus on value, flow, and people are the way to implement the principles of lean thinking in the software industry. This can really help to keep customers from changing their minds and raise the maturity of the organization to the level where it can deliver what customers want so fast that they have no time to change their minds.

6.5 REFERENCES

Abrahamsson, P., Salo, O., Ronkainen, J., & Warsta, J. (2003). *Agile software development methods: Review and analysis* (p. 478). Espoo, Finland: Technical Research Centre of Finland, VTT Publications.

Ambler, S. (2002). *Agile modeling*. Wiley.

Beck, K. (1999). *Extreme programming explained: Embrace change*. Addison-Wesley Professional.

Cockburn, A. (2004). *Crystal "clear": A human-powered software development methodology for small teams*. Addison-Wesley Professional.

Kilpatrick, J. (2003). *Lean principles*. UT: Utah manufacturing extension partnership.

Ohno, T. (1988). *Toyota production system: Beyond large-scale production*. Productivity Press Inc.

Palmer, S., & Felsing, J. (2002). *Practical guide to feature-driven development*. Prentice Hall.

Poppendieck, M., & Poppendieck, T. (2003). *Lean software development: An agile toolkit*. Addison-Wesley Professional.

Schwaber, K., & Beedle, M. (2001). *Agile software development with SCRUM*. Prentice Hall.

Stapleton, J. (1997). *DSDM: The dynamic systems development method*. Addison-Wesley Professional.

Section 2
Agile Software Practices for Open Source Development

Chapter 7
Testing

7.1 INTRODUCTION

Software testing is the process that controls the quality of software (Myers, 1979). Software testing is comprised in any development process and every method of development applies practices for software testing (Burnstein, 2003; Kaner *et al.*, 2002). Traditional methods of development, like the waterfall approach, allocate software testing in a given phase of the overall development process – e.g., toward the end of the software lifecycle. In modern methods, practices of software testing rather permeate the whole development process in an iterative and increasing way (Black, 2002; Spillner *et al.*, 2007) – e.g., in XP.

The goal of this chapter is to understand to what extent testing is embraced and applied in the OS projects. In particular, we discuss whether OSD adopts testing practices coming from AMs. In practice, we analyze OS repositories looking for information revealing the adoption of some testing practice. In other words, we analyze the existence, the date of creation, and the changes of test classes and their related code classes in the public version control systems available in the OS repositories.

DOI: 10.4018/978-1-59904-681-5.ch007

7.2 TESTING IN THE OPEN SOURCE DEVELOPMENT

The majority of OS projects combines the feedback from the community and an internal strategy of testing to release competitive and stable software products.

The most common practices of internal testing in the open source projects are the use of the nightly builds and the frequent releases. The frequent releases guarantees a fast and iterative reporting from all the community. The majority of the projects use Bugzilla or a modification of it to collect - from the internal teams or from the volunteers - reports on failures, request of modification, or enhancements. The same tool is used to divulgate solutions, patches, or occurrences of defects. Many of OS projects declare to use automated tools or agile practices for testing, like Test Driven Development (TDD). As we shall see, the reality is different: in many cases test classes are totally missing or appear in a very low percentage.In what follows we discuss the existence of test classes in projects stored in the following on-line repositories:

1. Tigris.org (http://www.tigris.org/)
2. Apache Foundation (http://www.apache.org/).
3. Mozilla Foundation (http://www.mozilla.org/)
4. OpenBSD (http://www.openbsd.org/)
5. XFree86 (http://www.xfree86.org/)
6. JBoss (http://www.jboss.org)
7. PostgreSQL (http://www.postgresql.org/)
8. KDE (http://www.kde.org/)

In Table 1 we report the number of classes (files), the programming language dominant in the project, the number of test classes (tests) and the percentage of test with respect to the files.

Among the 68 projects considered, 13 have no tests at all, or such tests are not stored in the version control system together with the source code. 32 have more than 10% of the files dedicated to test cases (Figure 1).

However, nearly all the projects that started in the last few years include a higher percentage of tests. This behavior could be caused by several reasons. However, it is interesting that the diffusion of the AMs started at the same time (2000 ca.). It is likely that the basic ideas of the AMs have affected the development of the projects that started from 2000 onwards.

Table 1. Test classes in the 68 projects analyzed

Project	Files	Tests	%	Language	Project	Files	Tests	%	Language
Ant	1,073	263	25	Java	Logging Log4cxx	316	93	29	C
Ant-Antidote	170	0	0	Java	Logging Log4j	380	93	24	Java
Apache 1.2	92	0	0	C	Maven	640	144	22	Java
Apache 1.3	222	18	8	C	Maxq	124	22	18	Java + Pyton
Apache 2.0	298	16	5	C	Mozilla Camino	2,035	838	41	C/C++
Apache-Apr	264	18	7	C	Mozilla Composer	1,971	838	43	C/C++
ArgoUML	1,372	103	7	Java	Mozilla Firefox	2,053	851	41	C/C++
Aut	74	51	69	C#	Mozilla Sunbird	1,988	839	42	C/C++
Avalon	1,945	353	18	Java	Mozilla Thunderbird	2,741	867	32	C/C++
Axion	658	95	14	Java	OpenBSD	303	3	1	C
Binarycloud	514	16	3	PHP	PostgreSQL	177	0	0	C
Cocoon 1.0	96	0	0	Java	RapidSVN	118	0	0	C++
Cocoon 2.0	76	1	1	Java	Scarab	1,328	300	22	Java
Cocoon 2.1	2,036	63	3	Java	Subversion	223	16	7	C/C++
Cocoon 2.2	562	25	4	Java	TortoiseSVN	26	0	0	C++
DB-ojb	1,004	337	34	Java	WS AXIS	2,414	654	27	Java
DB-torque	156	23	15	Java	WS FX	254	42	16	Java
Elmuth	172	0	0	Java	WS JAXME	726	0	0	Java
Eyebrowse	84	3	3	Java	WS jUDDI	502	17	3	Java
GEF	238	1	0	Java	WS SOAP	213	17	8	Java
Jakarta Hivemind	2,293	341	15	Java	WS WSIF	401	116	29	Java
Jakarta Jetspeed 2	609	66	11	Java	WS XMLRPC	67	8	12	Java
Jakarta JMeter	767	134	17	Java	XFree86 3.0	971	1	0	C
Jakarta Lucene	248	64	26	Java	XFree86 4.0	5,279	23	0	C
Jakarta ORO	86	0	0	Java	XML BATIK	1,579	176	11	Java
Jakarta POI	766	176	23	Java	XML Crimson	49	0	0	Java
Jakarta Taglibs	667	17	3	Java	XML FOP	605	17	3	Java
Jakarta Tapestry	1,035	212	20	Java	XML Forrest	28	0	0	Java
Jakarta Tomcat 3.0	349	80	23	Java	XML Security	532	28	5	Java

Table 1. continued

Jakarta Tomcat 4.0	799	135	17	Java	XML Xalan	1,905	151	6	Java/C/C++
Jakarta Turbine 2	464	66	14	Java	XML Xang	46	0	0	Java
Jakarta Turbine 3	93	8	9	Java	XML Xerces	1,938	71	4	Java/C/C++
JBoss	551	0	0	Java	XML Xindice	368	41	11	Java
KDE	2,670	217	8	C	XML XML-beans	1,188	362	30	Java

Figure 1.

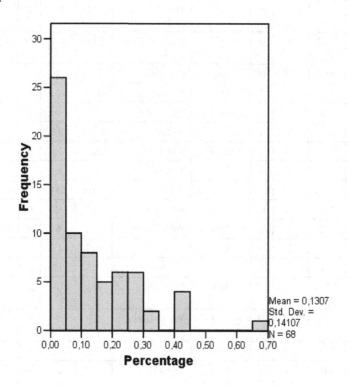

7.3 USE OF XUNIT IN AGILE AND OS DEVELOPMENT

There are several frameworks for implementing testing in various programming languages. They are called xUnit. There is JUnit for Java, SUnit for smalltalk, CPPUnit for C++ and so on. In general, these frameworks provide a simple and automated way to test specific areas of a program (Units). The developer may find predefined packages, classes, and methods from which to derive the test for a given unit. In this way, using xUnits helps to explicitly declare the expected results of a specific part of a program or execution path.

In particular, XUnit promotes the idea of testing before coding, also called *Test-Driven Development* (TDD) in AMs and *Test First* in the terminology of XP. The practice Test First is further extended in "test a little, code a little, test a little, code a little, ..." in an iterative manner. The code and the test case increment in parallel to assure the quality of the piece of software produced in each iteration.

7.4 A METHOD TO REVEAL THE ADOPTION OF TEST FIRST IN OS PROJECTS

In this section we discuss the adoption of Test First in some open source projects. We base our analysis on well-known repositories of OS projects from which we extract information about class size evolution and times to commit.

The method to inspect the repositories comprises two major activities.

1. Inspection of the documentation. This would tell whether any automated tools have been used in the open source project and if the project explicitly adopt Test First
2. Inspection of the versioning systems (CVS). This would tell the activity of a class / version of a project by its size evolution, the use of tests by the percentage of test classes, and the adoption of test first by the comparison of the dates to commit of class and test.

To select a sample of classes on which analyze the use of testing practices, we consider product releases having the highest percentile in the added, modified, deleted and total Lines of Code (LOC).

To have an indication of the use of the Test First practice in a project we analyze the time in which test classes are committed to the CVS. If we find that test classes have been committed earlier than their reference classes we may say that Test First has been adopted by OS project team. If this is not true we cannot deduce anything; in particular we cannot say that the team does not adopt Test First as time to commit might be different from the time of creation of a class (developers might have created test classes locally and committed together or later than the original classes). Of course to check the correct adoption of Test First we may need to have access to the local machine of the developer. Namely, Test First is correctly implemented when Test classes are implemented on *empty* regular classes – with no implemented methods. Furthermore, even in the case we find some test classes committed before their reference ones we are not done as we need to discuss the level of adoption of the practice by analyzing the extent to which this result permeates the classes of project. Hence, the percentage of classes following Test First will give the measure of the level of Test First adoption.

Further analysis may study the distribution of the LOC modification near the creation date of an original class. High number of modified LOC soon after the first version of a class may suggest an effort due to the implementation of the class and therefore a likelihood of the adoption of Test First.

7.5 ADOPTION OF TEST FIRST IN OPEN SOURCE PROJECTS: A MANUAL INSPECTION

The goal of this section is to evaluate the adoption of the practice *Test First* in OSD development. The analysis is based on a sample of tools selected in http://www.tigris.org/. Tigris is a popular web site that contains 537 medium sized projects. Projects in Tigris have a common mission: promoting software engineering in OSD. Thus, Tigris represents a well scoped OS project rather than a repository of projects. As team and project sizes are small/medium and projects fairly young, they fit the best environment for the application of the agile practices, Tigris represents a suitable *testbed* for the analysis of the connection between agile and OS development. In this context we can rephrase our first general research goal in:

Do open source projects hosted in a collaborative environment and with a common mission adopt Test First?

Results from the analysis may differ considerably from similar studies conducted in different OS repositories – like SourceForge. In the following sections we describe the data collection and the data analysis.

7.5.1 Data Collection

The data collection has been manually performed on the OS software in http://www.tigris.org/. This has been feasible thank to the small-medium size of the projects. Among all the projects we have selected the topmost featured one as appears in the web site (Table 2).

As first step we have analyzed the classes of each selected project to determine the correspondence between them and their test classes. This procedure gives a first idea of the percentage of test coverage. As a consequence we eliminate the projects: Lptools, Phpcreate, ReadySet, Sstree, Style, and Xmlbasedsrs, because either the projects were not developed with oriented-language or there were no xUnit suite available for testing.

Table 2. Projects considered in the analysis

Project	Language & license	Category[1]	Project	Language & license	Category
Ankhsvn	Visual Studio .NET, Apache License, v. 2.0	Student class projects	**Phpcreate**	Php, GNU GPL	Coding, testing, and debugging tools
ArgoUML	Java, BSD License	**Design tools**	**RapidSVN**	C++, Apache License, v. 2.0	Software Configuration Management
Aut	**C#.Net, GNU GPL**	Tools for software testing	**ReadySet**	XHTML with CSS, BSD License	Projects related to software development processes
Axion	**Java, Apache License, v. 2.0**	**Reusable components**	**Scarab**	Java, CollabNet/ Tigris.org Apache-style license	Defect and issue tracking tools
Binary-cloud	**Php, GNU LPL**	**Tools for technical communications**	**Sstree**	Java script, Apache License, v. 2.0	Reusable components
Elmuth	Java, BSD License	Student class projects	**Style**	CSS, Apache License, v. 2.0	Reusable components
Eye-browse	Java, CollabNet/ Tigris.org Apache-style license	Tools for technical communications	**Subversion**	C, Java, Pyton, CollabNet/Tigris. org Apache-style license	Software Configuration Management
Gef	Java, BSD License	Reusable components	**Tortois-eSVN**	C, GNU GPL	Software Configuration Management
Lptools	Ruby, Other OSI-certified license	Coding, testing, and debugging tools and Projects related to software development processes	**Xmlbased-srs**	C, GNU GPL	Software requirements management
Maxq	Java, Jyton, BSD License	Tools for software testing			

To analyze the adoption of the practice Test First we then analyze the source codes by sampling the classes in three specified versions of each project: the first, an intermediate and the final one. For each version we chose randomly 10 classes among the ones that have a test class. This procedure would guarantee the validity of the possible conclusion as it is conceivable that developers once started, adopt Test First continuously through the project. On the other hand not using Test First in some specific classes may be not so relevant or a standard procedure for specific kind of classes, which does not indicate a misuse of Test First. For each class considered – test or regular – we have collected the date of creation.

7.5.2 Review of the Data

At first we have analyzed the percentage of test classes within each project (Figure 2).

Then, we have studied whether automated tools have been used in the project and if the project explicitly requires the use of Test First. In our analysis, we have also taken onto account that xUnit were developed since November 2000, so projects with previously starting date could not use them at their beginnings (Table 3).

7.5.3 Analysis of the Results

The study has been conducted in a peculiar repository. Namely, Tigris is a collaborative project more than a repository for OS projects. OS projects hosted in Tigris have a common mission: developing quality software trough software engineering practices. Therefore, the analysis we report here may be more significant than in other repositories as the question is: do they also share practices from AMs?

Among the projects considered, Axion turns out to be the only project that fully adopted Test First. By its documentation we may also deduce that the project has been refactored and redesign with the use of Test First.

Among the remaining projects the answer is generally no; although, they tend to use automated tools for testing. The analysis may easily be extended to larger repositories perhaps with no common mission but with a wider spectrum of projects. This requires making the procedure automatic and will be discussed in the next sections.

Figure 2. Test classes percentage in the Tigris projects

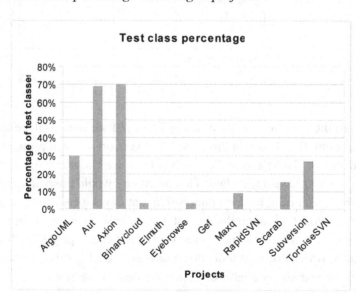

Table 3. Testing in the projects analyzed

Project	xUnit	Status of the project	Test First	# of classes	Test class percentage
ArgoUML	Yes, from September 2003.	Project started in 2000. Stable version	No	1372	30%2
Aut	Yes	Stable version	No	78	69%
Axion	Yes	Almost stable version	Yes – required in the project and verified on samples	658	70%
Binarycloud	Yes	Almost stable version	No	514	3%
Elmuth	No	Almost stable version	No	172	0%
Eyebrowse	No	In progress	No	84	3%
Gef	No, only one class has been automated tested	Stable version	No	238	0%
Maxq	Yes, but the minor part of the project	Almost stable version	No	124	9% in Java 0% and in Pyton
RapidSVN			N/A	118	0%
Scarab	Yes	Almost stable version	No	338	15%
Subversion	Yes, but the minor part of the project	Stable version. A consistent part is written in C	No	223	27% in Java and 2% in Pyton
TortoiseSVN			N/A	26	0%

7.6 TOOL SUPPORTING THE REPOSITORY'S INSPECTION

For every project we chose to analyze those three product releases having the highest percentile based on the added, modified, deleted, and total lines of code. To analyze the results of the diff operator in the version control system, we create a tool called CVSMetrics. To mark the evolution in time of a project we use the sequence of tags of a project. We call revision of a tag a new commit to the repository. For each tag there can be more revisions.

7.6.1 CVSMetrics Description and Implementation

To analyze and compare the quality of software developed by OS communities, we developed CVSMetrics, a tool that automatically extracts useful information from public CVS code repositories. CVSMetrics is written in Java and consists in a simple command line tool taking the information it needs, like repository path, module name, credential information etc., as command line parameters. The simple interface allowed us to run our tool in unattended batch-mode over several repositories, which often took several hours and even days and would have been cumbersome to do in another way. For every CVS repository our tool produces an XML file containing useful quality measurements concerning unit testing. This includes information like added, modified, deleted and total lines of code per CVS file revision and per CVS tag and some statistics about how many classes have associated unit tests and about the presence of test-first programming (i.e., test classes committed to the CVS before corresponding real class).

To count the different LOC metrics we implemented a LineCounter class, responsible to calculate the total lines of code. The pattern we used to define a real line is the semicolon. So only the lines containing a semicolon are counted.

```java
public LineCounter(){
    p = Pattern.compile(";");
}
public int getLOC(File javaClass){
    BufferedReader br = null;
    int lines = 0;
    try{
        br = new BufferedReader(new
FileReader(javaClass));
        String line;
        while ((line = br.readLine()) != null){
            if (isLOC(line)) lines++;
        }
    }catch(Exception e){}
    return lines;
}
public boolean isLOC(String line){
    if (line != null) {
        Matcher m = p.matcher(line);
if(m.find())return true;
    }
    return false;
}
```

This approach is commonly used and very fast, but it has some limitations. Some lines are not recognized in a correct manner.

Comments containing semicolons are counted, as well as all the lines of whole blocks which are commented out:

```
// this is a comment;
```

a *for loop* is counted as a single statement:

```
for (i = 1; i < 100; i++) {
}
```

an *if statement* does not contain any semicolon most of the times, and does not get counted at all:

```
    if (line != null) {
```

there are also other similar cases like the *try-catch statement*:

```
try{
          . . .
}catch(Exception e){}
```

or the *while loop*:

```
while(true){
}
```

or more than one declaration in one line:

```
int s, t;
```

and certain languages could not be parsed as they do not use semicolons:

```
e.g. Visual Basic
```

7.6.1.1 Detailed Definition of the Deleted, Added, Modified Lines and Limits

Class. A comparison of a class of two consecutive versions shows the definition of the three terms, add, modify, and delete. As basis the EclipseME project was selected. To be precise the class:

```
/eclipseme/EclipseME/src/eclipseme/model/impl/nokia/
Attic/NokiaWirelessToolkit.java
```

was chosen and a diff command between version 1.1 and 1.2 was executed. (see Table 4)

Table 4.

version 1.1, Tue Feb 10 00:49:06 2004 UTC	version 1.2, Sun Feb 22 03:12:03 2004 UTC
Line 7	**Line 7**
package eclipseme.model.impl.nokia;	package eclipseme.model.impl.nokia;
import java.io.File;	import java.io.File;
	import java.io.FileFilter;
	import java.io.FileInputStream;
	import java.io.IOException;
	import java.io.InputStream;
	import java.util.ArrayList;
	import java.util.Arrays;
	import java.util.Iterator;
	import java.util.List;
	import java.util.Properties;
	import java.util.StringTokenizer;
import org.eclipse.core.runtime.IProgressMonitor;	import org.eclipse.core.runtime.IProgressMonitor;
	import org.eclipse.core.runtime.IStatus;
	import org.eclipse.core.runtime.Path;
	import org.eclipse.jdt.core.JavaCore;
	import eclipseme.EclipseMEPlugin;
import eclipseme.model.IConfiguration;	import eclipseme.model.IConfiguration;
	import eclipseme.model.IEmulator;
	import eclipseme.model.IPlatformDefinition;

Legend

Removed from v.1.1	
Changed Lines	
	Added in v. 1.2

version 1.1, Tue Feb 10 00:49:06 2004 UTC	version 1.2, Sun Feb 22 03:12:03 2004 UTC
	import eclipseme.model.IPreverifier;
	import eclipseme.model.IProfile;
import eclipseme.model.InvalidWirelessToolkitException;	import eclipseme.model.InvalidWirelessToolkitException;
import eclipseme.model.impl.generic.WirelessToolkit;	import eclipseme.model.Version;
	import eclipseme.model.impl.generic.Configuration;
	import eclipseme.model.impl.generic.Profile;
	import eclipseme.model.impl.sun.AbstractSunWirelessToolkit;
/**	/**
* Wireless Toolkit implementation for the Nokia J2ME toolkit.	* Wireless Toolkit implementation for the Nokia J2ME toolkit.
Line 27	**Line 48**
* 	*
* @author Craig Setera	* @author Craig Setera
*/	*/
public class NokiaWirelessToolkit extends WirelessToolkit {	public class NokiaWirelessToolkit extends AbstractSunWirelessToolkit {
public static final String CLASSPATH_VAR = "NOKIA_ROOT";	public static final String CLASSPATH_VAR = "NOKIA_WTK";
/** Path to the devices within the wireless toolkit root */	/** Path to the devices within the wireless toolkit root */
public static final String DEVICES_PATH = "Devices";	public static final String DEVICES_PATH = "Devices";
	/** File filter to capture device directories */
	private class DeviceDirectoriesFileFilter implements FileFilter {
	/**
	* @see java.io.FileFilter#accept(java.io.File)
	*/
	public boolean accept(File pathname) {

Legend

Removed from v.1.1	
Changed Lines	
	Added in v. 1.2

version 1.1, Tue Feb 10 00:49:06 2004 UTC	version 1.2, Sun Feb 22 03:12:03 2004 UTC
	return pathname.isDirectory() && isDeviceDirectory(pathname);
	}
	/**
	* Return a boolean indicating whether the specified path
	* appears to be a device directory.
	*
	* @param pathname
	* @return
	*/
	private boolean isDeviceDirectory(File pathname) {
	return getDevicePropertiesFile(pathname) .exists();
	}
	}
	/**
	* Return the list of libraries that are defined by the specified
	* property.
	*
	* @param properties
	* @param propertyName
	* @return
	*/
	static List getPropertyLibraries(Properties properties, String propertyName) {
	ArrayList libs = new ArrayList();
	// Pull the libraries definition from the properties

Legend

Removed from v.1.1	
Changed Lines	
	Added in v. 1.2

version 1.1, Tue Feb 10 00:49:06 2004 UTC	version 1.2, Sun Feb 22 03:12:03 2004 UTC
	String librariesProp = properties. getProperty(propertyName, "");
	// Not sure if the path separators are changed by platform. Going to split
	// on either just to make sure we are covered.
	StringTokenizer st = new StringTokenizer(librariesProp, ";:");
	while (st.hasMoreTokens()) {
	String library = st.nextToken();
	// Not sure about the file separator either... convert to one
	// format
	library = library.replace('\\', '/');
	// Finally... All of these libraries are relative paths and yet
	// the props file has some with leading path separators. Remove
	// the leading path character to make sure it acts relative.
	if (library.charAt(0) == '/') {
	library = library.substring(1);
	}
	libs.add(library);
	}
	return libs;
	}
/**	/**
* Construct a new Nokia wireless toolkit.	* Construct a new Nokia wireless toolkit.
*	*

Legend

Removed from v.1.1	
Changed Lines	
	Added in v. 1.2

version 1.1, Tue Feb 10 00:49:06 2004 UTC	version 1.2, Sun Feb 22 03:12:03 2004 UTC
Line 47	**Line 126**
}	}
/**	/**
* @see eclipseme.model.impl.generic.WirelessToo lkit#getCLDCPreverifierParameters(eclipseme.model. IConfiguration)	
*/	
protected String[] getCLDCPreverifierParameters(I Configuration configuration) {	
// TODO Auto-generated method stub	
return null;	
}	
/**	
* @see eclipseme.model.impl.generic.WirelessToo lkit#getRootClasspathVariableName()	* @see eclipseme.model.impl.generic.WirelessT oolkit#getRootClasspathVariableName()
*/	*/
protected String getRootClasspathVariableName() {	protected String getRootClasspathVariable- Name() {
Line 65	**Line 136**
* @see eclipseme.model.impl.generic.Wireless Toolkit#initializeToolkit(org.eclipse.core.runtime. IProgressMonitor)	* @see eclipseme.model.impl.generic.Wireless Toolkit#initializeToolkit(org.eclipse.core.runtime. IProgressMonitor)
*/	*/
protected void initializeToolkit(IProgressMonito r monitor) {	protected void initializeToolkit(IProgressMonit or monitor) {
// TODO Auto-generated method stub	name = NokiaWirelessToolkitType.TOOL- KIT_NAME;
	version = NokiaWirelessToolkitType.TOOL- KIT_VERSION;
	// Gather the device directories
	File devicesDir = new File(getRoot(), Noki- aWirelessToolkitType.DEVICES_DIRECTORY);
	File[] deviceDirs = devicesDir.listFiles(new DeviceDirectoriesFileFilter());

Legend

Removed from v.1.1	
Changed Lines	
	Added in v. 1.2

version 1.1, Tue Feb 10 00:49:06 2004 UTC	version 1.2, Sun Feb 22 03:12:03 2004 UTC
	// Create the platform component lists
	ArrayList configList = new ArrayList();
	ArrayList profileList = new ArrayList();
	ArrayList platDefsList = new ArrayList();
	// Create the platform definitions
	for (int i = 0; i < deviceDirs.length; i++) {
	try {
	IPlatformDefinition def = createDevicePlatform(deviceDirs[i]);
	platDefsList.add(def);
	configList.add(def.getConfiguration());
	profileList.addAll(Arrays.asList(def.getProfiles()));
	} catch (IOException e) {
	EclipseMEPlugin.log(IStatus.WARNING, "initializeToolkit", e);
	}
	}
	// Set the configurations and profiles for this toolkit
	platformDefinitions =
	(IPlatformDefinition[]) platDefsList.toArray(
	new IPlatformDefinition[platDefsList.size()]);
	profiles =
	(IProfile[]) profileList.toArray(new IProfile[profileList.size()]);
	configurations =
	(IConfiguration[]) configList.toArray(new IConfiguration[configList.size()]);
	}

Legend

Removed from v.1.1	
Changed Lines	
	Added in v. 1.2

version 1.1, Tue Feb 10 00:49:06 2004 UTC	version 1.2, Sun Feb 22 03:12:03 2004 UTC
	/**
	* Add libraries to the profile based on the information as defined in
	* the device properties.
	*
	* @param profile
	* @param deviceDirectory
	* @param deviceProps
	*/
	private void addLibrariesToProfile(
	Profile profile,
	String deviceDirectory,
	Properties deviceProps)
	{
	// Pull the libraries definition from the properties
	Iterator libraries =
	getPropertyLibraries(deviceProps, "emulator.library").iterator();
	while (libraries.hasNext()) {
	String library = (String) libraries.next();
	// Build up the library path to be added to the profile
	StringBuffer sb = new StringBuffer(CLASSPATH_VAR);
	sb.append('/').append(DEVICES_PATH);
	sb.append('/').append(deviceDirectory);
	sb.append('/').append(library);
	Path path = new Path(sb.toString());
	profile.addLibrary(JavaCore.newVariableEntry(path, null, null));

Legend

Removed from v.1.1	
Changed Lines	
	Added in v. 1.2

version 1.1, Tue Feb 10 00:49:06 2004 UTC	version 1.2, Sun Feb 22 03:12:03 2004 UTC
	}
}	}
/**	/**
* @see eclipseme.model.IWirelessToolkit#getDeviceNames()	* Create a platform definition for the specified device directory.
	*
	* @param file
	* @return
*/	*/
public String[] getDeviceNames() {	private IPlatformDefinition createDevicePlatform(File deviceDir)
return getDeviceNames(new File(root, DEVICES_PATH));	throws IOException
	{
	Properties deviceProps = getDeviceProperties(deviceDir);
	String name = deviceProps.getProperty("device.model", "Unknown");
	IConfiguration config = getConfiguration(name, deviceProps);
	IProfile profile = getProfile(name, deviceDir.getName(), deviceProps);
	IEmulator emulator = new NokiaEmulator(deviceDir, deviceProps);
	IPreverifier preverifier = new NokiaPreverifier(deviceDir, deviceProps);
	return createNewPlatformDefinition(
	name,
	deviceDir,
	emulator,
	preverifier,
	config,
	new IProfile[] { profile });
}	}

Legend

Removed from v.1.1	
Changed Lines	
	Added in v. 1.2

version 1.1, Tue Feb 10 00:49:06 2004 UTC	version 1.2, Sun Feb 22 03:12:03 2004 UTC
/**	/**
* @see eclipseme.model.IWirelessToolkit#getEmulatorClassName()	* Get the configuration specified by the device properties.
	*
	* @param platformName
	* @param deviceProps
	* @return
*/	*/
public String getEmulatorClassName() {	private IConfiguration getConfiguration(String platformName, Properties deviceProps) {
// TODO Auto-generated method stub	Configuration config = null;
return null;	String configProp = deviceProps.getProperty("microedition.configuration");
	if (configProp != null) {
	int dashIndex = configProp.indexOf('-');
	if (dashIndex != -1) {
	// Create the configuration
	String configName = configProp + " (" + platformName + ")";
	String versionString = configProp.substring(dashIndex + 1);
	Version configVersion = new Version(versionString);
	config = new Configuration(this, config-Name, configVersion);
	// Do all of the registration stuff.
	config.addDependentComponent(this);
	config.setDerived(true);
	config.setSpecificationVersion(versionString);
	getRegistry().add(config);
	}
	}

Legend

Removed from v.1.1	
Changed Lines	
	Added in v. 1.2

version 1.1, Tue Feb 10 00:49:06 2004 UTC	version 1.2, Sun Feb 22 03:12:03 2004 UTC
	return config;
}	}
/**	/**
* @see eclipseme.model.IWirelessToolkit#getEmulatorJarFiles()	* Get the properties definition for the specified device directory.
	*
	* @param deviceDirectory
	* @return
	* @throws IOException
*/	*/
public String[] getEmulatorJarFiles() {	private Properties getDeviceProperties(File deviceDirectory)
// TODO Auto-generated method stub	throws IOException
return null;	{
	Properties props = new Properties();
	File propsFile = getDevicePropertiesFile(deviceDirectory);
	InputStream is = new FileInputStream(propsFile);
	try {
	props.load(is);
	} finally {
	try { is.close(); } catch (IOException e) {}
	}
	return props;
	}
	/**
	* Get the properties file for the specified device directory.
	*

Legend

Removed from v.1.1	
Changed Lines	
	Added in v. 1.2

version 1.1, Tue Feb 10 00:49:06 2004 UTC	version 1.2, Sun Feb 22 03:12:03 2004 UTC
	* @param pathname
	* @return
	*/
	private File getDevicePropertiesFile(File device-Directory) {
	String propsName = deviceDirectory.get-Name() + ".properties";
	return new File(deviceDirectory, propsName);
	}
	/**
	* Get the profile specified by the device proper-ties.
	*
	* @param platformName
	* @param deviceDirectory
	* @param deviceProps
	* @return
	*/
	private IProfile getProfile(
	String platformName,
	String deviceDirectory,
	Properties deviceProps)
	{
	Profile profile = null;
	String profilesProp = deviceProps.getProperty("microedition.profiles");
	if (profilesProp != null) {
	int dashIndex = profilesProp.indexOf('-');
	if (dashIndex != -1) {
	// Create the profile
	String profilesName = profilesProp + " (" + platformName + ")";
	String versionString = profilesProp.substring(dashIndex + 1);

Legend

Removed from v.1.1	
Changed Lines	
	Added in v. 1.2

version 1.1, Tue Feb 10 00:49:06 2004 UTC	version 1.2, Sun Feb 22 03:12:03 2004 UTC
	Version profilesVersion = new Version(versionString);
	profile = new Profile(this, profilesName, profilesVersion);
	// Do all of the registration stuff
	profile.addDependentComponent(this);
	profile.setDerived(true);
	profile.setSpecificationVersion(version String);
	getRegistry().add(profile);
	// Add the profile libraries defined by the device properties
	addLibrariesToProfile(profile, deviceDirectory, deviceProps);
	}
	}
	return profile;
}	}
}	}

Legend

Removed from v.1.1	
Changed Lines	
	Added in v. 1.2

Here is exactly visible what is meant by the lines removed, modified and added. Removed are those that are present in a previous version but not in the actual, a changed lines is a line that is different from the same line before and an added line was not present in the previous version. The tool takes the data from the check out command and for every CVSTag we have a collection of revisions, which is filled in the following way:

```
public void addRevision(CVSRevision revision) {
  revisionList.add(revision);
}
```

Afterwards the following methods sum the lines.public int getAddedLOC() { int addedLOC = 0;

```
  for (Iterator it = revisionList.iterator();
it.hasNext();)
    addedLOC += ((CVSRevision)it.next()).getLocAdded();
  return addedLOC;
  }
public int getDeletedLOC() {
  int deletedLOC = 0;
  for (Iterator it = revisionList.iterator();
it.hasNext();)
    deletedLOC += ((CVSRevision)it.next()).getLocDelet-
ed();
  return deletedLOC;
  }

 public int getModifiedLOC() {
  int modifiedLOC = 0;
  for (Iterator it = revisionList.iterator();
it.hasNext();)
    modifiedLOC += ((CVSRevision)it.next()).getLocModi-
fied();
  return modifiedLOC;
  }
```

7.6.1.2 Revisions

In terms of revisions, we have the following situation. Using the XML gathered from our tool (taken from junit.xml) we get the following XML. The file

"\junit\junit\awtui\AboutDialog.java"

with the revision ID 1.2 has 0 added, 1 modified and 8 deleted lines. Totally the file contains 50 lines of code and it is contained in the tags r381, r38, v2, v1, r37, r36 and r35.

```
<File Name="\junit\junit\awtui\AboutDialog.java">
        <Revision ID="1.1.1.1">
            <Added_LOC>0</Added_LOC>
```

```
            <Modified_LOC>0</Modified_LOC>
            <Deleted_LOC>0</Deleted_LOC>
            <Total_LOC>58</Total_LOC>
            <TagList>
                <Tag>r34</Tag>
                <Tag>start</Tag>
            </TagList>
        </Revision>
        <Revision ID="1.1">
            <Added_LOC>0</Added_LOC>
            <Modified_LOC>0</Modified_LOC>
            <Deleted_LOC>0</Deleted_LOC>
            <Total_LOC>58</Total_LOC>
            <TagList/>
        </Revision>
        <Revision ID="1.2">
            <Added_LOC>0</Added_LOC>
            <Modified_LOC>1</Modified_LOC>
            <Deleted_LOC>8</Deleted_LOC>
            <Total_LOC>50</Total_LOC>
            <TagList>
                <Tag>r381</Tag>
                <Tag>r38</Tag>
                <Tag>v2</Tag>
                <Tag>v1</Tag>
                <Tag>r37</Tag>
                <Tag>r36</Tag>
                <Tag>r35</Tag>
            </TagList>
        </Revision>
        <Revision ID="1.3">
            <Added_LOC>0</Added_LOC>
            <Modified_LOC>12</Modified_LOC>
            <Deleted_LOC>0</Deleted_LOC>
            <Total_LOC>50</Total_LOC>
            <TagList>
                <Tag>Root_Version4</Tag>
            </TagList>
        </Revision>
    </File>
```

7.6.2 Example of use of CVSMetrics: JUnit

Than, for each tag, we sum data as showed for the JUnit project in Table 5. This is done by summing up lines of the files of all revisions that belong to a tag (Figure 3). Afterwards the three tags with the most changes are listed separately (Table 6). This ranking is then used as basis to choose the tags to analyze deeper with the Excel Metric Analyzer tool.

7.7 EXCEL TOOL FOR THE ANALYSIS AND EVALUATION OF COLLECTED METRICS

For every project (JUnit, EclipseMe, CruiseControl) we chose to analyze those three product releases having the highest percentile based on the added, modified, deleted and total lines of code (LOC). For every release collect the software metrics and build for every metric a summarizing table with graph, which compares them with the added, modified and deleted LOC.

To achieve the creation of more than 300 graphs we implemented several macros in the Excel worksheet. The tool needs just the start-up required data in the right place. Therefore copy the data collected by the CVSMetrics tool to the corresponding tables. The tool will then generate all the tables and graphs automatically, and only the first part of the interpretation sheet is left to be filled out. Furthermore, it is necessary to specify the first part of the path (of the classespaths) that has to be cut to be able to compare the data collected with different paths by the tools.

7.8 EXAMPLE OF THE USE OF THE MACRO, CRUISECONTROL_2.1.1

The interpretation is constructed partially in automatic, as mentioned before. The calculation for the classes that have to be taken in consideration is as follows:

Summing up the values for each metric and divide the sum by the count of values to get the average metric value (Table 7).

The average is therefore $618/58 \sim 10.5$. As we want only the classes that are well above the average we decided to multiply $10.5 * 1.5$. This is the minimum value that a class must have as value to be taken in consideration for the analysis.

Table 5. Analysis of JUnit

Tag	LOC Deleted	LOC Added	LOC Modified	TLOC	a+d+m	percentile/tag
Start	21	47	184	1688	252	80.00%
r34	19	47	159	1688	225	70.00%
r35	21	18	93	2222	132	10.00%
r36	26	24	55	2273	105	0.00%
r37	32	28	115	2283	175	20.00%
v1	30	30	115	2285	175	20.00%
v2	30	30	115	2285	175	20.00%
r38	65	52	60	3013	177	50.00%
r381	81	49	58	3028	188	60.00%
Root_Version4	22	41	287	3147	350	90.00%

Figure 3. Analysis of JUnit

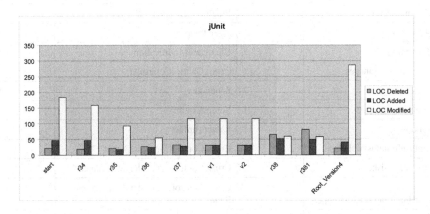

Table 6. Ranking of the revisions of JUnit

RESULT			
RANK	%	Name	Prom Upload
1	90.00%	Root_Version4	04.04.2005 at 21.44
2	80.00%	start	04.04.2005 at 22.07
3	70.00%	r34	04.04.2005 at 22.20

Table 7.

Name of the class	Added lines	Name of the class	Added lines
Main	8	Upgrader	20
CruiseControlException	4	StreamPumper	8
Builder	12	ProjectXMLHelper	24
FileSystem	8	ModificationSet	9
PVCS	21	Vss	8
P4	18	Modification	21
BuildQueue	8	VssBootstrapper	67
EmailPublisher	33	Commandline	14
ClearCase	10	Project	2
CVS	21	AntBuilder	7
CruiseControl	1	Publisher	4
ProjectControllerMBean	21	DefaultLabelIncrementer	24
ExecutePublisher	3	LabelIncrementer	13
P4Bootstrapper	11	ProjectController	3
SCPPublisher	14	XMLLogHelper	2
DateFormatFactory	2	PluginXMLHelper	5
PauseBuilder	7	Bootstrapper	13
ExitException	2	ClearCaseModification	14
NoExitSecurityManager	2	CruiseControlController	5
NullDate	2	Schedule	11
CVSLabelIncrementer	1	SourceControl	4
VssJournal	18	MavenBuilder	9
CurrentBuildStatusPublisher	4	CruiseControlControllerAgent	5
LinkEmailPublisher	2	CruiseControlControllerJMXAdaptor	5
CurrentBuildStatusBootstrapper	4	CruiseControlControllerJMXAdaptorM-Bean	18
ClearCaseBootstrapper	10	ArtifactsPublisher	10
CVSBootstrapper	8	HTMLEmailPublisher	1
Util	4	MKS	
EmptyLabelIncrementer	4	StreamConsumer	

7.9 MANUAL TEST FIRST ANALYSIS

To understand how our tools might work and which were the results that we could have expected we manually inspected the most active packages of 5 projects looking at the date of commit of the classes and the tests. The following section reports the results (Table 8).

7.9.1 XPlanner

As 52,38% of the classes in the package "xplanner\src\com\technoetic\xplanner\actions" have test classes and those are created earlier then their corresponding classes, we can say that the XPlanner developers are practicing only partly the test first methodology (Table 9).

7.9.2 Cruise Control

As about 72% of the analyzed classes have test classes, we can say that the Cruise Control developers uses testing and are practicing Test First as about 67% of the test classes have been made by test first (Table 10).

7.9.3 Prevayler

As about 70% of the analyzed classes have test classes, we can say that Prevayler developers use testing and are practicing Test First as about 53% of the test classes have been made by test first).

Table 8. Test classes in the package selected

Test first classes	22	52,38%
Test after classes	0	0,00%
No test classes	20	47,62%
Total classes	**42**	**100,00%**

Table 9. Test classes in the package selected

Test first classes	12	66,67%
Test after classes	1	5,56%
No test classes	5	27,78%
Total classes	**18**	**100,00%**

Table 10. Test classes in the package selected

Test first classes	9	52,94%
Test after classes	3	17,65%
No test classes	8	47,06%
Total classes	**17**	**100,00%**

7.9.4 EclipseME

No test classes found within the whole project, therefore no test first practiced.

7.9.5 Eclipse JavaCC

No test classes found within the whole project, therefore no test first practiced.

7.9.6 Eclipse Tomcat Plugin

No test classes found within the whole project, therefore no test first practiced.

7.9.7 Automated test first analysis

As we mentioned, CVSMetric also checks, whether the corresponding test classes for the different project classes exist and when they have been created. Therefore the following outputs in the XML file are possible:**Test not found**

```
<File Name="\junit\junit\extensions\RepeatedTest.
java">
          <Unit-Test>n.a.</Unit-Test>
...
</File>
```

Test first found

```
<File Name="\junit\junit\extensions\ExceptionTestCase.
java">
```

```
              <Unit-Test DaysCreatedBefore-
Class="1565.0">\junit\junit\tests\ExceptionTest-
CaseTest.java</Unit-Test>
...
</File>
```

Test found after

```
<File Name="\junit\junit\framework\ComparisonFailure.
java">
              <Unit-Test DaysCreatedBefore-
Class="-71.0">\junit\junit\tests\framework\Comparison-
FailureTest.java</Unit-Test>
```

To extend the manual inspection of the projects we have performed in the previous section we use CVSMetrics on Cruisecontrol - one of the projects that have showed the use of testing and Test First in particular – EclipseME – one of the projects that have not showed the use of testing and Test First in particular – and JUnit – the automated framework to create test suites.

7.9.8 CruiseControl

CVSMetrics confirms the results obtained with the manual inspection increasing the percentage of tests created before their classes. The developers use test classes for their project, as we can see that about 41% of the classes have test classes, and that 70% of them have been made with the test first methodology and only 30% with test after (Figure 4).

7.9.9 EclipseMe

The use of CVSMetrics on all the three tags of the project confirmed that are no test classes found within the whole project, therefore no test first practiced (Figure 5).

7.9.10 JUnit

The developers of JUnit have test classes for about 22% of their classes, whereas about 82% have been made with test first, and the other 18% with test after (Figure 6).

As for the JUnit project was no test framework, as JUnit available, the test percentage is low.

Figure 4. Tests in CruiseControl

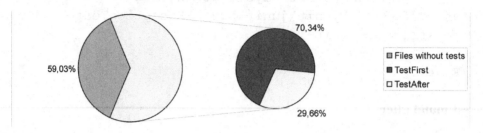

Figure 5. Tests in EclipseMe

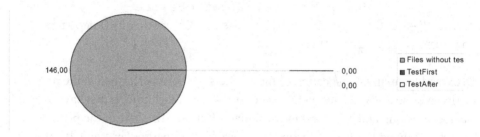

Figure 6. Tests in JUnit

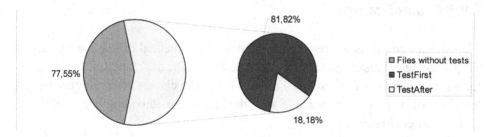

7.10 REFERENCES

Black, R. (2002). *Managing the testing process*. Wiley.

Burnstein, I. (2003). *Practical software testing*. Springer.

Kaner, C., Bach, J., & Pettichord, B. (2002). *Lessons learned in software testing*. Wiley.

Myers, G. J. (1979). *The art of software testing*. Wiley.

Spillner, A., Linz, T., & Schaefer, H. (2007) *Software testing foundations: A study guide for the certified tester exam*. Rocky Nook Inc.

ENDNOTE

[1]   Categories as defined in the Tigris web site.

Chapter 8
Code Ownership

8.1 INTRODUCTION

In many AMs, such as XP, the source code does not belong to the developer that wrote it. The common practice is that all the code belongs to the whole team; therefore every member can modify it. Collective Code Ownership encourages everyone to contribute new ideas to all parts of the project. Any developer can change any line of code to add functionality, fix bugs, or refactor. No one person becomes a bottle neck for changes. This could seem hard to understand at first. It is almost inconceivable that an entire team can be responsible for the architecture of the system (Beck, 1999; Feller & Fitzgerald, 2001).

In many traditional development methods, it is not possible to implement this approach, since a developer knows the details of a very limited part of the product. Usually, just the code he has written. On the contrary, in XP for instance, all the developers have a deep knowledge of the entire code base, since they have to participate in the development of all the code, not just a limited portion (Scotto *et al.*, 2007).

DOI: 10.4018/978-1-59904-681-5.ch008

8.2 PARETO ANALYSIS

Pareto analysis is a statistical technique in decision making that is used for selection of a limited number of tasks that produce significant overall effect. It uses the Pareto principle, the name derives from the Italian economist Vilfredo Pareto, who observed that 80% of income in Italy went to 20% of the population. Pareto later carried out surveys on a number of other countries and found to his surprise that a similar distribution applied.

Pareto analysis is a formal technique useful where many possible courses of action are competing for your attention. In essence, the problem-solver estimates the benefit delivered by each action, then selects a number of the most effective actions that deliver a total benefit reasonably close to the maximal possible one.

8.2.1 Example

Step 1: Frequency Analysis

The first step of the Pareto analysis is to gather data on the frequency of causes (Table 1).

Step 2. Ranking Causes

To identify the most important causes, we rank the causes based on the frequencies they found in their survey (Table 2).

Step 3: Pareto Graph

We draw a horizontal axis (x) that represents the different causes, ordered from the most to least frequent. Next, we draw a vertical axis (y) with cumulative percentages from 0 to 100% (Figure 1).

Now it is easy to see that approximately 7 factors are responsible for 80% of problem. The other 13 factors are responsible for only 20%.

8.3 ADOPTION OF CODE OWNERSHIP IN OPEN SOURCE DEVELOPMENT

To evaluate the adoption of Collective Code Ownership we performed a Pareto analysis on the source code repositories of some OS projects. The sample includes 53 products: 12 written in C/C++, 39 in Java, and 2 in C/C++ and Java, with a number

Table 1. Pareto analysis

Possible cause	%
A	1
B	1
C	2
D	2
E	13
C	2
D	2
E	2
F	6
G	2
H	1
I	1
J	16
K	1
L	2
M	1
N	14
O	12
Q	9
R	10
Total	**100**

of files between 28 (XML Forrest) and 5,279 (XFree86 4.0), and duration between 4 (XML Forrest) and 109 (OpenBSD) months. The considered products belong to very different application domains including: web and application servers, database, operating system, and windows manager. Major versions of the projects Apache, Tomcat, Cocoon, Turbine, and XFree86 are considered as separate projects, since they are very long projects and stored in different repositories.

Table 3 summarizes the contributions to the projects by different developers and points out that the Pareto rule is valid in most of the cases. A small number of the developers (about 20%) are able to commit code into the repositories provide most of the contributions (about 80%). This is true from the point of view of both the total number of commits and the total number of lines of code (added, removed, or modified).

Table 2. Ranking

Possible cause	%	Cumulative %
J	16	16
N	14	30
E	13	43
O	12	55
R	10	65
Q	9	74
F	6	80
C	2	82
D	2	84
C	2	86
D	2	88
E	2	90
G	2	92
L	2	94
A	1	95
B	1	96
H	1	97
I	1	98
K	1	99
M	1	100

In some cases (e.g., XFree86 3.0 and 4.0), most of the commits are made using a shared login in the CVS system (several users using the same account in the CVS system). For this reason, it is not possible to identify the actual developers from the CVS log. In this case, there is a single virtual contributor who has provided more than 95% of the code. Therefore, in such cases the Pareto rule cannot be verified. According to Table 3 only about 20% of the developers that are able to commit source code are the people who drive the development. This means that if the team is small the development is guided by a 2-3 gurus and the project is highly dependent on them. On the other hand, if the project is large enough, the dependency on gurus is reduced and the project is likely to survive even if some of the main developers decide to leave. Table 4 shows the behavior of the developers towards the access policy to source code files.

Excluding the XFree86 projects for the reasons explained above (shared CVS login), data show that most of the code was developed by several developers (Figure 2). In this sense, there is a collective code ownership, several developers are able to modify the same file.

Figure 1. Pareto chart

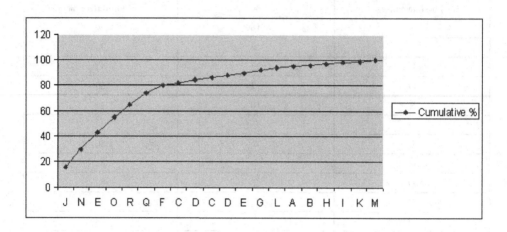

Table 3. People contributing to the projects

Product	People	People contributing to 80% of the commits	People contributing to 80% of the LOC
Ant	29	5 (17%)	6 (21%)
Ant-Antidote	5	2 (40%)	2 (40%)
Apache 1.2	16	8 (50%)	8 (50%)
Apache 1.3	50	11 (22%)	11 (22%)
Apache 2.0	53	12 (23%)	9 (17%)
Apache-Apr	10	2 (20%)	2 (20%)
Avalon	30	6 (20%)	5 (17%)
Cocoon 1.0	13	4 (31%)	5 (38%)
Cocoon 2.0	9	4 (44%)	4 (44%)
Cocoon 2.1	40	7 (17%)	7 (17%)
Cocoon 2.2	29	6 (21%)	6 (21%)
DB-ojb	16	5 (31%)	4 (25%)
DB-torque	18	6 (33%)	5 (28%)
Jakarta Hivemind	46	11 (24%)	11 (24%)
Jakarta Jetspeed 2	11	4 (36%)	4 (36%)
Jakarta JMeter	13	4 (31%)	5 (38%)
Jakarta Lucene	15	4 (27%)	4 (27%)
Jakarta ORO	2	1 (50%)	1 (50%)
Jakarta POI	11	3 (27%)	3 (27%)
Jakarta Taglibs	19	7 (37%)	7 (37%)

Table 3. continued

Product	People	People contributing to 80% of the commits	People contributing to 80% of the LOC
Jakarta Tapestry	7	1 (14%)	1 (14%)
Jakarta Tomcat 3.0	34	5 (15%)	4 (12%)
Jakarta Tomcat 4.0	31	6 (19%)	5 (16%)
Jakarta Turbine 2	19	5 (26%)	4 (21%)
Jakarta Turbine 3	11	6 (54%)	6 (54%)
JBoss	87	9 (10%)	10 (11%)
KDE	379	39 (10%)	38 (10%)
Logging Log4cxx	3	2 (67%)	2 (67%)
Logging Log4j	13	2 (15%)	2 (15%)
Maven	27	5 (18%)	5 (18%)
Mozilla Firefox	266	51 (19%)	37 (14%)
Mozilla Thunderbird	315	47 (15%)	37 (12%)
OpenBSD	66	8 (12%)	5 (8%)
PostgreSQL	13	2 (15%)	1 (8%)
WS AXIS	58	12 (21%)	9 (15%)
WS FX	11	3 (27%)	4 (36%)
WS JAXME	4	1 (25%)	1 (25%)
WS jUDDI	3	2 (67%)	1 (33%)
WS SOAP	12	5 (42%)	4 (33%)
WS WSIF	8	4 (50%)	3 (37%)
WS XMLRPC	11	4 (36%)	4 (36%)
XFree86-3	17	1 (6%)	1 (6%)
XFree86-4	19	1 (5%)	1 (5%)
XML BATIK	10	4 (40%)	4 (40%)
XML Crimson	2	1 (50%)	1 (50%)
XML FOP	12	4 (33%)	4 (33%)
XML Forrest	3	2 (67%)	2 (67%)
XML Security	8	3 (37%)	2 (25%)
XML Xalan	31	9 (29%)	8 (26%)
XML Xang	1	1 (100%)	1 (100%)
XML Xerces	34	9 (26%)	9 (26%)
XML Xindice	11	3 (27%)	2 (18%)
XML XMLbeans	9	3 (33%)	2 (22%)

Table 4. Number of developers per file

Product	Mean	Std. Dev.
Ant	5.36	3.14
Ant-Antidote	1.69	0.78
Apache 1.2	7.12	3.83
Apache 1.3	9.05	7.42
Apache 2.0	9.88	7.08
Apache-Apr	1.30	0.62
Avalon	2.46	1.54
Cocoon 1.0	2.29	1.27
Cocoon 2.0	1.14	0.45
Cocoon 2.1	2.62	1.66
Cocoon 2.2	2.28	1.57
DB-ojb	2.65	1.92
DB-torque	4.72	2.66
Jakarta Hivemind	2.09	1.48
Jakarta Jetspeed 2	1.89	1.17
Jakarta JMeter	2.40	1.51
Jakarta Lucene	2.69	1.49
Jakarta ORO	1.93	0.26
Jakarta POI	1.83	1.04
Jakarta Taglibs	1.96	0.92
Jakarta Tapestry	1.06	0.25
Jakarta Tomcat 3.0	3.51	2.68
Jakarta Tomcat 4.0	2.64	1.69
Jakarta Turbine 2	4.65	2.09
Jakarta Turbine 3	2.85	1.99
JBoss	4.67	4.62
KDE	7.28	8.17
Logging Log4cxx	1.86	0.57
Logging Log4j	2.11	1.41
Maven	2.15	1.46
Mozilla Firefox	3.17	4.58
Mozilla Thunderbird	5.06	7.56
OpenBSD	4.42	2.41
PostgreSQL	2.25	0.92
WS AXIS	3.17	2.63
WS FX	1.93	0.89

Table 4. continued

Product	Mean	Std. Dev.
WS JAXME	1.03	0.18
WS jUDDI	1.59	0.50
WS SOAP	2.72	2.01
WS WSIF	2.04	1.09
WS XMLRPC	2.51	1.57
XFree86-3	1.10	0.37
XFree86-4	1.02	0.16
XML BATIK	2.26	1.29
XML Crimson	1.02	0.14
XML FOP	2.50	1.54
XML Forrest	1.07	0.26
XML Security	2.70	1.29
XML Xalan	3.82	2.62
XML Xang	1.00	0.00
XML Xerces	3.48	1.90
XML Xindice	2.57	1.51
XML XMLbeans	1.40	0.85

Figure 2. Distribution of developers per file

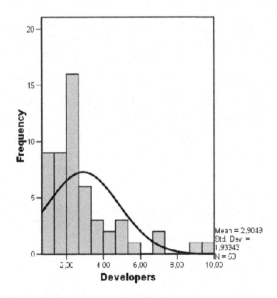

It is interesting to notice that the average number of developers per file is comparable to the number of core developers showed in Table 3.

8.4 REFERENCES

Beck, K. (1999). *Extreme programming explained: Embrace change*. Addison-Wesley Professional.

Feller, J., & Fitzgerald, B. (2001). *Understanding open source software development*. Addison-Wesley Professional.

Scotto, M., Sillitti, A., & Succi, G. (2007). An empirical study on the open source development process based on mining of source code repositories. [IJSEKE]. *International Journal of Software Engineering and Knowledge Engineering, 17*(2), 1–17. doi:10.1142/S0218194007003215

Chapter 9
Design Approaches

9.1 INTRODUCTION

In this chapter we compare agile and OS development in terms of the adoption of design practices.

We review the practices of AMs to identify the agile approaches to the design and we inspect the code of a set of open source projects to determine whether these approaches are undertaken by OS projects.

Software design is a process that defines the solutions to software implementation at the early stages of the software development process. It comprises software requirements and software architecture modeling. In the waterfall approach this process is in general realized with the Big Design Up Front (BDUF). The method consists in creating big structured models of design before any coding to ensure the transparence of the overall software development. In literature there are various models of software design. The most known are diagram specifying requirements, architecture of the system, components, technologies, classes and interfaces. In object oriented programming the design is implemented by the series of UML diagrams – the structure, the behavior, and the interaction diagrams (Ambler, 2004; Fowler, 1999).

DOI: 10.4018/978-1-59904-681-5.ch009

A modern concept of design modeling is performed through the design patterns. A design pattern is a solution to a problem of design that repeatedly occurs and that can be implemented in the code. The model in general is independent from a specific language and a given application domain, but it might be related to a type of programming like the object oriented programming. The design pattern is used to speed up the process of development reusing stable solutions to specific problems of development. A design pattern is not an algorithm though as is not related on computational solution of the conceptual system.

In object oriented programming the major reference on design patterns is the book of the *Gang of Four* (Gamma *et al.*, 1994). The design patterns are classified by the type of problem they solve. In Gamma *et al.* (1994), patterns are classified in three categories: structural, behavioral, and creational.

The structural patterns relate to class and objects and their composition, the behavioral patterns refer to class communication, and creational patterns concern class instantiations.

In the following section we describe the design practices and patterns used in the agile development.

9.2 AGILE APPROACHES TO DESIGN

Agile Methodologies focus on incremental development without a single and large upfront design. Namely, they adopt the Big Design Up Front Anti-pattern (BDUFA) that embrace changes adopting envisioning modeling of design (requirements and architecture) just when needed. The usual approach is to mix and refine with short iterations the design, coding, and the testing phases. Therefore, the code is subject to change frequently, whenever requirements change due to a deeper understand or because the customer has changed idea. As such the design approach in the agile methods can be readily identified in the source code. In this chapter we shall deduce whether the developers of OS adopt BDUFA by analyzing the code changes.

In the following we shall just give some examples and discuss the most famous facts related to design approaches in AMs.

In general, AMs use design patterns when the language of programming is object oriented. Namely, AMs share the common principle of reusing existing working objects from previous projects or project iterations to avoid waste and useless activities. This applies also to design objects proving the use of design patterns successful used in previous project's iteration or projects in AMs.

A design practice peculiar to development with the AMs concerns testing. Many of the AMs embrace testing in the early phase of the development and all across the development itself. In this sense, AMs extensively use the concept of *acceptance test*. The acceptance test is design object negotiated with the customer in which requirements are modified and accepted by both developers and customer.

In the following we briefly discuss the design approach in the some of the most known agile methods.

In XP, the initial light design is defined with the *System Metaphor*. The System Metaphor is a short description of the system describing how it works. It is written in a simple natural language that facilitates the communication among the stakeholders of the development. The design is further implemented with the use of models like user stories, acceptance tests, and CRC cards. These models are refined in each iteration. Namely, as the work is incremental the additions of new system components or user's requirements are also modeled iteratively.

SCRUM is a management, enhancement and maintenance methodology for an existing systems or prototypes. Therefore it assumes existing design and code that in the case of object-oriented development is supported by class libraries. Therefore SCRUM is more oriented to the orchestration of existing practices or model of design. In order to achieve this orchestration, SCRUM uses backlogs to organize and design the work. These are prioritized lists of tasks. Backlogs are dynamically and iteratively filled by the different stakeholders of the development. The priority is based on customer's needs and team ability. Backlogs are used in the SCRUM meetings to understand and predict the performance of the work.

In Test Driven Development (TDD) the stress is on testing. Design practices and pattern reflect this stress. In particular Test Driven Development includes design patterns like the Positive Feedback Loop, for which tests need to be isolated, to be written soon starting from the assert, to use realistic data, to relate input with output. Another diffused practice in Agile development is to use mock objects to simulate complex or external systems. In TDD the mock objects are used in testing. For example, the communication between two objects can be defined by implementing a method of one object working with the interface of the second.

9.3 ADOPTION OF BIG UPFRONT DESIGN IN OPEN SOURCE DEVELOPMENT

As patterns are then implemented into the code, in this chapter we analyze the source code of the OS projects to identify design patterns. We analyze the occurrences in time of the changes. Depending on the density of the changes we can derive whether the Big Design Up Front is implemented. Namely, an accumulation of non-cosmetic changes at a given phase of the development process is a sign of deep activity of design modeling.

Table 1. Classification of the modifications

Type	Code identifier
Structural	Any change to the source code that affects the structure of the product. It includes: class and function definitions, decision statements, loops, etc.
Non-structural	Any change to the source code that does not affect the structure of the product. It includes: variable definitions, inclusions, assignments, etc.
Comment	Any change to comments

Based on several studies on code evolution (Baxter *et al.*, 2004; Eisenbarth *et al.*, 2001; Klint, 2003; Lin & Holt, 2004; Maletic *et al.*, 2002) and on refactoring (Fowler *et al.*, 1999), we have developed the classification of the code changes showed in Table 1.

Moreover, for each type of modification, we identify whether they are additions, removals, or modifications of statements.

We discuss whether OS projects adopt Big Design Up Front by analyzing the behavior of the programmers in the changes they performed in the source code. In particular, in our classification we identify the structural patterns. If we find a predominance of one of the class in Table 1 (mainly structural and non structural changes) we can say that the programmers of the given OS project adopt Big Design Up Front.

The sample includes 53 products: 12 written in C/C++, 39 in Java, and 2 in C/C++ and Java, with a number of files between 28 (XML Forrest) and 5,279 (XFree86 4.0), and duration between 4 (XML Forrest) and 109 (OpenBSD) months. The considered products belong to very different application domains including: web and application servers, database, operating system, and windows manager. Major versions of the projects Apache, Tomcat, Cocoon, Turbine, and XFree86 are considered as separate projects, since they are very long projects and stored in different repositories.

9.4 TIME SERIES ANALYSIS

To identify patterns in the behavior of the developers, a time series analysis technique has been used. A sequence analysis identifies a set of phases of a model and evaluates their evolution in time. This kind of analysis is based on categorical data and its aim is to identify patterns. The considered technique is a sequence analysis that comes from the social sciences called gamma analysis (Pelz, 1985). We clas-

Table 2. Phases for the gamma analysis

Phase	Structural modifications	Non-structural modifications	Comment modifications
000	0	0	0
100	≠ 0	0	0
010	0	≠ 0	0
001	0	0	≠ 0
110	≠ 0	≠ 0	0
101	≠ 0	0	≠ 0
011	0	≠ 0	≠ 0
111	≠ 0	≠ 0	≠ 0

sify source code modifications into three categories (Table 1). Hence, the phases considered for the analysis are listed in Table 2.

The gamma analysis is able to describe the order of the phases in a sequence and provide a measure of the overlapping of the phases. It is based on the *gamma score*, which is a non-parametric statistic based on the ordinal relationship of Goodman and Kruskal (Pelz, 1985) defined as follows:

$$\gamma_{(A,B)} = \frac{P - Q}{P + Q}$$

where P is the number of A-phases preceding the B-phases and Q is the number of A-phases following the B-phases. The γ calculated in this way is symmetric and varies between -1 and +1. Its meaning is summarized in Table 3. The *gamma score* is used to calculate the *precedence score* and the *separation score*. The former one is the mean of the gamma scores:

$$\gamma_A = \frac{1}{N} \sum_i \gamma_{(A,i)}$$

Table 3. Meaning of gamma

	Meaning
$\gamma_{(A,B)} < 0$	A-phases following B-phases
$\gamma_{(A,B)} = 0$	A-phases and B-phases are independent
$\gamma_{(A,B)} > 0$	A-phases preceding B-phases

where N is the number of phases and $\gamma_{(A,i)}$ is the gamma score calculated between the phases A and i. The precedence score varies between -1 and +1. The separation score is the mean of the absolute value of the gamma scores:

$$s_A = \frac{1}{N} \sum_i \left| \gamma_{(A,i)} \right|$$

It varies between 0 and +1. A separation score of 0 means that the phases are independent, while +1 means that there is a separation among the phases. The values of γ and s are calculated for each file in the project. Then, their values for the whole project are calculated as a weighted average as follows:

$$\gamma = \frac{1}{N} \sum_i v_i \gamma_i$$

$$s = \frac{1}{N} \sum_i v_i s_i$$

where γ_i, s_i, v_i are the precedence score, the separation score, and the number of versions of the file i. Table 4 shows that most of the modifications made to the source code (more than 80%) belong to the phases: 000, 010, 110, 111.

According to the data, a large percentage of the modifications (Figure 1) involve the basic structure of the code (i.e., execution paths). This means that there is a continuous adaptation of the code without any large upfront design. In the case of a large upfront design, the modifications to the basic structure of the code should be a minimum amount.

9.4.2 Correlation Among Time Series

The visual inspection suggests that the distributions of the data are not normal. This hypothesis has been verified using the Kolmogorov-Smirnov test (Siegel & Castellan, 1988). Consequently, the analysis is based on non-parametric techniques. In particular, it is not possible to use the Pearson correlation coefficient because it is based on a linear model; hence, the correlation analysis is based on the calculus of the Spearman correlation coefficient.

The separation scores of the most relevant kind of contributions are negatively correlated with the number of versions of the files belonging to the projects (Table 5). All the values are significant at the 0.01 level (except the ones identified by *). This value is more conservative than commonly accepted in software engineering (El Emam *et al.*, 2001).

Table 4. Main modifications

Product	000, 010, 110, 111	Other
Ant	92% (42%, 25%, 14%, 11)	8%
Ant-Antidote	99% (54%, 26%, 8%, 11%)	1%
Apache 1.2	86% (24%, 27%, 21%, 14%)	14%
Apache 1.3	87% (25%, 31%, 18%, 13%)	13%
Apache 2.0	89% (25%, 30%, 20%, 14%)	11%
Apache-Apr	89% (16%, 33%, 28%, 12%)	11%
Avalon	93% (28%, 41%, 15%, 9%)	7%
Cocoon 1.0	84% (26%, 21%, 21%, 16%)	16%
Cocoon 2.0	89% (10%, 24%, 26%, 29%)	11%
Cocoon 2.1	89% (17%, 42%, 18%, 12%)	11%
Cocoon 2.2	90% (10%, 52%, 16%, 12%)	10%
DB-ojb	91% (13%, 32%, 23%, 23%)	9%
DB-torque	91% (13%, 39%, 23%, 16%)	9%
Jakarta Hivemind	89% (16%, 33%, 23%, 17%)	11%
Jakarta Jetspeed 2	88% (5%, 28%, 29%, 26%)	12%
Jakarta JMeter	77% (9%, 22%, 26%, 20%)	23%
Jakarta Lucene	89% (17%, 34%, 19%, 19%)	11%
Jakarta ORO	78% (15%, 55%, 4%, 4%)	22%
Jakarta POI	90% (26%, 32%, 16%, 16%)	10%
Jakarta Taglibs	93% (17%, 46%, 17%, 13%)	7%
Jakarta Tapestry	91% (51%, 12%, 20%, 8%)	9%
Jakarta Tomcat 3.0	86% (9%, 31%, 21%, 25%)	14%
Jakarta Tomcat 4.0	87% (11%, 31%, 21%, 24%)	13%
Jakarta Turbine 2	92% (35%, 28%, 18%, 11%)	8%
Jakarta Turbine 3	89% (16%, 38%, 15%, 20%)	11%
JBoss	88% (10%, 19%, 29%, 30%)	12%
KDE	83% (16%, 24%, 26% 17%)	17%
Logging Log4cxx	88% (34%, 30%, 18%, 6%)	12%
Logging Log4j	86% (14%, 32%, 22%, 18%)	14%
Maven	89% (11%, 29%, 29%, 20%)	11%
Mozilla Firefox	85% (30%, 20%, 18%, 17%)	15%
Mozilla Thunderbird	84% (19%, 24%, 23%, 18%)	16%
OpenBSD	88% (8%, 37%, 32%, 11%)	12%
PostgreSQL	94% (25%, 25%, 31%, 13%)	6%
WS AXIS	87% (16%, 34%, 21%, 16%)	13%
WS FX	88% (12%, 28%, 26%, 22%)	12%

Table 4. continued

Product	000, 010, 110, 111	Other
WS JAXME	90% (6%, 52%, 22%, 10%)	10%
WS jUDDI	98% (19%, 18%, 23%, 38%)	2%
WS SOAP	90% (13%, 37%, 21%, 19%)	10%
WS WSIF	90% (6%, 42%, 25%, 17%)	10%
WS XMLRPC	86% (6%, 37%, 19%, 24%)	14%
XFree86-3	80% (19%, 20%, 16%, 25%)	20%
XFree86-4	80% (28%, 13%, 18%, 21%)	20%
XML BATIK	91% (24%, 34%, 16%, 17%)	9%
XML Crimson	82% (13%, 15%, 20%, 34%)	18%
XML FOP	75% (9%, 28%, 23%, 15%)	25%
XML Forrest	86% (2%, 57%, 20%, 7%)	14%
XML Security	88% (26%, 32%, 15%, 15%)	12%
XML Xalan	87% (27%, 28%, 14%, 18%)	13%
XML Xang	97% (17%, 52%, 14%, 14%)	3%
XML Xerces	85% (19%, 31%, 18%, 17%)	15%
XML Xindice	92% (13%, 46%, 21%, 12%)	8%
XML XMLbeans	90% (23%, 37%, 17%, 13%)	10%

Figure 1. Modifications

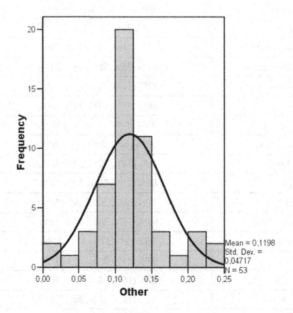

Table 5. Separation scores

Product	N, 000	N, 010	N, 110	N, 111
Ant	-0.425	-0.511	-0.578	-0.565
Ant-Antidote	-0.572	-0.560	-0.283*	-0.702
Apache 1.2	-0.631	-0.541	-0.502	-0.636
Apache 1.3	-0.695	-0.620	-0.719	-0.649
Apache 2.0	-0.314	-0.363	-0.593	-0.408
Apache-Apr	-0.563	-0.514	-0.479	-0.513
Avalon	-0.652	-0.628	-0.618	-0.579
Cocoon 1.0	0.007*	-0.361*	-0.466	-0.602
Cocoon 2.0	0.000*	0.000*	0.000*	-0.125*
Cocoon 2.1	-0.595	-0.615	-0.607	-0.547
Cocoon 2.2	-0.543	-0.588	-0.504	-0.651
DB-ojb	-0.605	-0.640	-0.590	-0.657
DB-torque	-0.422	-0.570	-0.686	-0.644
Jakarta Hivemind	-0.522	-0.712	-0.743	-0.614
Jakarta Jetspeed 2	-0.540	-0.637	-0.604	-0.698
Jakarta JMeter	-0.683	-0.631	-0.627	-0.629
Jakarta Lucene	-0.646	-0.680	-0.581	-0.464
Jakarta ORO	0.184*	0.180*	-0.764	-0.238*
Jakarta POI	-0.639	-0.580	-0.391	-0.531
Jakarta Taglibs	-0.399	-0.474	-0.636	-0.592
Jakarta Tapestry	-0.420	-0.466	-0.516	-0.454
Jakarta Tomcat 3.0	-0.524	-0.731	-0.688	-0.608
Jakarta Tomcat 4.0	-0.613	-0.554	-0.702	-0.689
Jakarta Turbine 2	-0.457	-0.438	-0.602	-0.533
Jakarta Turbine 3	-0.659	-0.660	-0.593	-0.431
JBoss	-0.463	-0.541	-0.599	-0.609
KDE	-0.662	-0.686	-0.663	-0.636
Logging Log4cxx	-0.341	-0.408	-0.386	-0.403
Logging Log4j	-0.559	-0.574	-0.549	-0.629
Maven	-0.613	-0.565	-0.649	-0.587
Mozilla Firefox	-0.675	-0.783	-0.683	-0.651
Mozilla Thunderbird	-0.597	-0.773	-0.678	-0.662
OpenBSD	-0.586	-0.462	-0.458	-0.368
PostgreSQL	-0.511	-0.505	-0.642	-0.622
WS AXIS	-0.469	-0.517	-0.635	-0.587
WS FX	-0.612	-0.497	-0.670	-0.462

Table 5. continued

Product	N, 000	N, 010	N, 110	N, 111
WS JAXME	-0.572	-0.621	-0.618	-0.544
WS jUDDI	-0.581	-0.660	-0.777	-0.682
WS SOAP	-0.485	-0.607	-0.710	-0.735
WS WSIF	-0.261	-0.434	-0.516	-0.706
WS XMLRPC	-0.566	-0.642	-0.846	-0.632
XFree86-3	-0.422	-0.523	-0.475	-0.512
XFree86-4	-0.475	-0.481	-0.448	-0.482
XML BATIK	-0.554	-0.551	-0.622	-0.701
XML Crimson	-0.707*	-0.709*	-0.717	-0.739
XML FOP	-0.727	-0.614	-0.715	-0.728
XML Forrest	0.000*	0.000*	-0.354*	0.000*
XML Security	-0.414	-0.417	-0.556	-0.593
XML Xalan	-0.715	-0.741	-0.580	-0.666
XML Xang	-0.791*	0.137*	0.000*	-0.396*
XML Xerces	-0.625	-0.633	-0.668	-0.636
XML Xindice	-0.189	-0.317	-0.303	-0.555
XML XMLbeans	-0.458	-0.598	-0.604	-0.734

This means that in every project, the separation among phases decreases with the increasing of the number of versions of the files of the project. Again, such data reveal that phases are mixed and this behavior increases during the project rather than decrease.

9.5 REFERENCES

Ambler, S. (2004). *The object primer: Agile model driven development with UML 2*. Cambridge University Press.

Baxter, I. D., Pidgeon, C., & Mehlich, M. (2004). DMS: Program transformations for practical scalable software evolution. *26th International Conference on Software Engineering*.

Eisenbarth, T., Koschke, R., & Simon, D. (2001). Aiding program comprehension by static and dynamic feature analysis. *IEEE International Conference on Software Maintenance*.

El Emam, K., Melo, W., & Machado, J. C. (2001). The prediction of faulty classes using object-oriented metrics. *Journal of Systems and Software, 56*(1), 63–75. doi:10.1016/S0164-1212(00)00086-8

Fowler, M. (1999). *UML distilled: A brief guide to the standard object modeling language*. Addison-Wesley Professional.

Fowler, M., Beck, K., Brant, J., Opdyke, W., & Roberts, D. (1999). *Refactoring: improving the design of existing code*. Addison-Wesley Professional.

Gamma, E., Helm, R., Johnson, R., & Vlissides, J. (1994). *Design patterns: Elements of reusable object-oriented software*. Addison-Wesley Professional.

Klint, P. (2003). How understanding and restructuring differ from compiling-a rewriting perspective. *11th IEEE International Workshop on Program Comprehension*.

Lin, Y., & Holt, R. C. (2004). Software factbase extraction as algebraic transformations: FEAT. *1st International Workshop on Software Evolution Transformations*.

Maletic, J. I., Collard, M. L., & Marcus, A. (2002). Source code files as structured documents. *10th IEEE International Workshop on Program Comprehension*.

Pelz, D. C. (1985). Innovation complexity and sequence of innovating strategies. *Knowledge: Creation Diffusion . Utilization, 6*, 261–291.

Siegel, S., & Castellan, N. J. (1988). *Nonparametric statistics for behavioral sciences*. McGraw-Hill.

Chapter 10
Case Studies

10.1 INTRODUCTION

AMs have been developed considering mainly environments that are limited such as companies. For instance, XP defines practices such as 40-hours per week and pair programming that make sense only inside companies. However, the basic principles and most of the related practices are not bounded to such environments and can be useful to organize Agile teams in different contexts such as in OS communities.

There are several OS tools that are developed using Agile techniques (e.g., JUnit, Eclipse, Funambol, etc.). The case of Eclipse is particular for several aspects such as:

- The development is lead by an organization (IBM at the beginning, the Eclipse Foundation at present)
- There is an active community contributing
- The system includes several sub-projects developed independently

Since the Eclipse IDE includes several sub-projects developed independently, it is not possible to talk about a general *Eclipse Development Process* applied to the entire system but we need to focus on specific sub-projects. The core part of

DOI: 10.4018/978-1-59904-681-5.ch010

the Eclipse IDE is the Eclipse Platform that defines the basic infrastructure used by all the other sub-projects. This part of the system has been developed using Agile practices adapted to the specific environment. This is an example of how Agile development can be customized to support the specific needs of a company or a community.

10.2 THE ECLIPSE SOFTWARE DEVELOPMENT PROCESS

Even if we focus only on the Eclipse Platform development team, it is difficult to define an Eclipse Development Process since it is not fixed but it is evolving continuously adding, removing, or modifying the practices used. In this way, the team is able to tune the process and improve its ability to:

- **Deliver quality software on time:** Quality and schedule are two main problems of software development (Brooks, 1995), in particular if the product is the base for several other projects that rely on it. The development process should help developers in accessing the quality of the software produced to avoid rework and problems that may generate schedule slips.
- **Be predictable:** Make reliable estimates of the time required to complete a set of tasks it is always difficult and requires a lot of experience and a

Figure 1. The Eclipse development process

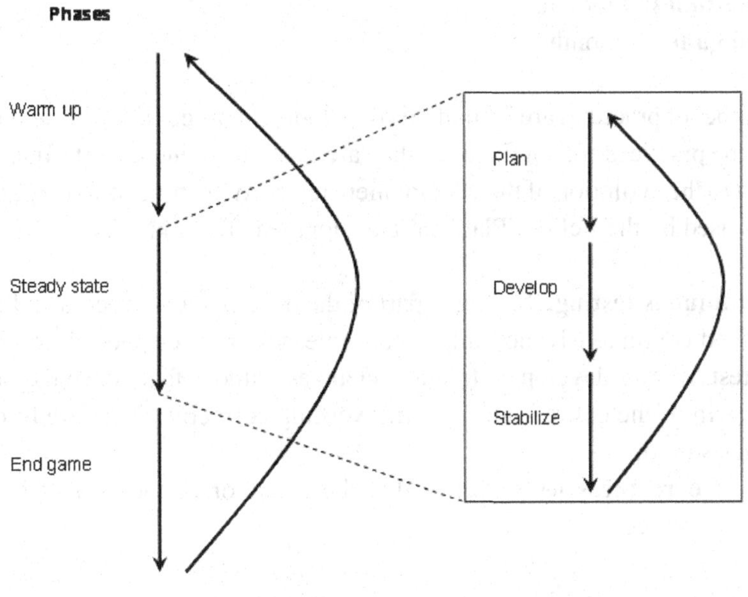

development methodology that helps in the definition of such estimates (DeMarco, 1982).

The development process is organized in cycles corresponding to releases of the platform. Each cycle includes three main phases (Figure 1): warm up, steady state, and end game.

In the *warm up* phase, the team recovers from the stress of the previous release (decompression) (often they schedule it in conjunction with holidays). When the developers are back to work and refreshed they do a retrospective of the previous cycle and define an initial release plan. The plan is not static but dynamic: it may change during the cycle according to the feedback (from the development team and from the community). The plan lists all the potential features to add and the team marks each item as committed, proposed, or deferred. The plan is public and the team likes to receive feedback on that. In particular, related to the proposed features.

In the *steady state*, the development is organized in milestones that are released at regular intervals (6 weeks). Milestones are organized in the same way as cycles, including a shorter version of the same phases called: plan, develop, and stabilize.

After the release of the last milestone, there is the *end game* phase. This is a sprint phase in which the goal of the team is to increase the quality level of the code through short fix-and-test cycles. At the beginning of the end game, they test for 2 days and fix for a variable number of days (usually 3-5 days).

The entire cycle for a release lasts about 12 months distributed as follows:

- **Warm up:** 1 month
- **Milestones:** 9 months
- **End game:** 2 months

A number of practices are behind this development process. As the development process, the practices are not fixed but they are evolving to increase the quality level and adapt to the evolution of the development team. At the time of writing, the main practices used by the Eclipse Platform Development Team include:

- **Continuous testing:** Testing is part of the development process and it is performed continuously, not only before releases or milestones. A complete set of tests allows developers to make changes without fear, since they are able to verify if the entire system is still working correctly. There are three kinds of tests used:
  - **Correctness tests:** Verify that the behavior of the system is the one expected.

- ○ **Performance tests:** Verify that the performance of the system is not decreasing comparing the execution times with the ones calculated in the previous executions and stored into a database.
- ○ **Resource tests:** Verify that the amount of resources used by the system (e.g., memory, CPU, etc.) is not increasing comparing the monitored data with the ones retrieved in the previous executions and stored into a database.

All the tests are executed automatically after every build (nightly, weekly, milestone). Weekly and milestone build are considered executed correctly only if all the tests are passed.

- **Continuous integration:** The status of the entire system is tested continuously to identify problems as early as possible and avoid quality problems and delays related to late integration. To implement continuous integration it is required that the entire building process is automated. Moreover, the quality of the build is verified by a set of automated tests. There are three levels of build:
  - ○ **Nightly builds:** These builds aim at identifying daily problems related to components integration. If building failures occur, it is not a major problem since a new build is done the day after.
  - ○ **Weekly integration builds:** These builds aim at providing a usable system that can be used by the development team to continue their development. It is required that in such builds all the automated tests run successfully. If building failures occur, the system is rebuild to create an acceptable version that can be used by the team.
  - ○ **Milestone builds:** These builds aim at being used by the community. Therefore, they have to be stable enough and include features to test. If building failures occur, the system is rebuild to create an acceptable version that can be used by the community.
- **Milestones:** Instead of using long release cycles (several months), the development is organized in short milestones (6 weeks). Each milestone is developed using a shorter version of the entire development cycle (warm up, steady state, and end game). One of the goals of the milestones is increasing the quality of the product keeping it high during the entire development and avoiding concentrating all the testing and fixing just before the release of the product. In this way, stress at the end of the development cycle is reduced and developers are more confident about the released product. The quality of the milestone is good enough to be used by the community. At the end of each milestone, there is a short retrospective to evaluate what went well and what did not.

- **Always beta:** The system is considered always in beta version. This means that each build is a release candidate and the team is expecting that it is working correctly (no building failures). The goal is producing release quality software every day.
- **End game:** It is the last iteration before a release in which the developers focus only on testing and fixing. The phase produces high level of stress, therefore it is effective only if it is performed only for a limited amount of time. There is a strong commitment and shared responsibility of the development team that aim at releasing software at the highest possible quality.
- **Community involvement:** The community is the best source of feedback on the product. To involve people is to enough to produce open source software but it is required that the development process is transparent to allow people to know what is going on. Lack of transparency reduces feedback because people do not know what are the new features included in a build discouraging its early adoption. Moreover, to encourage feedback is required to be open and discuss plans and decisions with the community.
- **Consume your own output:** Developers have to use their own code to develop. This allows developers to test extensively their own code and push them to produce high quality code since they have to use it to develop the day after.
  - ○ The team of a specific component uses every day the latest code available for their components.
  - ○ The team uses the latest weekly build for the part of the system they are not developing.
  - ○ The community is encouraged to use the latest milestone build and report feedback.
- **Publish new and noteworthy:** It is difficult to get feedback from the community about the most recent functionalities added (or modified) in a product if just a small number of people install the new version of the product. Publishing the new features (both the ones already developed and the ones planned) and the noteworthy stuff related to the product is a way to push the community to install milestones (not only releases), test the new features, and provide useful feedback to the development team.
- **Early incremental planning:** During the warm up, the development team defines the plan for the release considering the input from the community. The team defines a general plan that is detailed at component level by each team responsible for a specific component. At this stage, according to the requirements and the available resources, the team defines a list of features that they classify as committed, proposed, or deferred. The list is revised quarterly to identify progress on the ongoing items, new items, and use the

input from the community. The definition of the plan includes the evaluation of the risk of the items and it is defined according to the following criteria:

- Start with high-risk items and items with many dependences
- Keep a fixed schedule. If it is necessary, the team can drop items starting from the proposed ones and then drop committed ones only if really needed.
- High-risk items are serialized to minimize the integration effort.

- **Collective code ownership:** All the component leaders meet weekly to discuss the status, define plans, and identify cross-component issues. The minutes of such meetings are distributed to all the developers to allow them to know the status of the project and behave accordingly.
- **Component centric:** Eclipse is plug-in centric. Everything is a plug-in that exposes an interface and hides the implementation. In this way, developers can easily modify and extend the system limiting the effects on other parts that are not involved. Each team is responsible for one or more components.
- **APIs first:** Since the architecture is component-centric, the definition of a communication API is extremely important. The API should be consistent, concise, hide the implementation details, and be extensible. To build it the API implementation and a client for it should be developed at the same time.
- **Dynamic teams:** These teams are created to solve specific problems that are cross-component. When a cross-component issue arises, a dynamic team with the key developers of all the affected components is created to address the issue.
- **Build to last:** Every build of the system has to be considered as final from the point of view of the schedule and the quality. Deliveries have to be on time not only at the release but also at every build. The code has to meet quality levels (e.g., stability, scalability, performance, etc.) and continuously includes novelties. This does not mean that code cannot be modified. This means that modifications are required to build a system able to last in time but such modifications have to make the structure stronger not weaker adding bugs or reducing performance.
- **Retrospectives:** After developers have recovered after a release, the team analyzes the previous development cycle to improve the process. In particular, they focus on the following aspects:
  - **Achievements:** What was done well and what are the motivations for that. It is required to know them to be able to replicate them in the following cycle.
  - **Failures:** What and why something went wrong. The team has to identify actions to prevent repeating the same mistakes.
  - **Process:** How to improve the process (e.g., add/remove/modify

practices, tune procedures, etc.)
- ○ **Cross-team collaboration:** Evaluate how the collaboration among developers was carried out, identify potential problems and solutions.

10.3 THE ECLIPSE SOFTWARE DEVELOPMENT PROCESS AND THE XP VALUES AND PRACTICES

As stated in Chapter 1, XP defines in details a sequence of development principles and practices. However, these are not defined directly but they are derived from values and drivers that are the foundation of the methodology. The Eclipse Development process is mainly based on the same set of values and drivers (Table 1).

Table 1. Values and drivers of the Eclipse development process

	Drivers			Values			
	Focus on value	Constant flow	No defects	Communication	Simplicity	Feedback	Courage
Continuous Testing			✓		✓	✓	✓
Continuous Integration	✓	✓	✓			✓	✓
Milestones	✓	✓		✓		✓	
Always Beta		✓	✓			✓	✓
End Game	✓		✓			✓	
Community Involvement	✓			✓		✓	
Consume Your Own Output			✓		✓		✓
Publish New and Noteworthy	✓			✓			
Early Incremental Planning	✓	✓		✓		✓	✓
Collective Code Ownership	✓		✓	✓		✓	✓
Component Centric	✓		✓		✓		
APIs First	✓			✓	✓		
Dynamic Teams	✓			✓	✓		✓
Build to Last	✓		✓			✓	✓
Retrospectives	✓		✓	✓		✓	

Moreover, considering XP and Eclipse practices, it is possible to define a correspondence table (Table 2). This correspondence does not mean that the practice is the same (in some cases it is), but it means that their goals overlap.

In summary, the Eclipse Development Process implements the most important aspects of XP adapting it to the specific context and enabling many different teams to work together.

10.4 THE FUNAMBOL RELEASE LIFE CYCLE

Funambol (http://www.funambol.com/) is a software company producing mobile messaging systems. Their products are released under an OS licence and they encourage developers from all over the world to contribute. To do that they have formalized a development process that follows and Agile approach and includes several Agile practices.

The Funambol Release Life Cycle (RLC) is a development process that defines a set of guidelines for releasing products at Funambol. It defines phases and milestones of the releases and provides the requirements for each milestone. The process is intended in a way to support the developers not to limit their creativity. Therefore, the process is subject of revisions to accommodate new approaches and improve the productivity of the development team.

Table 2. Eclipse and XP practices mapping

Eclipse practice	XP practice
Continuous Testing	Testing
Continuous Integration	Continuous Integration
Milestones	Short Releases
Always Beta	-
End Game	-
Community Involvement	Customer On Site
Consume Your Own Output	-
Publish New and Noteworthy	-
Early Incremental Planning	Planning Game
Collective Code Ownership	Collective Code Ownership
Component Centric	Simple Design
APIs First	-
Dynamic Teams	-
Build to Last	-
Retrospectives	-

Figure 2. The Funambol release life cycle

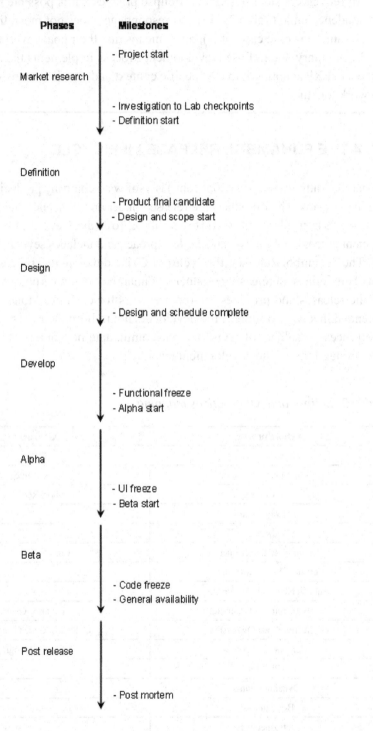

The Funambol RLC includes the following seven phases (Figure 2): market research, definition, design, develop, alpha, beta, post release. During each phase a set of milestones are defined:

- **Market research:** Project start, investigation to Lab checkpoint, definition start
- **Definition:** Product final candidate, design and scope start
- **Design:** Design and schedule complete
- **Develop:** Functional freeze (individual components), alpha start
- **Alpha:** UI freeze, beta start
- **Beta:** Code freeze, general availability
- **Post release:** Post mortem

At each milestone, the development team has to satisfy a checklist organized in five sections:

1. Development
2. Quality assurance
3. Documentation
4. Team

The development section includes items related to the development such as number of bugs present and fixed, functionalities implemented, etc. The quality assurance section includes items related to the number of test cases, testing plan and execution, etc. The documentation section includes items related to the status of the documentation available (including content and format). The product management section includes items related to the packaging of the product to be marketed. The team section includes items related to the commitment of the development team to go ahead with the development (eventually starting the subsequent development phase).

Besides these four standard sections, there are additional sections defined just for specific milestones.

The alpha phase focuses on internal testing and it lasts 2-6 weeks. The check list associated to the alpha start milestone is the following:

1. Development
    ◦   Release schedule updated
    ◦   All functionalities implemented
    ◦   No blocking bugs that prevent quality assurance testing
    ◦   Fix as many critical an major bugs as possible
    ◦   Collect test suggestions from the developers for the new features
2. Quality assurance
    ◦   Test plan completed
    ◦   Staff assigned
    ◦   Equipment available
    ◦   70% of the regression test and new feature tests passed
3. Documentation
    ◦   Outline of the documentation available for delivering to the development team for review
4. Team
    ◦   Development team ready to start the alpha phase

The beta phase targets external testing of the product even if it focuses on a selected number. In this phase the sales department evaluates the new features compared to the market demand and defines pilot installations. The phase lasts 2-6 weeks. The check list associated to the beta start milestone is the following:

1. Development
    ◦   Release schedule updated
    ◦   User interface frozen
    ◦   No blocking, critical, or major bugs
    ◦   Software and documentation delivered to quality assurance for acceptance
    ◦   Support people trained to support beta testers
2. Quality assurance
    ◦   Alpha testing completed
    ◦   Integration tests completed
    ◦   Acceptance tests completed
    ◦   90% of the regression test and new feature tests passed

3. Documentation
   ◦ Documentation and release notes completed and reviewed by the team
     5. Product management
   ◦ Product packaging
   ◦ Product name and version number finalized
4. Team
   ◦ Development team ready to start the beta phase

The general availability milestone provides the official release of the product shipped to customers. The check list associated to this milestone is the following:

1. Development
   ◦ Beta release deployed and widely used
   ◦ General availability release candidate deployed
   ◦ No blocking, critical, or major bugs. Many normal bugs fixed. All bugs fix planned have to be completed. The others are deferred to the following release
   ◦ Final release delivered to quality assurance
2. Quality assurance
   ◦ Final test cycle completed
   ◦ Final integration tests completed
   ◦ 98% of the regression test and new feature tests passed
3. Documentation
   ◦ Final documentation and release notes completed and reviewed by the team
4. Beta manager
   ◦ 2-4 weeks of beta testing at external sites without major problems
   ◦ Confirmation of readiness from the beta testers
5. Team
   ◦ Development team ready to release the product to all the customers

10.5 REFERENCES

Brooks, F. P. (1995). *The mythical man-month: Essays on software engineering, anniversary ed.* Addison-Wesley.

DeMarco, T. (1982). *Controlling software projects-management, measurement, & estimation.* Yourdan Press.

Section 3
Empirical Evaluations

Chapter 11
A Framework for Collecting Experiences

11.1 THE RATIONALE

An informed introduction to AMs requires the ability to determine whether and when AMs are better than traditional software development methodologies. The risk is that AMs are considered just like another tool. Altogether to accredit AMs we need to show the qualified evidence of their effectiveness, performance, productivity, in the different contexts where they can be introduced.

This analysis is difficult as such effectiveness varies with the development environment, depending on several aspects, such as skills, resources and culture. However, this analysis is a key ingredient for the creation of a comprehensive body of knowledge on AMs.

To achieve our objectives, we need to collect existence experience on AM and to formalize it. To such an end we need to define a common *experience framework* where we identify rules so that experience can be archived, compared, and used to create knowledge.

The experience framework for AMs would support such an initiative defining standards and general guidelines for an experimental process in AMs. Its structure would allow some degree of freedom to guarantee its adaptation to individual and working group cultures when used in a single specific experiment.

DOI: 10.4018/978-1-59904-681-5.ch011

The experience framework focuses on different issues including the ones presented in the research roadmap:

- Business
- Management
- Human factor
- Infrastructure
- Technical

Each AM consists of a set of operational practices and share a set of common features with all the other AMs. As AMs are emergent, their practices are often loosely defined and applied by a subjective selection of a few core ones. Therefore, there is a need for benchmarking on AMs that evaluates and identifies best practices, tools and approaches.

Furthermore, following Highsmith's idea (2002) of an ecosystem, an evaluation system for AMs would help interested and expert people in building their own agile method.

There are two main kinds of analysis we may perform on AMs: per single agile practice or per common features.

If we identify standards and guidelines per single agile practice, we model our experimental process to reveal practice, use and efficiency across different agile methodologies. On the other hand if we focus on common features of AMs, we analyze analogies and differences across different AMs or compare AMs with traditional approaches.

11.2 STRUCTURE OF THE EXPERIENCE FRAMEWORK

We have identified four main ingredients to build an experience framework (Figure 1),

1. Data collection
2. Data analysis
3. Set up of the experiment
4. Generalization and validation of the results

The four branches are strictly interconnected. Three of them, data collection, data analysis and generalization and validation of the results are independent from the single experiment. The fourth, set up of the experiment, models general standards to the single experiment to cope with the environment of the experiment.

Figure 1. The four phases of the experience framework

The structure is intended to be agile in the sense that would allow easy access, collective ownership, automated tools, iterative processes, easy reuse, iterative modifications and refinements.

11.3 STANDARDS FOR DATA COLLECTION

A solid analysis requires valid data. Data validation and collection is a continuous process following all the phases of software development. Data needs to be validated in the field, for example, interviewing experts of the project. Vice versa, one can increase accuracy of data validation providing the experts guidelines for data collection.

Following the approach of (Basili & Weiss, 1984), we organize the data collection process along six recommendations.

1. The data must contain information permitting identification of types of error and changes made
2. The data must include the cost of making changes
3. Data to be collected must be defined as a result of clear specification of the goals of the study
4. Data should include studies of projects from production environments, involving teams of programmers
5. Data analysis should be historical; data must be collected and validated concurrently with development
6. Data classification schemes to be used must be carefully specified for the sake of repeatability of the study in the sane and in different environment

A methodology in collecting data prevents subsequent misunderstanding and deviated results. Standards guarantee replication of data collection both in the same and in other experiments, reduction of effort of collection and traceability of data all along the development process.

Hereby we outline a guideline for gathering valid data following the previous recommendations. The first two aspects that should be taken into account are considering the material that is already available and doing a formative action on the environment.

Look at sources of information already available. A software company has several standard forms of control of the software development including the accounting department (for example if the Activity Based Cost (ABC) is used), an existing defects database, a customer service center or a configuration management system. (Succi, 2002).

For companies developing with an AM, extra information can be gathered. For example, in XP there might be a user's story cards collection history that describes not only the requirements themselves, but also the planning game with the customer. In this way, one may also trace the historical development of the requirements that have led to their final form documentation.

Do a formative action on the environment. Data may be stored and forgotten or simply not considered relevant to the project. A formative action on members should encourage identifying correct data and using appropriate tools for collecting and validating them.

From this guideline one may delineate the following strategy for data collection.

11.3.1 Strategy for Data Collection

We have identified four crucial ingredients to be specified in any data collection:

1. Data type and categories for quantitative analysis
2. Data type and categories for qualitative analysis
3. Techniques to extract data
4. Tools to extract data

11.3.1.1 Data type and Categories for Quantitative Analysis

At the beginning of our process analysis, we need to declare which kind of data we are going to collect.

We may refer to categories of data defined by the company, or we may choose external classification. At any rate, it would be useful to specify for each category, the focus of the collection, the tools to be used and the development phase in which that kind of data may be retrieved.

We may also consider the commonly used metrics to evaluate data per each chosen category, but always keeping in mind that they might be modified or substituted by more suitable or agile ones, at the experiment actuation.

11.3.1.2 Data Type and Categories for Qualitative Analysis

Categories of data for qualitative analysis are harder to identify than the quantitative ones. In particular ones related to the development process. Very often, they depend on factors related to the environment context, like motivations and involvement of the interviewees.

A formative action on the environment would help in this direction making aware to the participants the experimental goals. This would help increase the participants' motivation, making the data collection easier. But this might also cause bias in the experimental process, creating factors that influence the analysis. Therefore, it is necessary to balance the given information: goals and results would be public, but access on mechanisms of data analysis and evaluation would be more limited to experts. Strict rules would be avoided; so situations and environments would mostly regulate the access to the experimental process information.

Questionnaires and direct interviews are very often used in collecting this kind of data, as for example in evaluating the use of an AM practice.

11.3.1.3 Technique to Extract Data

Techniques to extract data may depend on the previous two phases, in particular on the context. A formative action on the environment would help the gathering of information on techniques already used by the corporation.

Some techniques may intrude on the individual working sphere and would conflict with privacy policy. Non-invasive techniques using suitable automated tools could cope with this problem.

11.3.1.4 Tools to Extract Data

Techniques to analyze a process are supported by tools subject to considerations similar to the previous ones.

Agile practices recommend the use of automated tools. One can find automated tools useful for any phase of the software life cycle, for example:

- To trace employee' activity, such as Hackystat (Johnson *et al.*, 2003), PROM (Sillitti *et al.*, 2003)
- To trace and relate user's story cards, such as XPSwiki (Pinna *et al.*, 2003)
- To trace modification requests, such as Starteam
- To test code – JUnit, CUnit, etc.

11.3.2 How to Collect Data in a Non Invasive Approach

PROM (Sillitti *et al.*, 2003) is a tool for automated data acquisition and analysis that collects both code and process measures, developed by the Center for Applied Software Engineering (CASE) of the Free University of Bolzano. The tool focuses on comprehensive data acquisition and analysis to provide elements to improve products. Collected data include a wide range of metrics including all Personal Software Process (PSP) metrics, procedural and object oriented metrics, ad-hoc developed metrics to trace activities rather than coding such as writing documents with a word processor.

The tool collects and analyzes data at different levels of granularity: personal, workgroup and enterprise. This differentiation takes a picture of the whole software company and preserve developers' privacy providing to managers only aggregated data.

Moreover, managers take advantage of the system accessing aggregated data that are useful to manage a project. The PROM system takes care of developers' privacy not providing to managers data related to a single developer but only project level data.

11.3.3 Data Collection in the Incremental Process

Data collection of an AM development process reflects its iterative and incremental features. Procedures of data collections can be refined through the analysis performed in the previous iterations. Figure 2 illustrates an iterative data collection. Note that we intentionally emphasize the overlapping of subsequent data collection iterations: their common part represents a refinement phase for data categories, metrics, and techniques.

11.3.4 Categories of Data for Evaluating an XP Process

In the following we suggest possible categories of data that can be collected for each practice of XP.

Together with each data category we suggest to identify

- The purpose of collecting them
- The possible metrics that can be used
- The tools used to extract them
- The phases in the life cycle in which we may collect them.

11.3.4.1 The Planning Game

- *Data categories:* User stories per iteration complete of priorities and effort
- *General focus:* Customer's satisfaction, requirement fulfillment and project management
- *Metrics:* Number of user stories per iteration, effort per user story, relations among user stories
- *Tools:* Automated tools to collect user story – e.g. XPSwiki
- *Phases:* Requirement specification

11.3.4.2 Small Releases

- *Data categories:* Releases, implemented functionalities, user stories
- *General focus:* Customer's satisfaction, requirement fulfillment and project management
- *Metrics:* Defects/warnings count and distribution per release, number of user stories per release
- *Tools:* XPSwiki
- *Phases:* Requirements analysis per iteration

11.3.4.3 Metaphor

- *Data categories:* Metaphors
- *General focus:* System understanding
- *Metrics:* Number of metaphors
- *Tools:* XPSwiki
- *Phases:* Design, integration

11.3.4.4 Simple Design

- *Data categories:* Code units, classes
- *General focus:* Software quality, reuse
- *Metrics:* Complexity, number of classes, number of methods per class, coupling, code unit size
- *Tools:* PROM, Hackystat
- *Phases:* Design, integration

11.3.4.5 Refactoring

- *Data categories:* Refactored code units
- *General focus:* Reuse, time consuming
- *Metrics:* Complexity, number of classes, number of methods per class, coupling, code unit size
- *Tools:* PROM, Hackystat
- *Phases:* Refactoring

11.3.4.6 Test-First Development

- *Data categories:* Test cases
- *General focus:* Quality, time consuming
- *Metrics:* Number of test case per iteration, effort of testing
- *Tools:* PROM, Hackystat
- *Phases:* Design, testing

11.3.4.7 Pair Programming

- *Data categories:* Qualitative data
- *General focus:* Knowledge exchange, quality, job satisfaction
- *Metrics:* Data coming from questionnaires
- *Tools:* Questionnaire
- *Phases:* All along the process

11.3.4.8 Collective Ownership

- *Data categories:* Versions, authoring
- *General focus:* Reuse, time consuming
- *Metrics:* Number of change per person
- *Tools:* Log files
- *Phases:* All along the process

11.3.4.9 Continuous Integration

- *Data categories:* acceptance test, versioning
- *General focus:* reuse, time consuming
- *Metrics:* as before
- *Tools:* as before
- *Phases:* all along the process

11.3.4.10 40-Hour Week

- *Data categories:* Effort
- *General focus:* Time consuming
- *Metrics:* Effort
- *Tools:*
- *Phases:*

11.3.4.11 On-Site Customer

- *Data categories:* Acceptance test, qualitative data
- *General focus:* Customer's satisfaction
- *Metrics:* Number of acceptance test per iteration
- *Tools:* XPSwiki, questionnaire
- *Phases:* Analysis of the requirements

11.3.4.12 Coding Standards

- *Data categories:* Classes, methods
- *General focus:* Reuse, quality, maintainability
- *Metrics:*
- *Tools:* Questionnaires
- *Phases:* All long the iteration

One may also capture data according to common features of AMs, following a similar template.

11.3.5 Example of the Application of the Strategy for Data Collection for an XP Process

Here we outline the strategy in the case of an XP developing process

As XP is an incremental and iterative methodology, the data collection procedure may follow the scheme in Figure 2. As we may collect the same kind of data in different iterations, a first analysis based on comparison among iterations may be promptly reported to the customer.

Furthermore, in the iterative processes we may more and more detail and refine data categories.

Figure 2. Data collection in an iterative development process

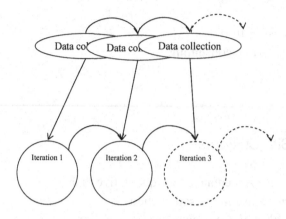

11.3.5.1 Data Type and Categories for Quantitative Analysis in XP

In XP quantitative data are mainly collected from code and user stories. This is because in XP the code would represent its documentation[1].

Moreover, data on the code are readily accessible through a code version system, which realize the XP practice of collective code ownership. Coding standards would help in the data classification.

User stories collections allow tracing the planning game with the customer also. In this way, all the history that led to the final version of the requirement documentation is traceable.

11.3.5.2 Data Type and Categories for Qualitative Analysis in XP

Qualitative data collections do not depart from the quantitative data collection procedure in XP. Due to the subjective nature of some qualitative data, they might be collected on predefined time intervals, more than in a continuous manner. As XP iterations last about four weeks, we may already have a valid amount of data once we collect them at the beginning and at the end of each iteration.

Particular involvement of the customer in XP helps in early detection of information specially the ones related to customer's satisfaction.

11.3.5.3 Technique to Extract Data in XP

XP is an incremental and iterative development method, therefore data collection would model on these features (Figure 2). For each XP iteration, the experts may access to a CVS that support the collective code ownership practice for retrieving code and tests information.

As in all the AMs, XP promotes automated tools and respect for the individual. It is therefore very natural to consider techniques that respect this policy.

11.3.5.4 Tools to Extract Data in XP

Non-invasive and automated tools to extract data are strongly suggested by the XP methodology. There are some agile tools already available, like PROM, XPSwiki, Starteam, etc.

Traditional tools for subjective information, like questionnaires or direct interviews, are also adopted.

In traditional development, the turnover of the employees is a complicating factor in data collection. In XP, thank to a CVS, retrieving historical information is not a big problem and agile databases help in this direction. Even if all the features of an agile database are still under discussion, there are some examples of them already in use – for example Prevayler[2].

11.4 STANDARDS FOR DATA ANALYSIS

An accurate analysis starts from valid data and gives findings that are expressed in a clear and well-defined language.

In this section standards must be categorized so that the data analysis may be:

a.   Replicable, ensuring robustness
b.   Comparable, enabling generalizations
c.   Coherent, in line with existing research

As in Poppendieck & Poppendieck (2003) we need to state the objectives of our analysis at a high level. Goals should be independent from the development process we are going to analyze, but still subject to agile values. Our analysis includes:

- Identification of patterns in the data
- Setting of statistical methods to make inferences
- Using automated tools for data analysis – statistics tools, algorithms for mining and identifying patterns of set of data.

11.4.1 Standards for Data Analysis

As for the data collection, we may consider two different types of analysis, namely according to common features and according to the (set) of practice(s).

If we choose the former, we may like to identify analogies and differences among AMs or compare traditional approaches with agile ones; if we perform the latter we may focus on practice use and efficiency across different AMs or we may be concerned with best patterns of practices for different environmental contexts.

We list some AMs together with their practices. We also suggest similitude among practices of different AMs. This may help in the analysis of common features and practices.

11.4.2 Example: An Example of How to Structure the Analysis in an Incremental and Iterative Process

In Figure 3 we display a possible analysis process for incremental and iterative development processes. Analysis is performed at the end of each iteration of the gathered data. A comparative analysis may be made based on the previous iterations results.

To outline the analysis flow we start with the lean management directives (Poppendieck & Poppendieck, 2003), which recommend the definition of high level objectives for the analysis conforming to the corporate requirements. Analysis processes would not aim at 100% of accuracy in each iteration of the developing process. The best accuracy and the most valid results should come out from several iterations or replications of the analysis process. In Figure 3 we outline an iterative and incremental analysis process that will be further discussed in the next section.

11.4.3 Statistical Techniques

Statistical techniques are mostly selected according to type of collected data and to the goals of the analysis.

Inferential analysis, regression models and best fit theory have been used for prediction and data timing, like defect detection, cost estimation etc.

Descriptive statistics and correlations may identify independent and significant variables of the experiment.

Data patterns have been used to design and re-factor. They help in identifying similarities and differences among experiments, contexts, environments.

Factorial analysis concerns sample groups characterized by specific differences, like the use of different development practices.

Figure 3. An analysis flow for an iterative and incremental process

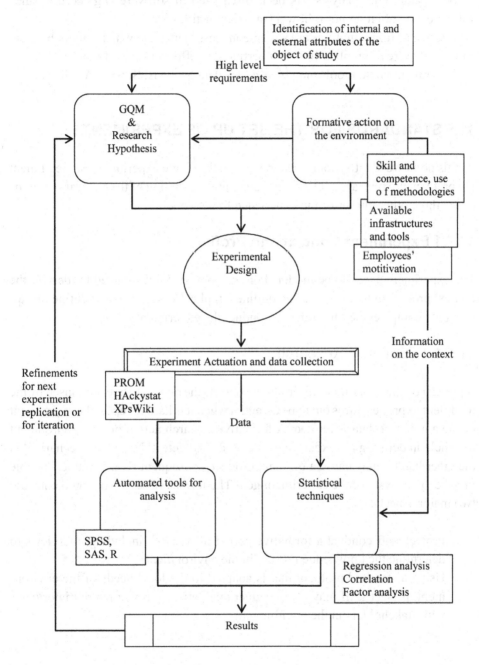

Non-parametric analysis has been often used in software engineering, since software data often do not follow a Gaussian distribution.

Interval or fuzzy analyses are suitable in classifying data which cannot be measured with a (real) number, like data pertinent to effort or cost estimation.

Several automated tools may be used for data analysis: SPSS, SAS, R, etc.

11.5 STANDARDS FOR THE SET UP OF EXPERIMENTS

At this point we identify standards specific to the single experiment. Some of them are pretty new, some are a refinement, adaptation or tuning of the general standards of the three other phases of the experience framework.

11.5.1 Experiment Context and Profile

The experiment needs to be modeled on the context. First we need to identify the context profile. In this way we can outline a replicable scenario and define the appropriate competencies and roles to conduct the experiment.

11.5.1.1 Formative Research

A pre-test on the experiment environment detects the rate of difference caused by the treatment. A pre-test turns out to be essential when it is hard to repeat the experiment or the amount of data is limited. A formative research action on the environment may help in defining the experiment standards and detect the pre-test scenario. On the other hand it may cause a bias and produce consequent rival variables: people may become aware of the experiment goal. The formative research would consider two major aspects:

1. Project staff conduct a formative period of research including interviews to determine the knowledge present in the environment
2. Using a standard protocol that is adapted to the local needs of the environment, project staff may also conduct qualitative, semi structured interviews with stakeholders in the environment.

We report here two scenarios that can be successful to collect context information in XP (Goldman, 2002).

11.5.1.2 A successful Software Practice

- Customer comes with a basic problem
- The customer and the developer sit down together and define the scope of the scenarios to be written
- They work together to write between 3 and 10 short scenarios (usually with between 4 and 12 steps in each scenario)
- They review the scenarios with the project stakeholders
- The scenarios are used to drive further analysis or design (CRC cards, UML class diagrams, etc.)

11.5.1.3 ...With Automated info Collection

- Developers create design a model with scenarios
- A tool parses the model and generates simple test scenarios
- Developers or testers add more test-level detail to the test scenarios, to guide the creation of actual test code
- Later, the design model changes, and the same tool is run again to update the list of tests

A formative research protocol would help in retrieving the following three kinds of information.

11.5.1.4 Background Information About the Industrial Circumstances in Which an Empirical Study Takes Place

The experiment context would involve software SMEs either competent or only interested in AMs.In this section the research should specify:

- Software company competence
- Software company standards – company standards process, quality assurance procedure, configuration management process
- Staff expertise and skills – with languages, AMs, tools and application domain
- Technical support and facilities – platforms, components etc.
- Automatic tools for data collection or analysis – metric tools, log files etc.
- Company standards for reporting research context:
- Specification of taxonomy or ontology of context – e.g. XP vocabulary: test first, customer on-site, coach, stand up meeting

- Knowledge management – knowledge documentation template, knowledge repository, automatic tool, post-mortem analysis, evangelist, interviews, questionnaire, XP customer's manual

11.5.1.5 Background Information About the Experiment

- Kind of projects - pilot project, exploratory experiment, comparative project, project converted to XP
- Project applicative domain
- Project staff composition – number of teams, number of team components, coaches, work environment and staff geographical distribution, turn over
- Agile Methodology considered – XP, SCRUM, Dynamic Systems Development Methodology, and Feature Driven Development, Crystal etc.
- Start up practice or sequential order of practices – process length and iterations decomposition, development iteration length
- Product type
- Possible confounding factors for the specific empirical study – non-complete adoption of all the practices, customer different approach, project early suspension, pressure to ship, turn over

11.5.1.6 Information About Related Research

To collocate the experiment in the appropriate research context one needs to consider the state of art of the related research. The entire research picture could help in defining data collection and storing standards.

11.5.2 Goal Question Metric (GQM) of the Experiment

To start an analysis process we need:

- To describe clearly the objectives of the research
- To identify of the internal and external attributes of the process that concern the above objectives
- To convert those attributes into measurable objects

We may then adopt Basili's Goal Question Metric paradigm (Basili & Rombach, 1988; Wholin *et al.*, 1999) displayed in Table 1.The Goal describes the objective of the research identifying:

Table 1. The GQM paradigm to declare the objective of the research

Goal	Question	Metric	Feedback
1. Action 2. Object of study 3. Purpose 4. Focus 5. Point of view 6. Context	List operational questions in order to achieve the Goal.	Set of metrics according to data features and questions	What has been learned here? In order to clarifying the research for future use of it, sum up results in a "learned lesson" section.

- Action {characterize, evaluate, predict, motivate, etc.}
- Object of study {process, product, model, metric, etc.}
- Purpose {understand, assess, manage, engineer, improve, etc.} it
- Focus {cost estimation, effectiveness, correctness, defects prediction etc.}
- Point of view {customer, developers, managers}
- Context (environmental factors, including process factors, people factors, problem factors, methods, tools, constraints, etc.)

The Question is a relation to be verified connecting the Object of Study with the Focus.

The Metric is a set of metrics for Object of Study, Focus and Question that leads to verify the Question. Identifying metrics for the Object of study, the Focus and the Question allows transformation of the Question in the more operational Research Hypothesis (RH).

The Feedback collects the lessons learned from the analysis.

11.5.2.1 Setting Metrics

Metrics are chosen to measure the Object of study and answer the Question. Three aspects may be considered in selecting them:

- Consider the most used metrics
- Identify appropriate metrics
- Consider metric integration

For example, in a XP process we would like to "measure the productivity in the development phase." Then the number of methods per class, the size of a method, the unit test per class, the complexity may be some suitable metrics. If instead we would "estimate productivity," then effort and velocity of user stories may be the correct ones.

Table 2. Example of GQM (Succi et al. 2002)

Goal	Question	Metric	Feedback
Analyze **pair programming** in order to **evaluate it** with respect to **job satisfaction** from the point of view of **software developers** in the **development of software systems**	Did the developers using pair programming experience higher job satisfaction than those not using pair programming?	Difference of rate of job satisfaction in groups using and not using pair programming	It appears that pair programming effects job satisfaction of developers

As we have seen in the data collection, metrics may be specified in that phase. Refinement or creation of new metrics may be considered afterwards, but still respecting the coherence with previous choices.

11.5.2.2 A Comprehensive Example

The example in Table 2 describes a possible GQM (Succi *et al.*, 2002) for an analysis on the use of pair programming.

The metric for the Object of Study is the use of pair programming, the Focus is the rate of job satisfaction and the Question is the difference of this rate in groups using or not using pair programming.

11.5.2.3 Research Hypothesis

The research hypothesis can be derived from the Question in the GQM model. It is its operational translation that can be built once metrics are identified for the Object of Study and Focus. Each iteration could refine the metrics and the RH to get more and more precise results.

11.5.2.4 Experiment Design

By the theory of experimental design (Campbell *et al.*, 1990), we can choose among several designs of an experiment according to the particular context in which the experiment is conducted.

Very often true experimental design cannot be adopted and quasi experimental design is more feasible. The choice may be connected with the amount of available data: quasi-experimental design is suitable for a limited amount of data or when a randomization process on the data is not feasible. Interested readers should refer to the aforementioned book.To determine the appropriate design, we need the following activities:

- Defining the experimental unit
- Identifying the population being studied
- Declaring the methods used to reduce bias and determine sample size
- Stating the rationale and technique for sampling from that population
- Defining the process for allocating and administering the treatments
- Identifying the possible rival variables to the interpretation of the experiment, which may cause bias
- Rejecting any inadequate hypothesis
- Identifying metrics in terms of their relevance to the objectives of the empirical study

11.5.2.5 Experiment Design in XP

Often development projects with XP are not large scale ones. Furthermore each iteration lasts for a few weeks and the amount of data gathered per iteration cannot be large. Hence in XP a quasi-experimental design is more advisable.

In the iterative processes one may consider either to change design from one iteration to the other or to stop the analysis at an intermediate iteration, as each iteration stands by itself. Data on processes, although not refined, are anyway completed. Changing design is not advisable if one does not want to change the objective of the research. Sticking to the same design allows comparison among data from the iterations.

Of course, analysis of the final software product should end together with its final release.

Iterations help in identifying rival variables to the experiment. That is variables (not controlled variables) that may influence the results. By repetition of the measurement significant variables may be found easier.

11.5.3 Standards for the Experiment Data Collection

Data collection is a rather delicate matter and a particular care to follow the standards should be taken.

11.5.3.1 Data Collection Tools

In this section we specify the tools used for the single experiment according to the general recommendations of section 1.

The more the data collection process is automated the more the data should turn out to be more objective. The use of questionnaires is commonly used, but it is subject to bias whenever an appropriate set up of the experiment has been neglected.

An emergent issue is to identify a strategy for implementing an agile database (Schuh, 2002; Wells, 2001), which therefore would supply an agile-oriented storage and access of the data.

11.5.3.2 Data Collection Schedule

Data collection is a continuous process concurrent with the development process. We need to identify phases of data collection according to the phases of the software life cycle. Each phase would give different categories of data.

In AMs we also may consider data divided per single practice.

The schedule should match with the iterative and incremental features of the AMs.

11.5.3.3 Data Collection Start Up

At this point a complete check of instruments is conceivable. We identified four major steps:

- Trial period to test forms
- Kick-off session
- Checking forms for correctness and completeness
- Storing form data

11.6 STANDARDS FOR GENERALIZATION AND VALIDATION OF THE RESULTS

11.6.1 Comparison

Comparison is a fundamental technique for the validation of the results. There are several types of comparisons one may perform, including:

- Among iterations of the same project
- Among projects in the same application domain
- Among projects using the same agile methodology

11.6.1.1 Among Iterations within the Same Project

Benefits of this analysis consist of fast refinements before the end of the development process.

Comparisons among iterations lead to more consolidated results giving us an extra instrument to analyze the process.

Furthermore, results may be readily available to the customer before the release of the product.

11.6.1.2 Among Projects with the Same Applicative Domain

In the same applicative domain we may compare products and development processes.

Very often we need to understand a more suitable approach or practice to develop a product for a precise target domain focusing on different aspects.

For example in real time domains, with high pressure of time to market, light development approaches and reliability are both important. In this case, one might need to evaluate agile approaches against traditional ones in order to evaluate effort and reliability.

11.6.1.3 Among Projects with the Same Agile Method

Different projects (in domain, size and rigidity) may perform differently under the same AM. For example in public administration, where a lot of documentation is required, AMs may not be the best approach.

With this kind of analysis, the advantages and disadvantages of an AM would be collected to provide cases history.

11.6.2 Refinements

In iterative processes, refinements may be performed within the process itself, among different iterations. Refinements in AMs are quite natural considering their iterative characteristic. Here we outline a few considerations on possible refinements.

11.6.2.1 Data Collection, Metrics and Analysis Techniques

To evaluate the RH we need to measure the relationships between metrics measuring the Object of Study and those measuring the Focus in the GQM. The wrong choice of a metric hampers our deduction process.

If for data accuracy we can replicate the measurement, for valid results we may use iterations. Metrics may be selected based on the conclusions of the previous iterations.

The incremental process may also determine the use of different metrics along the development process. For example, two OO metrics of the CK suite, Cyclomatic

Complexity (CC) or Number of Children (NOC), may give more accurate results in the later iterations rather than in the initial ones, when the number of classes and of methods are still limited.

Together with metrics we may decide to refine our data collection procedure and analysis techniques. They may depend on different tools used in the analysis process or on the evolving environmental context. Refinements detect rival variables of our analysis, such as history and mortality (Campbell & Stanley, 1990).

In XP, short iterations and continuous code ownership would also prevent the influence on the analysis of rival variables like mortality (negative effects caused by staff turnover may be limited).

11.6.3 Meta Analysis and Generalizations

There are two ways to create a body of knowledge: through meta-analysis or through the creation of theories and models.

The role of meta-analysis is to integrate research findings across statistical studies. A substantial number of case studies would consolidate meta-analysis results.

Whenever no formal assessment could be accomplished based on the relatively small amount of information gained in a limited period of time, a meta-analysis may be adopted.

In AMs where we still need to consolidate a body of knowledge, meta-analysis would help in establishing best approaches to further application and investigation

Meta-analysis has two serious shortcomings: it is based on information often a year or more old, and it is based on information typically biased towards the positive. The positive bias stems from the tendency to underreport negative results and the proponents' natural desire to share positive results.

A more stable approach consists in validating the data against an established theory. Unfortunately, the creation of theories passes through a process of generalization and validation of results against previous research. Often it comes after a meta-analysis process, which requires several studies and abstractions.

Depending on the history, the quality or the quantity of the data one may choose one or the other or both ways.

11.6.4 Storage of the Data and the Results

In our process we need to provide recommendations on identifying database profiles for data and for results.

Features of agile databases are still under discussion. Literature is scarce for agile databases for data, and it is null for agile database for results. Namely, managing information is quite a hard matter; it is hard to extract from the single and to store in suitable format in order to be reused.

For managing results we may consider to create a benchmark on AM similar to famous ones like TPC (Transaction Processing Performance Council), SPEC99 (for hardware).

Storing data and results we need to take into account three general recommendations:

- It should allow
- Continuous integration
- Collective ownership
- Collaborate with developers

In XP, working code documents itself. Therefore information and data gather in this process reflects the code structure which is modular and granular, allowing an easy access for reuse and re-factoring.

Tools for code versioning, strongly suggested by AMs, help in tracking history information.

11.7 HOW TO USE THE EXPERIENCE FRAMEWORK: AN EXAMPLE OF REPOSITORY

In this section we present an instance of the *experience framework put to work*. This instance will help the user to perform an experiment in AM following the experience framework guidelines. It consists of a repository accessible via web, which helps in gathering the right sequence of information and instruments to conduct an experiment and to store data and results according to a commonly agreed format. Therefore, it is more than a simple repository of data or results on AMs: it guarantees the validity of the experimental process and of all its outcomes. The main functionalities of the completed repository are:

- **Public multiple view of the meta-analysis results (solutions per practice, per AM, per applicative domain, per product type, etc.):** accessible to everybody. As meta-analysis results need a large amount of case studies and data to be valid.
- **Browse/Insert/update company data:** accessible to accredited users of the partner company
- **Browse/insert/update experiment data:** accessible to accredited users responsible of the experiment – the researchers

A future version of the Experience Framework (EF) web site should be able also to rank results by different points of view providing a benchmark on AMs.

11.7.1 Main Features of the Repository and its Structure

The repository consists of four main entities each corresponding to one section of the Experience Framework, plus an entity for the data (Figure 4).

Each entity corresponds to a major table in the database. The novelty is that each of those tables has more attributes than the expected ones. For example, the table Data would consist of several attributes: Name, Category, Focus, Phase, Tool and Metric and, lastly, the expected attribute, the data Value. This means, for example, that two different instances of Data may differ by the Phase of collection and may have the same values in the rest of the fields, including the value of the data. A similar idea is behind the construction of the remaining other branches.

The branch Generalization&Validation (intentionally highlighted in red) would be the bridge toward a benchmark in AMs.

Other fundamental features of this repository are "flow" and modularity.

There is a clockwise precise flow connecting the five branches (Figure 4.) of the repository starting from DataCollection. Before inserting Data attributes the researcher is advised to fill DataCollection, Data Analysis, and Set up of the Experiment. This would help the researcher have a clear mind about his/her method and about the required theoretical instruments, before performing an experiment.

Even though there is a suggested flow, entities (tables) are mutually independent: for example, the repository allows a researcher to fill in the table of Data without filling the table of DataCollection (for example, because he is inserting data previously stored in the local database) or vice versa, he/she may fill DataCollection without having filled Data.

In an advanced version of the repository, a researcher may also run the flow backwards starting from the entity Generalization&Validation. In the full implementation of this branch, the researcher may refine and replicate experiments towards the establishment of meta-analysis. To accomplish this objective, it is necessary to perform ad hoc modification in the other tables running against the standard flow.

Attributes in each major table will be populated by the accredited user through the corresponding graphic interface.

Each entity corresponds also to a graphic interface of the web site that is filled from the accredited user. After submitting the details of a branch, a summary report is popped out warning on the missing fields. As soon as the researcher submits their details, the four first major tables are linked and an all-in report is popped out to the researcher. To access the Generalization&Validation table, researchers have to complete all the fields of the other branches.

Figure 4. The EF repository

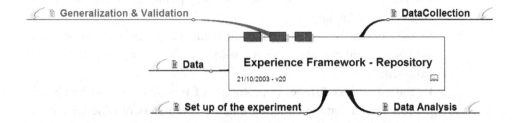

11.7.2 Users

There are two major distinct levels of access:

- To insert/update company data, which include information on employees, on projects,
- To insert/update experiment data, which deals with the experiment and the analysis performed on the project, and include details of data, data collection, data analysis and generalization.

Company's employees may access the former, whereas the researcher accesses the latter.

In Table 3., we display the possible users of our repository and their permissions

The following list represents the current and future permissions.

1. Any user
    a. **Currently and in the future:** He/she may navigate meta-analysis results. Information is stored in secure mode: data may not be modified

Table 3. Users of the system

User	Access
Administrator	He/she can modify the structure and manage users' profiles. He/she cannot modify any data of the company
Reference Person	He/She can access/manage to the stable data of a company, like credentials, list of employees, list of projects. He/she cannot access to the experiment section
Researcher	He/she can only access/modify data related to the experiment and the project
Project Manager	He/she can only modify data related to the project
Customer	He/she can only view/navigate public data

2. Single accredited user
   a. **Currently:** Restricted accredited user may populate the repository and access their own data
   b. **In the very near future:** Industrial/academic partners of the enlarged network would populate the repository with data coming from their experience
   c. **In the very next future:** A prototype of repository would be able to process simple data (as ranking data by parameters of efficiency or of use)
   d. **In the future:** Running an interactive repository with well established features for a wider accredited population, like TPC – Transaction Process Performance Council – web site). Any accredited user may access the full functionalities of the repository.

11.7.3 Graphic Interfaces for the Researcher

To insert the data the user accesses through some graphic interfaces (forms) according to the flow of the branches (see section 1). Each time he submits a form to the repository he gets a summary report on what he/she submitted, with red warnings for missing fields. To get the final branch, Generalization&Validation, the researcher has to have filled all the previous branches.

11.7.4 Scenarios of Usage

In this section we give a simple example of use of the instance of EF – repository. We would like to perform a

Monitoring of efficiency of Pair Programming in communication and knowledge exchange among students of an Internship project

Here we show only the major tables which mainly correspond to a branch (see section 1.3). We omit the Generalization&Validation table because that does not play any role here as the researcher has performed only one experiment.

For the reader's sake, we inserted in Table 4, Table 7, Table 9, and Table 11 the full name of the fields instead of the ID numbers.

The researcher starts filling the DataCollection table (Tables 4, 5):

One may note that DataCollection Technique includes all the tools that have been mentioned in Data.

Here *Iterative* means *according to the project iterations*.

Table 4. Table of DataCollection

DataCollection	
PK	DataCollectionID
FK	DataCollectionSchedule
FK	DataCollectionTechnique
FK	DataCollectionType
FK	FormativeAction

Table 5. A record of DataCollection- Counter =1

DataCollection
Automatic (1)
Periodical/Iterative Test and Questionnaire Incremental Yes

Table 6. A record of DataCollection- Counter =2

DataAnalysis
Automatic (2)
Periodical/Iterative Test and Questionnaire Incremental No

Table 7. A record of DataAnalysis

DataAnalysis	
PK	DataAnalysisID
FK	ObjectofStudy
FK	AnalysisKind
FK	DataAnalysisType
FK	StudyFormat
FK	DataAnalysisDetail

Here s/he decides which Analysis is going to be performed after the data collection:

From Table 8, we see that he/she has chosen to perform the data collection of Table 6 (DataCollectionID=2).

One may note that Object of Study includes DataName of. Table 11.

Table 8. A record of DataAnalysis

DataAnalysis
Automatic
Use of communication tools Experimental By Practice Statistical (Statistics Type) Correlation, (Statistic) Spearman's index, (Significance) Yes, (Value of significance), (Variable 1) Adoption of Pair Programming, (Variable 2) Rate of Use of Instant Messenger, (Model) Linear, (Value of the best fit model parameters), (Ranking) rank in the list of other comparable regression models

Table 9. Table SetUp of the experiment

SetUp	
PK	SetUpID
FK FK FK FK FK FK	ContextInfo Project GQM HR Experiment ExperimentalDesign ExperimentSchedule

Finally, he/she sets up the experiment.

Note that ContextInfo field is not available because a formative action (we have chosen Table 6) has not been performed.

The researcher is now ready to fill the Data table (Tables 11, 12)

All the fields have been filled. The researcher is able to access the Table Generalization&Validation.

11.7.5 An Example of Insert Data flow

The flow to insert data in the repository follows a clockwise route round the branches of Figure 4 starting from Data. The user must be accredited and logged onto the system. However as we have seen, data may be inserted starting from each single branch; missing a whole branch will be reported in the intermediate/final summary.

Table 10. A record of set up of the experiment

SetUp		
Automatic		
Not available		
4		
Goal	Question	Metric
Object of Study: use of instant messengers Purpose: monitoring it Focus: Pair Programming adoption Point of View: students Context: Summer Internship	Is there any relation between the use of instant messengers and the adoption of Pair Programming	Index of Spearman's correlation between Rate of use (ordinal) and Adoption of Pair Programming (boolean)
The use of instant messengers is negatively correlated to the adoption of Pair Programming		
4.1		
Pretest-Posttest Control group Design		
Iterative		

Table 11. Table of data

Data	
PK	DataID
FK FK FK FK FK	DataDescription Phase Tool Metric Focus DataValue

Table 12. A record of data (counter=1)

Data
Automatic (1)
Use of instant messenger
Development
Questionnaire
Rate of use
Practice Adoption
daily

Table 13. An example of insert data flow

User	Researcher
Preconditions	The researcher is logged into the section of the experiment. The company has been registered. The project has been added to the list of viewable projects. The Project Manager and all the information on the project team(s) have been updated.
Main Flow	1. The researcher inserts values in DataCollection. A summary report is popped out (S1) 2. The researcher inserts values in DataAnalysis. A summary report is popped out (S2) 3. The researcher inserts values in SetUp Of the Experiment. A summary report is popped out (S3) 4. The researcher inserts values of the table Data. A summary report is popped out (S4) 5. The researcher inserts the results of the experiment. A summary report has popped out (S5) 6. A final summary result is popped out. All the missing fields are highlighted (S6)

Alternative Flows	1.
	    a. Values for DataCollection have been already inserted. The researcher skips it and starts with M2
	    b. Values for DataCollection have not been inserted. The researcher skips it and starts with M2. The summary report S2 inform of the missing M1 action
	2.
	    a. Values for DataCollection have been already inserted. DataAnalysis has been already filled. The researcher skips both and starts with M3
	    b. Values for DataCollection have been already inserted. DataAnalysis has not been filled. The researcher skips both and starts with M3. The summary report S3 inform of the missing M2 action
	    c. Values for DataCollection have not been inserted. DataAnalysis has been already filled. The researcher skips it and starts with M3. The summary report S3 inform of the missing M1 action
	    d. Values for DataCollection have not been already inserted. DataAnalysis has not been already filled. The researcher skips both and starts with M3. The summary report S3 inform of the missing M2 and M1 actions
	3.
	    a. Values for DataCollection have been already inserted. DataAnalysis has been already filled. SetUpExperiment has been already filled. The researcher skips all of them and starts with M4
	    b. Values for DataCollection have been already inserted. DataAnalysis has been already filled. SetUpExperiment has not been filled. The researcher skips both and starts with M3. The summary report S3 inform of the missing M3 action
	    c. Values for DataCollection have been already inserted. DataAnalysis has not been filled. SetUpExperiment has not been filled. The researcher skips both and starts with M3. The summary report S3 inform of the missing M2 and M3 actions
	    d. Values for DataCollection have not been inserted. DataAnalysis has not been already filled. SetUpExperiment has not been filled. The researcher skips it and starts with M3. The summary report S3 inform of the missing M1, M2, and M3 actions
	    e. Values for DataCollection have been already inserted. DataAnalysis has not been filled. SetUpExperiment has been already filled. The researcher skips it and starts with M3. The summary report S3 inform of the missing M2 action
	    f. Values for DataCollection have not been inserted. DataAnalysis has not been filled. SetUpExperiment has been already filled. The researcher skips it and starts with M3. The summary report S3 inform of the missing M2 and M1 actions
	    g. Values for DataCollection have not been inserted. DataAnalysis has been filled. SetUpExperiment has been already filled. The researcher skips it and starts with M3. The summary report S3 inform of the missing M1 actions
	4. Similar combination of cases

Post Conditions	The database has been updated. A final document visualizes the data that have been inserted to the Researcher; the document highlight eventual missing fields. The four tables are linked.

Table 14. Characteristics of agile development

Modularity	Each table stands by itself. May be accessed independently and may be updated independently. The first four branches are linked only when all their fields have been filled
Reuse	Each populated table may be reused in different experiments
Security	Different profiles of access
Simplicity	The user inserts fields strictly needed for the table. Upload of Access or Excel files help the researcher to insert data all in once
Scientific	To insert data in the branch Genarilization&Validation, the researcher has to fill up all the other branches. The researcher is suggested to follow a prescribed flow. This guarantees the validity of the data and the results stored in the database. The user need not modify many fields. Only the required fields have to be filled in before the next step, these are displayed in the graphical interface.
Public Availability	The web site in its final shape will be full available to accredited users, whereas eventual established results will be of public domain since the beginning.

In Table 13 we mean for data values, numerical values or discovery/fix dates. For qualitative values we mean all the other *nominal* fields as displayed in Table 11.

11.7.6 Some Features of the EF repository

The EF repository is our main instrument to address analysis experimentation in AMs and to answer the open issues listed in the Research Roadmap. In building it, we focused on the following features that characterize the research in agile development (Table 14).

11.8 REFERENCES

Basili, V. R., & Rombach, D. (1988). The TAME project: Towards improvement-oriented software environments. *IEEE Transactions on Software Engineering, 14*(6), 758–773. doi:10.1109/32.6156

Basili, V. R., & Weiss, D. M. (1984). A methodology for collecting valid software engineering data. *IEEE Transactions on Software Engineering, 10*(6), 728–738.

Campbell, D. T., & Stanley, J. C. (1990). *Experimental and quasi-experimental designs for research*. Houghton Mifflin Company College Division.

Goldman, R. (2002). Scenarios. *OOPSLA Workshop on Distributed eXtreme Programming, Tackling the Discovery Costs of Evolving Software Systems, and Pair Programming Explored*.

Highsmith, J. (2002). *Agile software development ecosystems*. Addison-Wesley Professional.

Johnson, M. P., Kou, H., Agustin, J., Chan, C., Moore, C., Miglani, J., et al. (2003). Beyond the personal software process: Metrics collection and analysis for the differently disciplined. *25th International Conference on Software Engineering*.

Pinna, S., Mauri, S., Lorrai, P., Marchesi, M., & Serra, N. (2003). XPSwiki: An agile tool supporting the planning game. *4th International Conference on XP and Flexible Processes in Software Engineering*.

Poppendieck, M., & Poppendieck, T. (2003). *Lean software development: An agile toolkit for software development managers*. Addison-Wesley Professional.

Schuh, P. (2002). Agility and the database. *3rd International Conference on XP and Flexible Processes in Software Engineering*.

Sillitti, A., Janes, A., Succi, G., & Vernazza, T. (2003). Collecting, integrating, and analyzing software metrics and personal software process data. *EUROMICRO*.

Succi, G. (2002). A lightweight evaluation of a lightweight process. In M. Marchesi, G. Succi, D. Wells & L. Williams (Eds.), *Extreme programming perspectives*. Addison-Wesley Professional.

Succi, G., Marchesi, M., Pedrycz, W., & Williams, L. (2002). Preliminary analysis of the effects of pair programming on job satisfaction. *3rd International Conference on XP and Flexible Processes in Software Engineering*.

Wells, D. (2001). *XP and databases*. Retrieved on November 11, 2008, from http://www.extremeprogramming.org/stories/testdb.html

Wohlin, C., Runeson, P., Höst, M., Ohlsson, M. C., Regnell, B., & Wesslén, A. (1999). *Experimentation in software engineering: An introduction*. Kluwer Academic Publishers.

ENDNOTES

[1]   Manifesto for Agile Software Development, http://www.agilemanifesto.org/ (accessed on November 11, 2008)

[2]   http://www.prevayler.org/ (accessed on November 11, 2008)

Chapter 12
Improving Agile Methods

Barbara Russo
Free University of Bozen-Balzano, Italy

Marco Scotto
Free University of Bozen-Balzano, Italy

Alberto Sillitti
Free University of Bozen-Balzano, Italy

Giancarlo Succi
Free University of Bozen-Balzano, Italy

Raimund Moser
Free University of Bozen-Balzano, Italy

12.1 MOTIVATION

Apart from personal experience, anecdotal evidence and demonstrations are still the most prevalent and diffused methods on which software engineers have to base their knowledge and decisions. Although – by searching on line databases such as the ACM[1] or IEEE[2] libraries – we find numerous papers for example on software quality or cost estimation many of them either do not perform any empirical validation at all (they are mostly experience reports or base ideas more on personal opinion than hard data) or the performed validation has limited scientific value as it exhibits one or more of several drawbacks:

DOI: 10.4018/978-1-59904-681-5.ch012

- Data collected and used for analysis are not characterized properly. In particular, it is not always clear how data have been collected, what is their granularity and what statistical properties (kind of distribution, outliers, etc.) it possesses.

- Often studies use the same set of rather old and/or artificial data (Mair *et al.*, 2005), thus risking to be biased towards that data sets and not represent current industrial practices and environments.

- Scarcity of data from industrial settings is a key problem in empirical software engineering and thus experiments most of the times are not replicated by other researchers – limiting their validity.

- Data are often collected manually by developers or dedicated people (for example quality assurance department) within an organization: A manual data collection process is not only costly (it requires a lot of resources) but also error prone as any human activity. Moreover, if the activity of data collection is not conform with development practices – such as in AMs – there is a high risk that data are biased as developers tend not to collect them at all or to collect data in a way that promotes their personal development practices (Johnson *et al.*, 2003).

Statistical methods are not always used in a correct way by software engineering researchers: Data coming from software engineering environments often are messy and show distributions, which do not allow simple statistical analysis such as ordinary least square regression or Pearson correlation (Meyers & Well, 2003). Moreover, statistical analyses and/or data mining techniques should always define a clear methodology for model selection, accuracy assessment, and predictive performance. For example most of the papers in empirical software engineering use the Magnitude of the Relative Error of the Estimate (MRE) as accuracy indicator and selection criterion for prediction models. However, Myrtveit *et al.* (1999) show that a model fitted using MRE as error function and which uses at the same time MRE as selection criterion tends to underfit since it fits to some values below the central tendency of the dependent variable. Tichy (1998) analyzes the status of experimentation in Computer Science and concludes that there is a significant lack of experimentation compared to other fields in science. According to him the main reasons for this fact is the cost factor. While it is true that experimentation in software engineering consumes considerable resources and not negligible costs Tichy emphasizes the advantages and values of experimentation:

- Experimentation can help to build a reliable base of knowledge and thus reduce uncertainty about which theories, methods, and tools are adequate.

- Observation and experimentation can lead to new, useful, and unexpected insights and open whole new areas of investigation. Experimentation can push into unknown areas where engineering progresses slowly, if at all.
- Experimentation can accelerate progress by quickly eliminating fruitless approaches, erroneous assumptions, and fads. It also helps orient engineering and theory in promising directions.

We agree completely with these points and think that effort spent in experimentation in software engineering as in any other field of engineering is worth its value. Being cognizant of the problems and difficulties of experimental, data driven methods in software engineering research with this research we aim at proposing some solutions and overcoming some shortcuts identified earlier, in particular for agile development environments:

- We use a novel measurement framework targeted to agile environments, which enables the automatic and non-invasive collection of reliable and fine grained process and product data.
- We propose methods for selecting and comparing predictors that are easy to collect and still good indicators for assessing software quality.
- We evaluate the impact of agile programming practices such as refactoring on both productivity and quality using real data collected in agile environments.
- We show the feasibility of an automatic effort prediction model, which is highly adaptable to an organizations context and suitable for iterative development processes.

Today software development processes and technologies change faster than ever. Moreover, many software firms operate in highly volatile domains (as for example web development or in the telecommunications sector) and often have to adapt fast to new and unfamiliar business domains. This not only requires huge investments in human resources (people with appropriate technological and social skills) and technology but imposes also a lot of constraints on any measurement program set up in a software organization: First of all, resources for data collection are limited, thus it has to be done in an automatic way. Second, models should reflect short technology and product cycles: It is risky to develop models based on old data and apply them in a completely different context – it is likely that they will fail if between data collection and model application for example development teams, technology or processes change (Cohn, 2006). Third, it is also essential to evaluate and update continuously measures (we refer to them sometimes as features or metrics) used as input (predictors) and output (dependent) variables for models. Since such measures in general depend highly on programming languages/paradigms or specific processes a change of the latter has an impact on the meaning and impact of the further. While statisticians and data miners (Hubert & Verboven, 2003; Bishop, 1994) are well aware of these issues, in particular that multicollinearity leads to models with high variance (thus high predictive errors) software engineers sometimes neglect or ignore such concerns. Being cognizant of the peculiarities of statistical properties of software engineering data in this thesis we over and over emphasize and propose techniques to circumvent or solve possible problems for proper statistical analysis such as multicollinearity of input variables or skewed data distributions.

The context of the two case studies of this research belongs to the family of agile development processes. We recapitulate the ideas and principles of agile methodologies for the unfamiliar reader in order to give her/him an understanding of the challenges of measurements and application of data analysis for process and product control in such environments. Agile software development is an approach for building systems that emphasizes evolutionary development and design, short cycles, incremental planning, customer-centricity, low-documentation/specification overhead, and its ability to response to changing business needs. It strongly relies on oral communication, and uses tests and source code to communicate system structure and intent. AMs are often further defined with respect to what they are not, traditional, rigid, plan-based approaches typified by the so-called waterfall model. A high-level set of attributes of AMs is provided as part of the Agile Manifesto[3] and consists of the following four dichotomies:

1. Individuals and interactions over processes and tools
2. Working software over comprehensive documentation
3. Customer collaboration over contract negotiation
4. Responding to change over following a plan

Though there are numerous methodologies that fit loosely under the agile umbrella (Marchesi & Succi, 2003), in this work we focus mostly on a method called XP (Beck, 1999). XP is light-weight methodology for small teams that promotes the following development practices: test first development, acceptance tests, continuous integration, small and frequent releases, refactoring, pair programming, collective code ownership, on-site customer, planning game, simple design, 40-hour-week, system metaphor, coding standards.

The body of substantially detailed and rigorous studies of AMs in practice is still relatively small and immature (van Deursen, 2001). The many writings by industry commentators that do exist suggest that agile methods are in fact succeeding in practice, but these claims have yet to be substantially corroborated with reliable studies. Many of the empirical studies that have been done were performed using students as the participant sample or using subjective surveys rather than hard data coming from industrial settings (one exception is the study run by Layman *et al.* in 2004). The results of these studies, while interesting from the perspective of higher education, lack some of the validity required to generalize their results to the domain of professional software development. One of the most compelling arguments for the agile approach to developing systems is that given the fact that most software projects run out of budget or even fail, developers should focus on delivering working functionality in the shortest possible increments of time so that project sponsors quickly receive some return on their development investment. Diminishing the time between analyses and fielding of a system also helps to manage the fact that organizational requirements change rapidly and that the best way to meet evolving requirements is through a development approach that is able to evolve in parallel. The challenge to developers and managers is to create a development team culture capable of adapting to shifting organizational priorities while at the same time maintaining a commitment to high-quality processes and delivery of sound software system products. From the statements before it is clear that it is difficult to introduce and apply data collection programs in agile environments: Developers focus on implementing features required by a customer for the next development iteration and are not willing to *waste* any time for other activities such as documentation or filling in time sheets (for the purpose of data collection) unless those activities contribute to the final goal. Moreover, if forced to invoke data collection tools manually they are distracted from their core activity, which is development and thus it is likely that such tools decrease productivity or even change usual developers' behavior. Nevertheless, as more and more companies aim at reaching level three of the Capability Maturity Model (CMM) (Humphrey, 1995), which means that the development process needs to be defined using both product and process measures, even for agile companies a measurement program is a must. In particular governmental organizations more often require that a software company is certified according to some defined CMM level in order to accept a contract; in short, if agile companies want to be competitive (in particular with their non-agile competitors) they need to invest resources and install some kind of – preferably light-weight – measurement program. By careful analysis of the specific needs and characteristics of agile development projects we defined properties and constraints that agile, lightweight measurement frameworks need to have in practice. We implemented those requirements in the PROM tool (Sillitti *et al.*, 2003), which we use for noninvasive data collection in agile development projects. While automatic data collection is for sure a precondition for data analysis in agile contexts it has to be complemented by appropriate analysis techniques:

- Traditional models of software engineering are based on assumptions that are not anymore given in agile environments and therefore questionable. A common, traditional approach for building for example effort·or quality prediction models can be outlined as follows: Data from several old projects are collected and used for model building. Such model is used to predict future effort or quality of projects, which have similar characteristics with the projects used for model construction (often *similar* is not defined well by some objective metric but rather by subjective opinion). Usually such process takes a long time as the completion of several projects is needed in order to build a reliable model. The problems of such approach in agile development can be summarized as follows:

- From the time of data collection to the application of the model technologies and processes may change. This is even more likely in agile environments since developers may easier change technology or processes in response to changing requirements and market demands. Such changes potentially invalidate any models built on historic data; moreover, it is not clear if it is possible to recalibrate them and an organization risks to waste resources for collecting data and building unusable and outdated models.

12.2 DATA COLLECTION

As said in the previous section a non-invasive measurement framework for automatic collection of reliable, fine-grained data is a precondition for a successful application of quantitative techniques for modeling and improving both software processes and products. However, such framework is not easy to build – in particular if, as in our case, used with and targeted to AMs – and use. Most of available commercial or OS tools for data collection in software engineering lack the following characteristics, which are essential for their usage in agile development environments: Mostly, they deal with product measures; (semi)automatic collection of process measures is nearly always ignored. Often, they are not integrated in the usual working context of developers and managers; the developer is required to invoke such tools explicitly. This lack of integration affects the precision of the collected data. Sometimes, it even happens that measures are collected later in the process than expected, just to comply with given process guidelines; this results in spurious data. Even when some of the tools a developer or a manager use support the collection of a few, mostly product-oriented measures, such measures are not combined with the measures collected from other tools the user or the manager use. Moreover, such activities could potentially distract developers and alter the nature of the development process itself (Poppendieck & Poppendieck, 2003). Finally, if collected data is used to evaluate programmers' performance or working habits it is likely that it will be biased – if not collected without any human intervention.

12.2.1 The PROM Architecture: An Overview

The architecture design of PROM has three main constraints: The architecture should be extensible to support new Integrated Development Environments (IDEs), kind of data, and analysis tools. IDE and third party applications dependent plug-ins need to be as simple as possible. Developers can work off-line, i.e. without Internet connection. All these main constraints are satisfied by the PROM architecture. The PROM core is completely written in Java using open source technologies and standard protocols such as XML and XML-RPC. XML-RPC is a lightweight protocol based on XML that implements remote procedure calls (RPC) over HTTP channels. Developers can write plug-ins in any language but they have to communicate to the PROM Transfer (Figure 1) using the XML-RPC protocol. PROM exposes a set of functions that are available inside an Intranet or over the Internet as web services. Moreover, PROM provides secure communications and data are encrypted using RSA algorithm with 1024 bit keys. PROM has a modular, component based design. It has four main modules (Figure 1):

- The PROM server is the core of the PROM system and installed either locally within an organization that uses PROM for data collection or remotely on some server that can be reached via Internet (for example within a research institute), it consists of four major components: the XML-RPC server, which is responsible for communicating with the PROM Transfer tool and encrypted data transfer; a web-server used for administration and data visualization; several tools for data processing (integration with process metrics and data cleaning) and finally the PROM data warehouse storing integrated and cleaned data.
- The PROM Transfer tool is installed on a client machine and its main purpose is to collect data coming from various sources and send it to the PROM Server using XML-RPC calls and HTTP as transport protocol. Moreover, it provides data caching in case a client machine is not connected to the Internet and provides facilities for user authentication and some basic administration.
- Client tools: The PROM Trace is a generic tool for collecting effort spent on various activities (it records the time a window is on focus and the screen saver is not activated, thus it does not distinguish between reading, editing, or other activities), while PROM plug-ins are application specific plug-ins that retrieve effort data and – in some cases – also product data for specific applications such as Integrated Development Environments or Office productivity tools.

Figure 1. Schematic PROM architecture

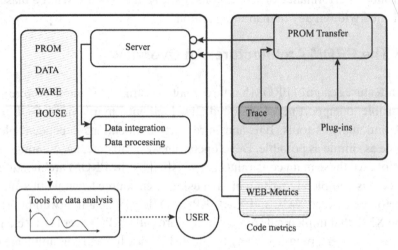

- Web-Metrics is an extensible tool able to extract code metrics from source code repositories. Currently procedural and object-oriented metrics for the following programming languages are extracted: Java, C#, and C/C++.

12.2.2 Data Collection with PROM

PROM is designed to collect different set of software data: product metrics (Chidamber & Kemerer, 1994; Fenton & Pfleeger, 1997 and Personal Software Process data (Humphrey, 1995). The former set includes code length, inter-class and inter-function dependencies, reusability etc. The latter includes time spent in each activity, number of classes per class, etc. Regarding product metrics PROM is able to collect both procedural metrics and design metrics. Some of the procedural metrics collected by PROM are:

- Lines Of Code (LOC) counted as non-commented source code instructions
- McCabe Cyclomatic Complexity defined as linearly independent paths of a procedure flow graph (McCabe, 1976)
- Halstead Volume (Halstead, 1977), which is basically a size measure and combines software size with measures from psychology in order to estimate implementation effort
- Fan-In and Fan-Out, which is used to describe the amount of information flow within procedures (Henry & Kafura, 1981)

In addition, there are also metrics for designs, especially object-oriented (OO) designs that are collected by PROM. Since OO designs can be well defined and specified, as with a language like the Unified Modeling Language (UML), measures about a system's class structure, coupling, and cohesion can be easily derived.

The most cited OO metrics are the Chidamber and Kemerer (CK) suite of OO design metrics. This is a set of six metrics, which captures different aspects of an OO design, including complexity, coupling, and cohesion. These metrics were the first attempt at being OO metrics with a strong theoretical basis. The metrics are listed below:

- Weighted Methods per Class (WMC)
- Depth of Inheritance Tree (DIT)
- Number Of Children (NOC)
- Coupling Between Objects (CBO)
- Response For a Class (RFC)
- Lack Of Cohesion in Methods (LCOM)

Once PROM is installed and configured properly source code metrics are extracted daily from a company's source code repository; moreover, PROM enables the automatic collection of effort associated to different developer tasks such as reading documents, browsing the web, and coding. In particular, plug-ins for Integrated Development Environments (IDEs) such as Eclipse or Microsoft Visual Studio collect the time spent by developers for coding activities at a method and class level: effort data for coding is collected as soon as the developer enters the cursor in the source code editor of the IDE in place and ends if the editor is off focus, the IDE is closed or the screen saver is activated. Moreover, PROM allows the user to specify if one or two programmers are sitting in front of a machine (this feature is needed when a company is using the practice of pair-programming). The notion of effort adopted in the context of this thesis is strongly related to only coding activities and does not include for example time spent discussing the design/code on a white board or other activities; however, in agile processes which themselves assign to coding activities the highest importance we think that the proposed measure is a reasonable measure for total development effort. Both source code metrics and effort data are integrated and stored automatically in a data warehouse, from where we access data for analysis and model building (Figure 1). Table 1 summarizes the measures we collect using the PROM tool: effort data is collected and stored in real-time during development, while product metrics are extracted once a day (preferably during night as it requires a considerable amount of processing time) from a source code repository.

Table 1. Measures collected by PROM and used for data analysis

	Date	Entity (file, class, method)	Effort	Procedural metrics	Object-oriented design metrics
Collection of process (effort) metrics during development	2006-12-17 14:05	UserStories.doc (MS Word)	17 min	---	---
	2006-12-17 14:13	Main.java (Eclipse)	4.8 min	---	---
	2006-12-17 14:15	computeTime(int) (Eclipse)	1.2 min	---	---
	...	...	...	---	---
Extraction of source code metrics once a day	2006-12-8, 00:10	Main.java	---	345 LOC, 1451 HV, 23 MCC, ...	23 WMC, 12 CBO, 30 RFC, 2 DIT, 1 NOC, 10 LCOM
	...	...	---	...	...

Since we integrate product and process measures in the PROM data warehouse, we can aggregate them easily in several ways: for example sometimes we are interested in development effort and changes of source code metrics for one class per day or per development iteration or we may aggregate measures at a package or system level and for different time windows.

12.3 CASE STUDY I

12.3.1 Context and Descriptive Statistics of Data

The object under study is a commercial software project – referred to as project A - developed at VTT in Oulu, Finland. The programming language in use was Java. The project was a full business success in the sense that it delivered on time and on budget the required product, a production monitoring application for mobile, Java enabled devices. The development process followed a tailored version of XP practices (Abrahamsson *et al.*, 2004), which included all the practices of XP but the *System Metaphor* and the *On-site Customer*; there was instead a local, on-site manager that met daily with the group and had daily conversations with the off-site customer. Two pairs of programmers (four people) have worked for a total of eight weeks. The project was divided into five iterations, starting with a 1-week iteration, which was followed by three 2-week iterations, with the project concluding in a final 1-week iteration. The developed software consists of 30 Java classes and a total of 1770 Java source code statements (denoted as LOC). Throughout the project mentoring was provided on XP and other programming issues according to the XP approach.

Table 2. Descriptive statistics for project A. The first row for each iteration indicates the mean and standard deviation, the second row the range.

Iteration	Data points	CBO	WMC	RFC	DIT	Effort (H)
2	21	8.5±4.2	9.2±7.1	19.7±10	2.6±1.1	6.2±6.2
		[1, 17]	[3, 36]	[10, 59]	[1, 4]	[0.3, 26.9]
3	27	9.5± 6.4	14.5±14	24.1±17	2.3± 1.2	8.4±12.2
		[1, 25]	[3, 60]	[3, 77]	[1, 4]	[0.2, 56.6]
4	29	9.6 ±7.3	16.4±19	25.5±19	2.3±1.2	9.8±15.2
		[1, 33]	[0, 81]	[0, 92]	[1, 4]	[0.2, 70]
5	30	9.8±7.1	17.8±22	25.7±19	2.3±1.2	10.1±16.
		[1, 32]	[0, 102]	[0, 91]	[1, 4]	[0.2, 76.2]

Three of the four developers had an education equivalent to a BSc and limited industrial experience. The fourth developer was an experienced industrial software engineer. The team worked in a collocated environment. Since it was exposed for the first time to the XP process a brief training of the XP practices, in particular of the test-first method was provided prior to the beginning of the project.

To collect the data listed in Table 2, we used the tool PROM. Not to disrupt developers we set up the tool in the following way: every day at midnight automatically a checkout of the CVS repository was performed, the tool computed the values of the CK and complexity metrics and stored them in a relational database. In this way we obtained directly the daily evolution of the CK metrics, LOC and McCabe's cyclomatic complexity. The total coding effort recorded by the PROM tool was about 305 hours. Table 2 shows a descriptive statistics of the collected design metrics and coding effort at the end of each development iteration. The effort values in column 7 of Table 2 are cumulative values, i.e. the effort of iteration n is the total effort from the start of the project to the end of iteration *n*.

12.3.2 Research Questions

The goal of this analysis is to determine whether refactoring supports ad-hoc reuse of software. Our objective is to present evidence that will allow us to reject the null hypothesis:

- H_0: The changes of reusability metric M_i induced by refactoring (ΔR_i) are not different from the average changes during development (ΔM_i) for classes that are likely to be reused in an ad-hoc manner.

And to accept the alternative hypothesis:

- H_1: The changes of reusability metrics M_i induced by refactoring (ΔR_i) are different (preferably lower) from the average changes during development (ΔM_i) for classes that are likely to be reused in an ad-hoc manner.

In the following section we explain what we mean by reusability metrics and what approach we take for data analysis.

12.3.3 Analysis Method

In defining suitable reusability metrics we follow the approach of Dandashi and Rine (2002). Their set of reusability metrics consists of the metrics listed in Table 3: they include the CK set of design metrics, lines of source code statements and McCabe's cyclomatic complexity.

However, we do not know a priori the range of values of these metrics that would indicate good or bad reusability. Analyzing historical data or several similar projects can only – if at all – derive such thresholds. We follow a different strategy, as we do not seek to associate absolute values of the metrics in Table 3 to different classes of reusability, but rather analyze the changes of them during development. Our approach is the following: First, we identify a set of candidate classes that are likely to be considered for reuse. Afterwards, we monitor the daily changes of our reusability metrics for each class during development. Finally we compare the average of these daily changes with the change each class gains after it has been refactored. This allows us to quantify the impact of refactoring on reusability metrics compared to their overall evolution during development.

Table 3. Selected internal product metrics as indicators for reusability

Metric name	Level	Definition
MAX_LOC	Class	Maximum number of Java statements of all methods in a class
MAX_MCC	Class	Highest McCabe's cyclomatic complexity of all methods in a class
CBO	Class	Coupling Between Object classes (CK)
LCOM	Class	Lack of Cohesion in Methods (CK)
WMC	Class	Weighted Methods per Class (CK)
RFC	Class	Response Of a Class (CK)
DIT	Class	Depth of Inheritance Tree
NOC	Class	Number Of Children

A bit more formally we can define our method as follows.

Let $M_i \in M = \{MAX\_MCC, MAX\_LOC, CBO, RFC, WMC, DIT, NOC, LCOM\}$ be one of the reusability metrics listed in Table 3. In a first step we average their daily changes for each candidate class over the whole development period not including days when the class has been refactored. We denote this average value for metric Mi by ΔM_i. N in the equation below is the total number of development days; Δt is a time interval of 1 day and R is the set of all days during which developers have refactored a particular class.

$$\Delta M_i = \frac{\sum_{\substack{k-1 \\ k \notin R}}^{N} M_i(k \cdot \Delta t) - M_i((k-1) \cdot \Delta t)}{N}$$

By ΔR_i we denote the average of the daily changes of reusability metric M_i only for the days ($k \in R$) in which a class has been refactored. To assess whether refactoring improves reusability of a class we compute its ΔR_i and ΔM_i values and compare them with each other: If ΔR_i is negative and significantly lower than ΔM_i we may conclude that refactoring improves reusability metric M_i compared to its standard evolution during development.

To apply our method to a real system we not only need to collect the daily evolution of source code metrics but also to identify a set of candidate classes and refactoring activities. Regarding the first issue we proceed as follows: we analyze the design document and use the description provided by developers and our own experience to find classes, which are either explicitly developed for reuse or at least are promising to be reused in the same or similar products. We exclude any classes that are highly dependent on the specific application such as classes dealing with the user interface, product specific data representation/processing or classes holding hard coded data (constants). The identification of candidate classes is a subjective process and therefore we may not identify all relevant classes. However, in an XP process development is not targeted specifically to reusability and in principle every class that is not tightened too much with a particular application feature could be reused in an ad-hoc manner.

The second issue we have to address is: How can we identify days in which a class has been refactored? Currently we are working on a method that extracts such information automatically from a CVS repository by using source code change metrics information (Demeyer *et al.*, 2000). This work is still in an early phase and cannot be used for this research. However, for the case study we present here developers have created user stories for refactoring activities and by analyzing them we know which classes have been refactored when.

To summarize our method for assessing the impact of refactoring on reusability we stress again that it has to be taken cum grano salis, as we do not include many important factors such as experience of developers, development tools, or the stability of the application domain. However, we think that by analyzing the change of important internal reusability metrics induced by refactoring we can indicate whether refactoring - by delivering easy to reuse code - supports ad-hoc reuse or not.

12.3.4 Results

We were able to collect the daily evolution of the metrics in Table 3 for the entire period of development, which was 8 weeks, apart from 3 days. In these days developers apparently did not check-in the source code and therefore we had to omit them from our analysis. The design of the developed system is based on the MVC pattern (Buschmann *et al.*, 1996), the Broker architectural pattern (Buschmann *et al.*, 1996) and several standard design patterns described in (Gamma *et al.*, 1995). We think that some basic classes of these patterns – their importance is also emphasized by the design document – are particularly interesting to be considered for reuse. Out of them we choose a subset of classes, which have been refactored during development. We can infer this information from two user stories that have been implemented specifically for refactoring tasks and comments added in the respective classes. We select in total five candidate classes and compute in a first step the daily changes of the metrics for each of them omitting the days when they have been refactored. We denote the five classes by A, B, C, D, and E. After we compute the average of these changes for all days in which a class has been refactored (the considered classes have been refactored at most on two different days during development). Table 2 shows the results: For each metric and candidate class we indicate the average changes during development (without refactoring), ΔM_i, the average changes induced by refactoring, ΔR_i, and whether or not we can reject our null hypothesis, H_0. We accept or reject H_0 by applying a one-sample Wilcoxon rank sum test (Hollander & Wolfe, 1973): We test whether a sample of changes for metric M_i has a median ΔR_i or not. For the test we use a significance level of $\alpha=0.05$.

The interpretation of the numbers in Table 4 is straightforward: for every candidate class there are at least two reusability metrics that improve significantly after it has been refactored (compared to the average evolution during development). In particular classes A and E show a notable enhancement: These two classes provide general interfaces to the user interface and database and it is likely that they will be reused in a similar application.

By investigating the different metrics we notice that not all of them are affected in the same way by refactoring: The metrics related to inheritance and cohesion for example are not at all or only in a negligible way changed by the refactorings

Table 4. Average daily changes of reusability metrics in case of refactoring (DR) and development (DM). A 1 in the column with heading H means that we can reject the null hypothesis for the particular class and metric, 0 means that we cannot reject the null hypothesis. Values are rounded to their closest integer.

Class	CBO			RFC			WMC			LCOM		
	ΔM	ΔR	H	ΔM	ΔR	H	ΔM	ΔR	H	ΔM	ΔR	H
A	0	0	0	0	1	1	1	-1	1	0	-1	1
B	1	-4	1	1	-4	1	0	0	0	0	0	0
C	1	0	0	2	-5	1	4	0	0	1	0	0
D	1	-1	1	1.4	-2	1	2	0	0	1	0	0
E	1	-1	1	3.5	-2	1	2	3	1	0	0	0
	MAX_MCC			MAX_LOC			DIT			NOC		
A	0	-1	1	0	0	0	0	0	0	0	0	0
B	0	0	0	2	-2	1	0	0	0	0	0	0
C	3	0	0	6	-46	1	0	0	0	0	0	0
D	3	-2	1	0	0	0	0	0	0	0	0	0
E	1	0	0	10	-20	1	0	0	0	0	0	0

applied in the project. This could be explained by the fact that the software under scrutiny is relatively small: It does not use deep inheritance hierarchies and only in a limited way inheritance as a mechanism for reuse. Therefore, it is quiet obvious that no refactoring dealing with inheritance has been applied (it was not necessary to restructure code due to complexity caused by inheritance). As for LCOM several researchers have questioned its meaning and the way it is defined by Chidamber and Kemerer (Counsell *et al.*, 2002) the impact of LCOM on software reusability is little understood by today and therefore we do not analyze it further in this research.

The highest benefit of refactoring show the CBO and RFC metrics: They express the coupling between different classes and the complexity of a class in terms of method definitions and method invocations. We believe that these two metrics are strong indicators for how difficult it is to reuse a class: A high value of RFC makes it difficult to understand what the class is doing and a high value of CBO means that the class is dependent on many external classes and difficult to reuse in isolation. Both situations prevent it from being easily reused. For three out of the five candidate classes refactoring improves significantly both the RFC and CBO values and as such clearly makes them more suitable for ad-hoc reuse. Refactoring seems also to lower method complexity: in all the classes either the method with the maximum lines of code or the one with the highest cyclomatic complexity have gained a notably improvement after refactoring. Again, classes with less complex methods are easier to reuse.

Summarizing our results we can reject hypothesis H_0 for several metrics M_i (in particular for the RFC and CBO metric) but not for all of them (like the inheritance related metrics) and not for all classes we selected. We can conclude that refactoring improves for every class we analyze at least two internal metrics that are important for reusability; moreover, for most of them it lowers significantly coupling and method invocation complexity – two *code smells* (van Emden & Moonen, 2002) that often prevent classes from being reused in an ad-hoc manner. Overall the results of this case study give strong evidence that refactoring supports ad-hoc reuse in an XP-like development environment.

12.3.5 Summing Up

Although agile processes and practices are gaining more and more importance in the software industry much more work has to be done to convince managers to introduce new and innovative development concepts in their companies. Software reuse is a key success factor for software development and should be supported as much as possible by the development process itself. We believe that refactoring supports and enhances ad-hoc reuse in a software project, which does not address reusability as one of its primary goals.

Refactoring seems to improve significantly important internal measures for reusability of object-oriented classes written in Java. Therefore, we can sustain our claim that refactoring has a positive effect on reusability and for sure promotes ad-hoc reuse in an XP-like development environment.

Of course refactoring as any other technique is something a developer has to learn and to train. First, managers have to be convinced that refactoring is very valuable for their business; this research should help them in doing so as it sustains that refactoring – if applied properly – intrinsically delivers code, which is easier to reuse than code which has not been refactored. Afterwards, they have to provide training and support to change their development process into a new one that includes continuous refactoring. AMs already use refactoring as one of their key practices and could be a first choice for developing code in a way that supports – among other benefits such as good maintainability – also reusability.

12.4 CASE STUDY II

12.4.1 Context and Descriptive Statistics of Data

The analysis concerns a commercial software project – we refer to it as project B - developed at VTT Technical Research Centre of Finland in Oulu, Finland. The programming language used was Java and the IDE was Eclipse 3.0. Project B delivered a project management tool for agile projects. The software is programmed with Java and Flash and is a standard web application for desktop computers. The development process followed a tailored version of the XP practices: three pairs of programmers (six people) have worked for a total of eight weeks. The project was divided into five iterations, starting with a 1-week iteration, which was followed by three 2-week iterations, with the project concluding in a final 1-week iteration. The working time for the dedicated project was 6 hours per day, 4 days a week. Beside the mentioned XP practices (pair programming, small releases, continuous integration, planning game) also the practices of refactoring and in part test-driven development have been adopted. Throughout the project mentoring was provided on XP and other programming issues according to the XP approach. Four developers were five 6th year university students and the two remaining employees of VTT and as such experienced industrial software engineers. Project B has 3426 lines of code (Java statements in source code) and 52 classes. The total coding effort for project B is about 664 h. Table 5 reports the descriptive statistics for project B.

Table 5. Descriptive statistics for project B. The first row for each iteration indicates the mean and standard deviation, the second row the range.

Iteration	Data points	CBO	WMC	RFC	DIT	Effort (H)
2	40	9.9±6.1	6.4±3	21.7±13	2.1±1	3.7±4.8
		[0, 20]	[2, 14]	[2, 62]	[1, 4]	[0.04, 20.9]
3	47	11.5±8.5	9.9±9.4	28.2±18	2.3±1	7.5±8.3
		[0, 26]	[3, 61]	[1, 90]	[1, 4]	[0.04, 30.8]
4	48	12.9±8.9	14.1±14.2	35.4±29.	2.3±1	11.1±14
		[1, 27]	[3, 68]	[5, 155]	[1, 4]	[0.04, 57.6]
5	52	15.0±10	14.4±15.7	36.5±29	2.4±1	12.7±15.2
		[1, 32]	[3, 72]	[5, 160]	[1, 4]	[0.04, 64.6]

12.4.2 Research Question

We analyze the impact of refactoring on development productivity and internal code quality. For this goal we first study how the selected productivity and quality measures evolve during the development of the project. By laws of software evolution (those of Lehman), a software is naturally subjected to continuing change (law 1), increasing complexity (law 2) and declining quality (law 3) (Lehmann *et al.*, 1997). In particular, during traditional development by adding new features to a system the internal quality metrics tend to show an increase in complexity and coupling and a decrease in cohesion. More complex code is more difficult to manage and to modify; therefore, we expect that the development productivity will show a decreasing trend over time. In contrast, in XP-like processes, thanks to its constant refactoring, the complexity of the code and the effort for adding new functionalities is claimed to remain about constant or to grow very slowly. Unfortunately, we were not able to run a formal experiment where we could analyze two projects, one with treatment (application of refactorings during development) and one without, and compare directly the evolution of the respective quality and productivity metrics. We have to content ourselves with a simpler approach: we compare productivity before and after big refactorings and use such comparison as criteria for assessing the impact of refactoring on it. For quality we determine the changes of several quality metrics after a big refactoring has been applied to the software and compare them with the average daily changes per iteration. If they are significantly different (improved) we may conclude that refactoring has a positive effect on code quality.

Framed in terms of research questions, we aim at presenting evidence that will allow us to reject (or accept) the following two null hypotheses H_{0i}:

- H_{00}: After a big refactoring the productivity (averaged over four consecutive days) is the same as before refactoring.
- H_{01}: The considered internal quality metrics (complexity, coupling and cohesion) do not show any improvement after a big refactoring with respect to their average daily changes per iteration

To obtain more reliable results we do not simply compare the changes of productivity and quality metrics before and after refactoring. Such changes could happen by chance or some other factors we do not control within this case study. In order to minimize the influence of random and uncontrolled changes we compare the average productivity the week before a big refactoring has been applied with the average productivity the week after. Also for the quality metrics we compute their average daily changes per iteration and compare them with the changes induced by a big refactoring.

Our research design is to some extent a one-factor, repeated-measures design: The treatment (in our case refactoring) is applied one or more times to the same subjects. However, we do not perform a true experiment and therefore we will not consider sophisticated analysis techniques that are available for such experimental design; instead, we use the most common method for comparing the means of different populations, namely the analysis of variance (ANOVA). Our samples are very small (less than 6 subjects per group) and we cannot assume a normal distribution and homogeneity of variance, as it is required by the standard ANOVA method. Therefore, we perform the so-called Brown-Forsythe test (Meyers & Well, 2003), which is similar to the ANOVA analysis, but more suited for our case (heterogeneous variance, small sample size). For the quality metrics we proceed in the following way: first, we compute their daily changes after a big refactoring has been applied. Then, we use a Wilcoxon Signed-Rank (Lehmann, 1986) test to determine whether these changes are lower than the average daily changes per iteration or not. Our final goal is to disprove the null hypotheses by using the Brown-Forsythe and the Wilcoxon Signed-Rank tests to determine (a) if the development productivity is higher after refactoring than before, and (b) if quality metrics are significantly improved by refactoring with respect to their medial changes. We use as significance level $\alpha=0.5$, as it is common in empirical software engineering research (Mišić & Tešić, 1998).

12.4.3 Productivity and Quality

Refactoring is an activity, which in more traditional development processes is – if at all – only present during the maintenance phase in order to improve software maintainability (Kataoka *et al.*, 2002). The context of our analysis however is an agile development process, namely a tailored version of XP; in such environment refactoring is an integral part of software development. Kent Beck illustrates the principle of agile development with the two hats metaphor: one is adding new functionality (coding) and the other is refactoring. The developer should swap frequently between these two hats but wear only one at a time. Therefore, we assume that developers apply small refactorings like Extract Method, Rename, Simplify Conditional, Move Method/Field, and so on throughout development – without even documenting it. We believe that all these small refactorings improve slightly the quality of the code and increase development productivity compared to a development process, which does not use the practice of refactoring. However, due to lack of empirical data (of two comparable software projects, one developed using an agile and one using a traditional method) such comparison is out of scope of this research. Instead, we analyze the effect of big refactorings on productivity and quality within the same project. By big refactoring we do not mean a big refactoring composed of several basic refactorings (sometimes in a predefined sequence) as described for example in the book of Fowler (2002. In this analysis, big refactoring means that developers devote one or more user stories (in XP a user story is a kind of informal requirement document developed at the beginning of each iteration) to refactoring and that the implementation of such user stories takes a considerable amount of time – from some hours to a whole day. For the time being, we do not identify different kinds of refactorings and analyze separately the impact of each refactoring category on productivity or quality (Fowler defines the following categories: composing methods, moving features between objects, organizing data, simplifying conditional expressions, dealing with generalization, making method calls simpler). Such coarse grained analysis could bias our results: Developers may for example only apply a limited subset of refactorings – due to their inexperience or other reasons – and in such case we can probably not generalize the implications for all other types of refactoring. We plan to take into account different categories of refactorings in a more refined, future study.

Now that we know what we mean by refactoring we have to define the other variables of interest for this research, namely development productivity and software quality.

Lots of work has been done on how to measure developers' productivity (Fenton & Pfleeger, 1997). Still, no definite measure has been defined and perhaps such measure does not exist. A very simple measure of productivity is the ratio of the lines of code (LOC) produced and the effort spent in producing them. Several objections has been raised against this measure as a malicious developer could artificially inflate the number of lines of code; only coding is considered ignoring all the other phases of development – analysis, design, etc; code reuse and automatically generated code are not taken properly into account; and other. Despite all its criticism, this equation is by far the most used in industry, as it is very easy to understand and gives clear and absolute numbers, which are easy to compare and to use in statistical calculations. Needless to say, these numbers have to be taken with a grain of salt. In this analysis, we use this equation because of its simplicity and expressiveness. In addition, programmers are all working in good faith – they volunteered for this experiment, the effort spent in activities other than coding has been closely monitored and evenly distributed, code reuse has been closely scrutinized also via the CVS repository, and no code generators have been used.

Software quality is a composite property of many internal and external software attributes. There has been a lot of discussion on the meaning of software quality (McCall, *et al.*, 1977; Boehm *et al.*, 1978). It is now commonly agreed (Fenton & Pfleeger, 1997) that software quality is a property defined by several small-scaled and directly measurable attributes. In this research we use object-oriented complexity, coupling, and cohesion design metrics, as defined by Chidamber and Kemerer

Table 6. Selected product and process metrics for assessing quality and productivity

Metric	Level	Definition
CBO	Class	Coupling Between Object classes
LCOM	Class	Lack of Cohesion in Methods
WMC	Class	Weighted Methods per Class
RFC	Class	Response For a Class
LOC	Method	Number of Java source code statements per method
Effort	Method	Time in seconds spent for coding a method

(Table 6); such measures are widely accepted both by practitioners and researchers and validated by several previous studies (Basili *et al.*, 1996). In addition, such measures are easy to collect and to understand, a precondition for their effective use (Johnson & Disney, 1998).

12.4.4 Summing Up

As mentioned, the Lehman laws evidence that throughout software development the productivity tends to decrease while the code becomes more complex and difficult to understand, classes become more and more coupled with each other, and therefore changes in addition or modification of functionality require more effort as the time progresses (Boehm, 1981). Figure 2 shows the evolution of the average productivity per iteration over the whole development period. It seems that the productivity follows Lehman's laws: It is high in iteration two and three and lower in the last two iterations. In iteration one it is also low, which could be explained by the fact that at the beginning of the project there was more work for setting up and getting familiar with the environment.

The first refactoring user story has been implemented towards the end of iteration 2. We compute the daily productivity of the 4 consecutive days before this first big refactoring and the daily productivity of the four consecutive days after it. In this way we get two, although small, samples of the productivity before and after refactoring, which we then compare by applying the Brown-Forsythe test. We use the same strategy for the second big refactoring, which has been applied towards the end of iteration 4. We choose a period of 4 days (almost one week of development) for comparison mainly for two reasons: On one hand a shorter time period as for example one day increases the probability that the productivity simply changes by chance (or some uncontrollable events) and not due to refactoring. On the other hand we do not have productivity data for more than four consecutive days after

Figure 2. Average development productivity per iteration

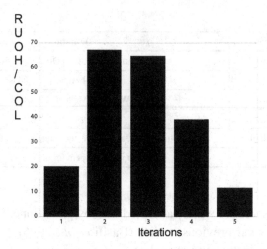

the first big refactoring, since – as mentioned before – some data from the CVS repository are missing. Moreover, an analysis of the second refactoring indicates that the effect of refactoring on productivity is not visible anymore after one week of development.

By applying a Brown-Forsythe test (Meyers & Well, 2003) we cannot reject H_{00} neither for refactoring 1 nor for refactoring 2. However, we can observe that a simple ANOVA test (which is less restrictive) would have allowed us to reject H_{00} for refactoring 1. Overall, we can conclude that the productivity data sustain the claim that refactoring raises the development productivity in the short-term, thus nullifying to some extent the complexity naturally added during development. However, this conclusion is more a confirmation of a suspicion and not a clear affirmation based on statistical inference from experimental data. To consider the long-term effects of refactoring, we have compared the medians of the daily productivity of each iteration using non-parametric Kruskal-Wallis test (Meyers & Well, 2003). The result is that the medians of the daily productivities of each iteration are not statistically different from each other: this means that productivity does not decrease significantly towards the end of the project. Altogether, our findings strongly advocate that refactoring of a software system raises subsequent development productivity and prevents in a long-term its deterioration.

Findings of prior studies qualitatively claim that refactoring improves some low-level quality metrics like coupling and cohesion measures (Bois & Mens, 2003). A visual inspection of the plots of CBO, WMC, RFC, and LCOM metrics (Figure 3) evidences that their average daily changes per iteration tend to decrease starting from the second iteration (1st big refactoring) for the CBO and RFC metric,

Figure 3. Evolution of the average daily changes of LCOM, CBO, RFC, and WMC per iteration

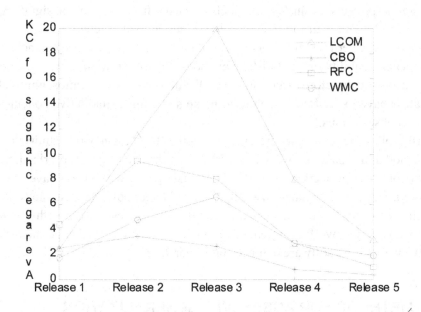

and from the third for the LCOM and WMC metrics. This is a first indication that refactoring could limit the overall increase of cohesion, coupling and complexity metrics that should occur, according to the current software engineering knowledge, as it is synthesized in the work of Lehman.

Visually inspecting the plot of the average daily changes of LCOM, CBO, RFC and WMC per iteration, we also notice an interesting phenomenon: After an initial phase of remarkable growth of these metrics, they start to decrease, most likely thanks to refactoring. We interpret this as the people gathering a more comprehensive view of the application to develop, and thus being able to better refactor the system, creating simpler, less coupled, and more cohesive code. Still, this is an interpretation based on a visual inspection not on a statistical test: only future research will be able to assess its statistical significance.

12.5 GENERALIZATION

Generalization of results obtained by single experiments or case studies is not an easy task. First, experiments in software engineering are conducted in unique environments and therefore data that are collected within such environments are also unique. This is in particular a problem in software engineering as many project specific factors (for example human factors and development environment) are not known or cannot be easily quantified. In this chapter we have seen that even for the two very similar projects we analyzed models extracted from data can be significantly different and do not work in the respective other context. Second, even if we can encode many experimental factors in hard data it is not easy to derive conclusions about generalizability using statistical methods. Moreover, we have analyzed only two projects and therefore a rigorous generalization procedure is almost impossible. We rather have to confine ourselves to make some more qualitative conclusions based on observations.

In the following section, we present some method to assess generalizability properties of models and statistics we used for analyzing the two projects described. Since we have only two projects in particular the Bootstrapping method and leave-one-out are useful for assessing generalizability. We could not apply the meta-analysis approach due two the limited size of experiments. Nevertheless we report this method here as it is very powerful for generalizing results across several experiments and hardly ever used by software engineering researchers.

12.6 METHODS FOR ASSESSING GENERALIZATION

12.6.1 Meta-Analysis

Statistical meta-analysis is the branch of statistics that studies how it is possible to combine statistical indexes across different experiments (Hedges & Olkin, 1985; Rosenthal, 1991; Hunter & Schmidt, 1990). Statistical meta-analysis has already been used in software engineering. Hu (1997) is probably the first researcher attempting to combine results from different studies. His study evaluates four alternative production models that have not been applied widely in software engineering: linear, quadratic, Cobb-Douglas, and translog. The performances are checked using the P-test. The comparison of the four alternative models suggests that quadratic software production model could be applied to a wide variety of projects, while the other three have limited practical applicability.

The method usually employed for estimating a common correlation from several studies – we use it to estimate a common correlation between software complexity measures and productivity – is the meta-analytical technique called *Weighted Estimators of a Common Correlation* (Hedges & Olkin, 1985). The technique assumes that:

- Sample data come all from normally-distributed populations with the same correlation;

• Sample correlations are computed according to Pearson's definition of correlation.

Since in our case we cannot assume any particular distribution of the samples, we compute the non-parametric Spearman's correlation coefficients of the samples. Such correlation is independent from the distribution of the population. From Spearman correlation coefficient *rs* one can approximate Pearson correlation coefficient by using the coefficient *rc* computed by the following formula (Pearson, 1907):

$$r_c = 2\sin\left(\frac{\pi}{6}r_s\right)$$

Studies show that *rc* generally underestimates Pearson correlation coefficient, though the error is usually very small: In simulation studies the largest error found between the converted correlation coefficient and the actual correlation was -0.005. The error decreases when the sample size and the actual population correlation increase (Kendall & Gibbons, 1990).The steps of the Weighted Estimators of a Common Correlation technique are:

1. Normalization of the sample correlations with the Fisher *z* transformation.
2. Computation of the required confidence interval for the transformed correlations, in our case the 95% confidence interval.
3. Application of the inverse Fisher *z* transformation on the resulting range.

At the end, a check is performed on whether the results disprove the original assumption on homogeneity of the data. For this purpose, an extension of the chi-square test is used. Given below, there is the summary of the three steps as described by Hedges and Olkin (1985). Suppose that samples of size $n_1, ..., n_k$ are taken from k studies; we compute the sample correlations $r_1, ..., r_k$ (in our case we compute the Spearman correlations and then we transform them with the formula above). The sample correlations are then transformed by the Fisher *z* transform:

$$z(r_i) = \frac{1}{2}\log\frac{(1+r_i)}{(1-r_i)} = z_i$$

Given a set of transformed correlation coefficients $z_1, ..., z_n$, we can now compute the mean transformed value as a weighted average of the z_is:

$$\bar{z} = \sum_{i=1}^{k} w_i z_i$$

where the weight for the i-th experiment is computed over the size n_i of sample i as:

$$w_i = \frac{(n_i - 3)}{\sum_{j=1}^{k} (n_j - 3)}$$

The 95% confidence interval in the transformed space, $[z^-, z^+]$, is then determined using the rule for normal distributions:

$$z^- = \bar{z} - \frac{1.96}{\sqrt{\sum_{i=1}^{k}(n_j - 3)}}, z^+ = \bar{z} + \frac{1.96}{\sqrt{\sum_{i=1}^{k}(n_i - 3)}}$$

To determine the 95% confidence interval on the original correlation coefficient, $[r^-, r^+]$, we have to compute the inverse Fisher z transform, z^{-1}, on z^- and z^+:

$$z^{-1}(x) = \frac{(e^{2x} - 1)}{(e^{2x} + 1)}$$

At the end, we have to check if the original data is indeed homogeneous. To do so, a chi-square test against the null hypothesis of homogeneity is performed. Given the sample size and the power of the test, a non-rejection of the null hypothesis amounts to its acceptance. The Q statistics used in our case is:

$$Q = \sum_{i=1}^{k} (n_i - 3)(z_i - \bar{z})^2$$

We compare it with the chi-square threshold value for k-1 degrees of freedom. If it is lower, then the dataset is considered homogeneous, otherwise not (Hedges & Olkin, 1985).

12.6.2 Bootstrapping

When applying statistical methods on small sample sizes we run into two kinds of risks: Either some statistical tests may not be applied at all or significance levels will not be high and thus results are not reliable. The central limit theorem states that the mean of k random variables tends to be distributed normally in the limit that k tends to infinity. And although in practice, convergence tends to be very rapid, so that for computing confidence intervals and other statistical properties of random variables one can assume that their means are distributed normally and thus benefit from the analytical properties of the normal distribution, in software engineering data samples often are too small for using any normal approximation. In such cases the computation of reliable confidence intervals is not trivial (there are no analytical expressions) and involves some tricky strategies that increase in an artificial way sample size in order to enable the application of traditional statistical techniques.

One such approach is the bootstrap method.

In short, through the re-sampling of existing observations, bootstrapping enables the estimation of any sample statistic distribution, e.g., mean, median, standard deviations to mention some common examples. Although computationally intensive, it has been shown that bootstrapping works well with small samples (Mooney & Duval, 1993). The basic assertion behind bootstrapping is that the relative frequency distribution of a sample statistic (correlation statistic in our case) calculated from the *resamples* is an estimate of the sampling distribution of this statistic. Theoretical work and simulations have shown this is the case when the number of re-samples is large (1000 is a standard number). The Bootstrap method for estimating confidence intervals for a statistic S and a data sample X requires the following steps:

- Repeat N times: Randomly sample, allowing replacement, the original data set, i.e. take randomly some of the original observations (allowing some of them to be included several times or missing) and construct a new (bootstrap) sample. This step yields N samples, each randomly and slightly different from the original sample, as some of the original observations will not have been sampled whereas others will have been sampled several times. That form of sampling is sometimes called *resampling*.
- For each of the newly generated samples compute S(X*), where X* is a (bootstrap) sample and S our statistic of interest, for example the correlation coefficient.
- Estimate the standard error by the sample standard deviation of the N replications. The multiple estimates of the mean and the standard error are used to define the confidence interval around the mean (Efron & Tibshirani, 1993). In

general, for each parameter we get a distribution whose we are able to compute the standard deviation, the mean and the 95% confidence interval.
• Another possibility is to compute the 2.5% and 97.5% percentiles of the distribution obtained by the computation of S(X*), which represent, based on bootstrapping theory, a good estimate of the 95% error interval for the statistic S, so called Efron's percentile confidence limit (Bontempi, 2003; Efron & Tibshirani, 1993).

12.6.3 Generalization and Over-Fitting

In general, the performance of neural networks depends highly on the chosen network architecture (number of layers, number of neurons, activation function, number of receptive fields, spread etc.). In constructing such models for software engineering purposes – as in general for any type of modeling – the two most important criteria are parsimony and generalization ability of the model, i.e. the model should have as few parameters as possible and should also provide good predictions for future inputs. In other words, the model has to find the optimal balance between bias and variance, also known as bias-variance dilemma. To make this issue more clear and explain how it is addressed in machine learning we make an artificial example. Assume we have a data set with 30 data points and want to build a model with five input features $\{x_i, i=1\ldots5\}$ and one output variable $\{y\}$ using a RBF network. Our first attempt could be to choose parameters of an RBF network in such a way that the root mean square error defined as

$$RMSE = \sqrt{\frac{\sum (y - y')^2}{30}}$$

(y' is the output predicted by the model) will be minimized: It turns out that it is not that difficult to build an architecture that not only minimizes the RMSE criterion but is able to fit our fictitious data set (almost) exactly. It is sufficient to choose a suitable set of 30 basis functions and then compute weights by solving a system of linear equations. However, the problem with this solution is clearly that while it fits exactly the so-called training data it will give poor predictions when used on a different data set (problem of over fitting or high variance). Therefore, in machine learning a common approach to evaluate the performance of a network is to split data into training, validation and test set: Various networks are trained by minimizing an error function defined with respect to a training set. The performance of the networks is then compared by evaluating the error function using an independent validation set, and the network having the smallest error with respect to the validation set is selected. This procedure is called hold out method. Since this procedure itself leads to some over fitting of the validation set, the performance of the selected network should be confirmed by measuring its error on a third independent set of data called a test set. This approach guarantees that the minimum of the sum of bias, which measures the ability of a model to approximate the true relationship, and the variance, which is an indicator of the generalizability of a model, is reached as it coincides with the minimum of the validation error. Figure 1 shows that while the RMSE value for the training data decreases as a model is using more and more parameters for fitting (for example number of radial basis functions for RBF networks or number of layers and neurons for MLP networks) this is not the case for the RMSE value evaluated on the validation data: while at the beginning it is decreasing (as the model's bias since the approximation of moderately complex target functions presupposes a certain number parameters) at some point it starts to increase. At this point a model is enough complex to approximate a target function fairly well and starts memorizing training data loosing its capability for generalization as more parameters are added and used for fitting. On the right side of this *validation boundary*, which we may use for defining the optimal complexity of a model, we enter the *over-fitting region* where a model will exhibit high variance and give poor predictions for new data.

The approach for model validation outlined so far works well if data samples are not very small. However, in our example we have only 30 data points and if we split them randomly in three equal sets we end up with a training set of 10 points. This is not enough for training a model if a target function is moderately complex. Since it is common that data samples in software engineering are of very limited size we are not able to afford the luxury of keeping aside part of the data for validation purposes. In such cases we can adopt the procedure of cross-validation (Bishop, 1994). Here we divide the whole data set at random into S distinct segments. We then train a model using S-1 segments and test its performance by evaluating an error function on the remaining segment. This is repeated for the S possible choices for the segment, which is omitted from the training process, and the validation errors are averaged over all S results. If data is very scarce we can go to the extreme limit of S=N for a data set with N data points, which involves N separate training runs per model, each using (N-1) data points. This limit is known as leave-one-out method. While it allows us to use almost all data points for training it requires the training process to be repeated N times, which under certain circumstances could involve large amount of processing time. Another advantage of the leave-one-out method is that when splitting data at random in S sets we could run into the risk that these sets do not reflect well overall data distribution, i.e. some sets for example could be populated only by data with specific properties. Imagine the following scenario: 50% of the data from a software system have one or more defects while the remaining 50% is defect-free (we may assume that one data point corresponds to a software module and the target variable encodes a two-class membership). In such case – if we split data into 2 sets and by chance such split separates perfectly data with zero and one or more defects – then any model using cross-validation and aiming at predicting whether or not a module is defect free will have a relative error of 50% (independent of how complex such model may be).

While there is no general theory behind the structural optimization of the topology of neural networks used in this work, they are developed as a result of some trial and error process. For each set of parameters, that specify a model, we compute the cross validation error. We keep the set that produces the lowest error and this topology of the network is deemed optimal. For the MLP we start with 2 neurons in the hidden layer and keep adding one neuron at a time until the leave-one-out cross validation error (LOOV-RMSE) stops decreasing. Its minimum value determines the optimum number of neurons to choose for the hidden layer. For RBF we do exactly the same: We start with one receptive field and add one at a time until the cross-validation error stops decreasing. We repeat this procedure for a range of spread parameters and keep the spread and number of receptive fields that return the absolute smallest cross-validation error. The same applies to GRNN: we minimize again the LOOV-RMSE by optimizing the spread parameter of the network.

12.7 LIMITATIONS OF THE EXPERIMENTS

It is needless to say that in order to consolidate the findings of this analysis and transform them into usable models and recommendations to developers and managers several replications are required. Moreover, we use a novel approach for data collection, which does not require an active involvement of developers and thus is well suited for agile environments. This approach is able to provide a high granularity of product and process data but a quantification of the improvement compared to manually collected data has to be carried out in a future experiment. All models for effort prediction and quality evaluation proposed and validated in this research have been built using two software projects in a particular XP environment and all possible threats to external validity have to be considered carefully. In particular we are faced with the following threats:

- Generalizability of the settings of the case studies: since the development process is a specific version of XP we cannot conclude that the results obtained from this study also hold in different XP or agile environments.
- Generalization with respect to subjects: the participants of the case studies are in part master students; it is questionable whether or not they represent

the average software developer in industry. Thus, further investigation with a randomized sample of developers is needed to analyze to which degree our findings are biased by the selection of the subjects.

- Most of the participants of the study have been exposed to XP for the first time. We do not control the impact of a learning curve on our results. It is referred to a future study if experienced XP developers would have performed in the same way.

As for the construction to validity of this research there remain some important issues we have to be aware of and clarify in the future:

- We observe that for both case studies effort data tend to form clusters; it would be interesting to develop prediction models for single clusters and to analyze whether such approach is superior to the one proposed in this work. Due to small sample sizes we could not perform this analysis in the current study. Such clusters could indicate that prediction models depend for example on single developers and/or different parts of a software system. With our approach we could easily develop models customized for single developers/ development teams and/or parts of a project. This idea is interesting as it addresses the heavy dependence of estimation models on many human factors and definitely deserves more exploration in the future.

- We develop regression models and neural networks for comparing global with incremental approaches. However, there are other promising modeling techniques in effort estimation such as Bayesian networks, classification and regression trees or hybrid models. They could possibly give different results and limit the validity of our findings to a subset of possible models.

- The choice of the CK design metrics as predictor variables may also have a crucial impact for the results obtained by incremental and global models. Other choices could favor one approach over the other and give again different conclusions.

- To do justice to global models we have to note that we use only one project for model building and use such model for effort prediction on a second project. In real life settings one would possibly use more past projects for the purpose of model building. Such model may be more reliable and stable as it averages data from several projects and becomes less influenced by characteristics of one particular dataset. Some researchers argue that in order to calibrate and stabilize properly an estimation model they need at least 10 (Boehm, 1981) or 15 (Shepperd & Schofield, 1997) projects. It remains to future experiments to determine whether a global model derived from a bunch of historic projects would be competitive to the proposed incremental approach.

- The conclusions we draw depend strongly on the definition we give of productivity and internal software quality and its usefulness and validity in industry. As discussed, the definition we used for productivity is adequate for the context of this case study. Needless to say, it would be interesting to run other studies using this definition but also a definition based on other parameters, for instance function points. The internal quality metrics we use are also widely used in other studies. However, it would be important to take into account also other, high-level quality measures, for instance number of defects.

12.8 SUMMING UP

As said in the introduction we cannot perform a statistical analysis to check whether or not the results we obtain from the two experiments generalize. However, we made a number of interesting observations, which provide some evidence that the findings we obtain may generalize to other Agile contexts. First, in both experiments the trends we observe are similar. For example, agile practices such as refactoring improve internal code quality metrics and development productivity for both projects. Also the proposed incremental effort prediction models outperform traditional estimation techniques in both case studies. Second, both projects have been developed using a customized version of XP, which includes most of common Agile practices. We expect that other Agile contexts, which use a similar set of development practices would yield similar results. We have also learned that while the findings of the two projects are quite similar one has to be cautious when applying models built for one project to another project. It seems that there exist no – at least for Agile development – *universal* laws that govern the process of software production. The best we can do is to seek for models, which can be easily adapted for a specific development context. We think that due the Agile nature of projects (fast changing requirements, technology, and business domain) we cannot use *static* models that work across spatial and temporal boundaries, but rather have to derive context specific models (for example the incremental effort estimation models we propose).Overall, the findings of this research can be summarized as follows:

- Refactoring improves important internal measures for reusability. Therefore, refactoring has a positive effect on reusability and for sure promotes ad-hoc reuse in XP-like development environments.
- Refactoring improves both development productivity and code quality. This confirms and is in line with claims that refactoring is a *best practice* for developing and maintaining software systems.

- XP projects tend to confine *entropy* of software systems as we can see a moderate growth (or even decrease) of maintainability indicators during project evolution.
- Given the availability of data collected in real-time during development we propose incremental effort prediction models. In practice such models can be used to estimate effort for future development iteration and prove to be more accurate than traditional estimation methods.

It seems to be rather difficult to build general purpose models and recommendations that work across different application domains and organizations; in particular, it appears that there is no global or universal type of model or set of predictor variables for a specific problem, but they rather change from one project to the next (Nagappan *et al.*, 2006). In this light, the task of a good modeler is not to seek developing a *universal* model, but to come up with a methodology for building auto-adaptive, project specific models in a fast and automatic way during project evolution.

Specific models built individually for a specific project and extracted from an organization's own data pool and targeted to its development process show very promising results. It remains an open question whether or not we are able to build a general *software engineering theory*, which may explain underlying principles of software engineering (Hannay *et al.*, 2007).

The particular challenge in empirical software engineering lies in the fact that on one hand experimentation is extremely difficult – due to high costs and the presence of many factors that are hard to control – and on the other hand domain knowledge is very limited. This has two implications:

First, due to the lack of massive experimentation and therefore availability of – both qualitative and quantitative - data theories cannot be validated in a sufficient and scientifically acceptable way, thus implying that little knowledge has been developed so far.

Second, data analysis is particular difficult in software engineering as it is constrained by a lack of domain knowledge and at the same time limited amount of available data. Thus, for a researcher often the only choice is develop in a trial and error manner some models that work for a particular environment, but lack either statistical strength or expressiveness and generalization capabilities.

12.9 FINAL CONSIDERATIONS

12.9.1 Difficulties

Here we propose a wrap-up of lessons learned:

1. **Do a thorough readiness assessment.** Before committing to help any organization transition to XP, thoroughly assess how prepared the organization is to make the transition.
    1. **Obtain high-level executive support.** Executives with the most power in the organization need to be recruited from day one to help make an XP transition run smoothly.
    2. **Ensure interdepartmental cooperation.** Managers and employees in different departments must cooperate. If they don't, someone with power (such as an executive) must step in to establish the necessary level of cooperation.
    3. **Increase communication with management.** Executive management must communicate regularly with everyone who is implementing XP within the organization.
    4. **Define success.** We must define what success on a project means and report our findings, on a regular basis, to management. This is particularly important when trying to show how a new process is better than an older process.
    5. **Make collaboration explicit.** We must be explicit in how we expect customers to collaborate with developers before we begin the transition.
    6. **Ensure committed resources.** Before the project begins, everyone who is critical to the success of the project must commit to spending sufficient time on it. This includes ensuring that customers and analysts have enough time to write user stories, help prioritize work, and assess whether features have been programmed acceptably.
    7. **Ensure sufficient control.** Programmers must have the ability to continuously integrate and evolve whatever is essential to the system (such as an enterprise database).

12.9.2 New Practices Proposed

These new practices resulted primarily from needing to properly include management on projects and ensure that project communities live up to XP spirit of continuous improvement. Like many of the ideas in XP, most of these practices are not new, though some have names that may be new to the reader. The six new practices proposed are:

1. **Readiness assessment.** Continuously evaluate whether an organization and project community are ready to do XP.
2. **Project community.** Identify and include people who affect a project or are affected by the project.
3. **Project chartering.** Ensure that what a project community will build is in harmony with the organization needs.
4. **Test-driven management.** Inspire, compel, enlighten, and align a project community by defining SMART (specific, measurable, achievable, relevant, and time-based) objectives.
5. **Retrospectives.** Include a rigorous, future-focused process for capturing lessons learned, best practices in a context, and multiple perspectives on how to improve a software development environment.
6. **Continuous learning.** Continuously improve team skills to deliver greater value and enjoy at the same time.

Readiness Assessment

Readiness assessments typically last one to two days and are conducted by experts in XP. An expert begins an assessment by talking to a project or process sponsor: someone who can describe a project, the people involved in the project (or those likely to be involved), and how those people fit into the organization. Following this meeting, the expert meets with individuals in small groups of three to five people. During each meeting, the expert explains how XP works and both ask and answer many questions.Below are questions an expert commonly asks during an assessment:

- Can we establish the kind of programming environment XP requires (staging machines, pair-programming workstations, a database we can actually evolve, version control that is under our control, etc.)?
- Will subject matter experts (SMEs) be available for the project? Can we expect to get ongoing feedback from end users of the evolving software?
- Is there a dedication to continuous improvement? Is there a commitment to doing retrospectives both during and at the end of the project?
- What is the organizational culture and structure like? Will other departments within the organization support change or construct barriers to change? What is the history of other changes that have taken place within the organization?
- Will the project community for this project have the right people?

During a typical assessment, an expert will meet with project sponsors, programmers, analysts, testers, database administrators (DBAs), project and product managers, domain experts, version control (or source control management) managers, software security people, architects, facilities workers (who will be in charge of setting up an open workspace), and process people. When necessary, an expert will also meet with auditors (or folks involved in compliance endeavors) and members of human resources (HR) and legal departments.

Project Community

A few years after publishing *Extreme Programming Explained*, Beck introduced the term *whole team* into the XP vocabulary. The notion is that software teams need the right people in order to be successful. It is found to be useful to replace the term *whole team* with *project community*.

While the idea connected with the term *team* is being a constrained set of people, the term *community* implies something broader. Communities have active members who may be at the center of an effort and less active members who may be on the periphery of the effort. Lawyers, auditors, and facilities folks are often on the periphery of an XP project community, yet they may play important roles on a project. If a project community fails to include important people inside or outside the organization, it will often face numerous problems that can delay or even stall a project.

David Schmaltz (Kerievsky, 2004) says, "The primary issue facing every project is the lack of awareness of its own *community-ness*. That's why the first steps are well focused upon increasing this awareness within the community."

Awareness of a project community begins during project chartering. An XP coach leads people through a session to identify everyone within the project community. This exercise nearly always leads to a list of names that fills up several whiteboards. Schmaltz points out that a project community is "always bigger than you think." During or after a project, most project communities realize that they failed to include someone important. So the practice of defining the project community is an ongoing endeavor that people improve at over time.

Project Chartering

After seeing XP work successfully on small projects and unsuccessfully in a number of great project, emerged the need of finding tools able to provide chartering for XP projects.Project chartering helps people answer questions, such as:

- Is the idea for the project worthwhile?
- How does the project further the organization's vision/mission?

- How would we know if the project is a success?
- Who is part of the project community?

Like many XP technical practices, project chartering is an ongoing endeavor. Writing and revising a charter helps establish the following project characteristics:

- **Vision**: A desired future
- **Mission**: The strategy for obtaining the vision
- **Project community**: The people involved in the endeavor
- **Values**: Concepts to guide decision making and conduct
- **Management tests**: Measures of success or failure that align and inspire a project community
- **Context diagram**: A depiction of key events flowing into or out of a software system or community
- **Community agreements**: Agreements shared and practiced by a project community

Test-Driven Management

How does a project community learn whether its project work is successful? The same way programmers learn whether their code works: tests.

Test-driven management directs the specification of management tests, which are statements that indicate a measurable, time-limited goal, framed in a binary manner. We either achieve the management test or we fail. Good management tests are SMART.

Management tests are statements about the world external to the project, treating the project as a boundary of responsibility and authority. They avoid specifying ways in which external effects (i.e., things that occur outside the boundary of the project and the software) should be achieved. In other words, good management tests set a destination, but don't specify how to get there.

Management tests provide an excellent way for a project community to understand what unites it. This echoes Tom DeMarco and Timothy Lister's observation (DeMarco & Lister, 1999): "The purpose of a team is not goal attainment, but goal alignment". Management tests create goal alignment by delineating how and when success will be measured, enabling individuals to understand the effects of their own actions.

Retrospectives

Unlike a more typical review session, a retrospective does not yield a list of items but continues on to establish next steps, accountabilities, and measures for making improvements happen. The XP approach to retrospectives is based on the work of Norman Kerth (2001).

XP retrospectives are conducted at the end of every iteration and release. An iteration retrospective is a study of what is working well, what needs improvement, and who will take ownership of an issue to help find its resolution. If a project community iterations are one or two weeks long, iteration retrospectives will last between a half hour and two hours. Members of a project community, including the coach and project manager, help facilitate iteration retrospectives.

Release retrospectives focus on issues, events, and lessons learned across an entire release. Typical release retrospectives look at either one release (generally three months long) or two releases (generally six months long). Release retrospectives tend to last anywhere from a half day to two days. It is best to have someone who is not part of the project community facilitate the retrospective.

One of the most popular ways for a project community to review and learn from its collective experience of a release is to create a timeline. Timelines are made by listing the months of a release on posters (which span the length of a large wall) and then letting participants write up their experiences on cards and attach those cards to times on the timeline when their experiences occurred. Timelines provide a wealth of information that can uncover new insights and ideas for improvement.

Continuous Learning

Continuous learning means actively and regularly learning new techniques and skills. While pairing helps people acquire new skills from others within the project community, continuous learning focuses individuals and groups on important technical and nontechnical subjects that can help them improve at their jobs.

XP project communities usually hold weekly or biweekly study sessions. Typical sessions often involve studying an important piece of literature or some significant items in a code base.

In environments where people are not encouraged to learn new skills or improve on existing skills, resume-based development (RBD) often takes hold. A learning-deprived employee wants to get some technology or experience on his or her resume so badly that he or she finds some way to convince the project community to use that technology, even if it isn't actually a good fit. This is bad, as it often leads to overly complicated and costly solutions that developers are afraid to change. Continuous learning provides an effective way to manage this risk and also helps a project community find enjoyment in personal growth.

12.10 ACKNOWLEDGMENT

The authors would like to thank Prof. Pekka Abrahamsson of the University of Helsinki, previously at VTT, for providing part of the data used in the analyses presented in this chapter.

12.11 REFERENCES

Abrahamsson, P., Hanhineva, A., Hulkko, H., Ihme, T., Jäälinoja, J., Korkala, M., et al. (2004). Mobile-D: An agile approach for mobile application development. *19th ACM Conference on Object-Oriented Programming, Systems, Languages, and Applications (OOPSLA'04)*.

Basili, V. R., Briand, L., & Melo, W. L. (1996). A validation of object-oriented design metrics as quality indicators. *IEEE Transactions on Software Engineering, 22*(10), 751–761. doi:10.1109/32.544352

Beck, K. (1999). *Extreme programming explained: Embrace change*. Addison-Wesley Professional.

Bishop, C. M. (1994). *Neural networks for pattern recognition*. Oxford University Press.

Boehm, B. W. (1981). *Software engineering economics*. Prentice-Hall.

Boehm, B. W., Brown, J. R., & Kaspar, J. R. (1978). *Characteristics of software quality. TRW series of software technology*.

Bois, B. D., & Mens, T. (2003). Describing the impact of refactoring on internal program quality. *International Workshop on Evolution of Large-scale Industrial Software Applications (ELISA)*.

Bontempi, G. (2003). *Resampling techniques for statistical modeling*. Retrieved on November 11, 2008, from http://www.ulb.ac.be/di/map/gbonte/ecares/boot1.pdf

Buschmann, F., Meunier, R., Rohnert, H., Sommerlad, P., & Stal, M. (1996). *Pattern oriented software architecture*. Wiley.

Chidamber, S., & Kemerer, C. F. (1994). A metrics suite for object-oriented design. *IEEE Transactions on Software Engineering, 20*(6), 476–493. doi:10.1109/32.295895

Cohn, M. (2006). *Agile estimating and planning*. Pearson Education.

Counsell, S., Mendes, E., & Swift, S. (2002). Comprehension of object-oriented software cohesion: The empirical quagmire. *10th International Workshop on in Program Comprehension.*

Dandashi, F., & Rine, D. C. (2002). A method for assessing the reusability of object-oriented code using a validated set of automated measurements. *17th ACM Symposium on Applied Computing (SAC 2002).*

DeMarco, T., & Lister, T. (1999). *Peopleware: Productive projects and teams*. Dorset House Publishing Company.

Demeyer, S., Ducasse, S., & Nierstrasz, O. (2000). Finding refactorings via change metrics. *15th ACM Conference on Object-Oriented Programming, Systems, Languages, and Applications (OOPSLA'00).*

Efron, B., & Tibshirani, R. J. (1993). *An introduction to the bootstrap*. Chapman and Hall.

Fenton, N. E., & Pfleeger, S. H. (1997). *Software metrics: A rigorous & practical approach*. PWS Publishing Company.

Fowler, M. (2002). *Refactoring improving the design of existing code*. Addison-Wesley Professional.

Gamma, E., Helm, R., Johnson, R., & Vlissides, J. (1995). *Design patterns: Elements of reusable object-oriented software*. Addison-Wesley.

Halstead, M. (1977). *Elements of software science*. Elsevier.

Hannay, J. E., Sjoberg, D. I. K., & Dybå, T. (2007). A systematic review of theory use in software engineering experiments. *IEEE Transactions on Software Engineering, 33*(2), 87–107. doi:10.1109/TSE.2007.12

Hedges, L. V., & Olkin, I. (1985). *Statistical methods for meta-analysis*. Academic Press.

Henry, S., & Kafura, D. (1981). Software structure metrics based on information flow. *IEEE Transactions on Software Engineering, 7*(5), 510–518. doi:10.1109/TSE.1981.231113

Hollander, M., & Wolfe, D. A. (1973). *Nonparametric statistical inference*. Wiley.

Hu, Q. (1997). Evaluating alternative software production functions. *IEEE Transactions on Software Engineering, 23*(6), 379–387. doi:10.1109/32.601078

Hubert, M., & Verboven, S. (2003). A robust PCR method for high-dimensional regressors. *Journal of Chemometrics, 17*(8-9), 438–452. doi:10.1002/cem.783

Humphrey, W. (1995). *A discipline for software engineering*. Addison-Wesley Professional.

Hunter, J. E., & Schmidt, F. L. (1990). *Methods for meta-analysis: Correcting error and bias in research findings*. Sage.

Johnson, P. M., & Disney, A. M. (1998). Investigating data quality problems in the PSP. *6th International Symposium on the Foundations of Software Engineering (SIGSOFT'98)*.

Johnson, P. M., Kou, H., Agustin, J., Chan, C., Moore, C., Miglani, J., et al. (2003). Beyond the personal software process: Metrics collection and analysis for the different disciplined. *25th International Conference on Software Engineering, Portland*.

Kataoka, Y., Imai, T., Andou, H., & Fukaya, T. A. (2002). Quantitative evaluation of maintainability enhancement by refactoring. *International Conference on Software Maintenance*.

Kendall, M. G., & Gibbons, J. D. (1990). *Rank correlation methods*. Oxford University Press.

Kerievsky, J. (2004). *Refactoring to patterns*. Addison-Wesley Professional.

Kerth, N. L. (2001). *Project retrospectives: A handbook for team reviews*. Dorset House Publishing Company.

Layman, L., Williams, L., & Cunningham, L. (2004). Exploring extreme programming in context: An industrial case study. *Agile Development Conference*.

Lehman, M. M., Ramil, J. F., Wernick, P. D., Perry, D. E., & Turski, W. M. (1997). Metrics and laws of software evolution-the nineties view. *4th International Software Metrics Symposium*.

Lehmann, E. L. (1986). *Testing statistical hypotheses*. Springer-Verlag.

Mair, C., Shepperd, M., & Jørgensen, M. (2005). An analysis of data sets used to train and validate cost prediction systems. *1st International Workshop on Predictor Models in Software Engineering (PROMISE 2005)*.

Marchesi, M., & Succi, G. (2003). *Extreme programming and agile processes in software engineering*. Springer.

McCabe, T. (1976). Complexity measure. *IEEE Transactions on Software Engineering, 2*(4), 308–320. doi:10.1109/TSE.1976.233837

McCall, J. A., Richards, P. K., & Walters, G. F. (1977). *Factors in software quality*. US Rome Air Development Center Reports.

Meyers, J. L., & Well, A. D. (2003). *Research design and statistical analysis*. Lawrence Erlbaum Associates Inc.

Mišić, V. B., & Tešić, D. N. (1998). Estimation of effort and complexity: An object-oriented case study. *Journal of Systems and Software, 41*(2), 133–143. doi:10.1016/S0164-1212(97)10014-0

Mooney, C., & Duval, R. (1993). Bootstrapping. A nonparametric approach to statistical inference (p. 95). In *Quantitative Applications in the Social Sciences*. Sage Publications.

Myrtveit, I., & Stensrud, E. (1999). A controlled experiment to assess the benefits of estimating with analogy and regression models. *IEEE Transactions on Software Engineering, 25*(4), 510–524. doi:10.1109/32.799947

Nagappan, N., Ball, T., & Zeller, A. (2006). Mining metrics to predict component failures. *28th International Conference on Software Engineering*.

Pearson, K. (1907). *Mathematical contributions to the theory of evolution. XVI. On further methods of determining correlation. Drapers' Company Research Memoirs (Biometric Series 4)*. Cambridge University Press.

Poppendieck, M., & Poppendieck, T. (2003). *Lean software development: An agile toolkit for software development managers*. Addison-Wesley Professional.

Rosenthal, R. (1991). *Meta-analytical procedures for social research*. Sage.

Shepperd, M. C., & Schofield, C. (1997). Estimating software project effort using analogies. *IEEE Transactions on Software Engineering, 23*(11), 736–743. doi:10.1109/32.637387

Sillitti, A., Janes, A., Succi, G., & Vernazza, T. (2003). Collecting, integrating, and analyzing software metrics and personal software process data. *EUROMICRO*.

Tichy, W. (1998). Should computer scientists experiment more? *IEEE Computer*, *31*(5), 32–40.

van Deursen, A. (2001). Program comprehension risks and opportunities in extreme programming. *8th Working Conference on Reverse Engineering (WCRE 2001)*.

van Emden, E., & Moonen, L. (2002). Java quality assurance by detecting code smells. *9th Working Conference on Reverse Engineering*.

ENDNOTES

[1]   http://portal.acm.org/ (accessed on November 11, 2008)
[2]   http://www.ieee.org/ (accessed on November 11, 2008)
[3]   http://www.agilemanifesto.org/ (accessed on November 11, 2008)

Chapter 13
Effort Estimation

Barbara Russo
Free University of Bozen-Balzano, Italy

Marco Scotto
Free University of Bozen-Balzano, Italy

Alberto Sillitti
Free University of Bozen-Balzano, Italy

Giancarlo Succi
Free University of Bozen-Balzano, Italy

Raimund Moser
Free University of Bozen-Balzano, Italy

13.1 EFFORT ESTIMATION IN AGILE ENVIRONMENTS USING MULTIPLE PROJECTS

As in more traditional development processes also in agile and iterative methodologies, estimation of development effort without imposing overhead on the project and the development team is of paramount importance. This analysis proposes a new effort estimation model aimed at iterative development environments, which are not suitable for description by traditional prediction methods. We propose a detailed development methodology, discuss a number of detailed architectures of such models (including a wealth of augmented regression models and neural networks) and include a thorough case study of XP carried out in two real semi-industrial projects. The results of this research evidences that in the XP environment under

DOI: 10.4018/978-1-59904-681-5.ch013

study the proposed incremental model outperforms traditional estimation techniques most notably in later iterations of development. Moreover, when dealing with new projects, the incremental model can be developed from scratch without resorting itself to historic data.

Effort prediction has always been perceived as a major topic in software engineering. The reason is quite evident: many software projects run out of budget and schedule because of an underestimation of the development effort. Since the pioneering work by Putnam (1978), Boehm (1981; 200) and Albrecht & Gaffney (1983), there have been many attempts to construct prediction models of software cost determination. An overview of current effort estimation techniques, their application in industry, and their drawbacks regarding accuracy and applicability can be found in (Lederer & Prasad, 1995; Boehm *et al.*, 2000; Sauer & Cuthbertson, 2003; Moløkken-Østvold *et al.*, 2004). The most prominent estimation model comes in the form of the so-called COCOMO family of cost models (Boehm *et al.*, 1995). While capturing the essence of project cost estimation in many instances, they are not the most suitable when we are faced with more recent technologies and processes of software development such as agile approaches and small development teams. Moreover, models such as COCOMO II depend quite heavily on many project-specific settings and adjustments, whose impact is difficult to assess, collect, and quantify (Menzies *et al.*, 2005). What makes the situation even worse, is the fact that in agile processes an effective collection of such metrics and the ensuing tedious calibration of the models could be quite unrealistic. As in other fields of software engineering a major problem in the development of effort estimation models is scarcity of experimental data. Most case studies, surveys and experiments on effort prediction found in the literature suffer from at one or more of several drawbacks:

*   In general, data coming from industrial environments are very limited and difficult to collect. Therefore, different studies have used the same dataset (for example the COCOMO'81 or Kemerer dataset) for analysis and validation raising concern on the generalization capabilities and/or bias of the findings (Mair *et al.*, 2005).
*   Most of the studies conducted in industrial environments, in particular for agile development processes, use data gathered by post-mortem surveys, and this may raise concerns about their soundness (Layman *et al.*, 2004).
*   The collected data are often very coarse-grained and sometimes of low quality. This is mainly because data collection is performed manually by developers and researchers and, as any human activity, error prone and unreliable. Moreover, developers do not like to spend their time on other activities than development; therefore, asking them to trace their own development effort is likely to produce data of very poor quality (Johnson & Disney, 1998; Johnson

et al., 2003). As an example, due to this fact the Personal Software Process (PSP) methodology is difficult to implement in industrial settings.

• Any manual data collection process introduces an artifact in the development process that is particularly serious in agile environments where all the "non-directly productive activities" should be banned (Poppendieck & Poppendieck, 2003).

• Traditional effort estimation models are static as they are built at one point in time using historical data and used for prediction of future projects. However, in agile development with its fast plan-implement-release cycle there is a risk that such models are outdated and not able to adapt to high volatility of requirements, technologies, personnel or other factors.

As far as we know, no specific models have been developed for agile and iterative development processes. Only a few studies deal with the idea of updating or refining prediction models during project evolution and using effort of previous development phases as predictor variable. Closest to our work is a recent study by (Trendowicz *et al.*, 2006) who incorporates into a hybrid cost estimation model feedback cycles and possibility for iterative refinement. MacDonell and Shepperd (2003) use project effort of previous phases of development as predictor for a simple regression model and show that it yields better results than expert opinion. However, both studies do not address the peculiarities of agile processes, use a different approach for model building and do not provide any comparative studies with traditional models. Alshayeb and Li (2003) investigate the correlation between object-oriented design metrics and effort in agile environments, but do not consider iterative model building or refining.

In general, traditional effort estimation models work as follows. Some predictor metrics are collected or estimated at the beginning of a project and fed into a model. The model, which is usually built upon historic data using similar projects, predicts the total development effort. While this approach is reasonable for traditional, waterfall-like development processes where common predictor metrics such as function or feature points, software size, formal design specifications, design documents, etc. are known at the beginning of a project and typically do not change too much throughout the overall project this is not the case for agile development processes. In agile development, a project is realized in iterations and requirements usually change from one iteration to another. At the end of each iteration, developers release the software to the customer who will eventually require new features, and change or removal of already implemented functionalities. At the beginning of the next iteration developers will negotiate with the customer about requirements and develop a plan (design document) for the next iteration (in XP this process is referred to as planning game). Therefore, standard predictor metrics proposed in the literature, in particular the ones derived from design documents, are the only known at the beginning of the next development iteration and not a priori for the whole project.

Being cognizant of the existing challenges as outlined above, the key objectives of our study are outlined as follows:

- We use a novel, non-invasive, tool-based approach for collecting fine grain effort data in a close-to an industrial, XP-like environment and integrate them with design metrics (Sillitti *et al.*, 2003). In particular, our non-invasive data collection process ensures: High reliability of data, as the collection is done automatically and does not involve manual activities. Absence of bias: in agile processes manual data collection on effort (such as done with spreadsheets) may alter the nature of the method itself resulting in biased data.
- We consider a proposal for a new, incremental effort prediction model for iterative software development processes.
- We carry out a thorough experimental validation of the incremental models and offer a comparative analysis with the existing monolithic (global) prediction models.
- We exploit the effectiveness of two main categories of realization of the models such as regression (linear as well as a number of modifications including its robust version) and neural networks. The performance of these models is discussed along with a detailed comparative analysis.

Given the objectives above we aim at answering the following research questions:

- Out of two classes of prediction models based on neural network respective regression techniques, which is the best model for predicting effort in iterative development?
- Given iterative software development processes, are incremental effort prediction models more efficient than global, monolithic models?

The results of this research are of interest for managers, developers, and customers. Developers can use the proposed incremental model for estimating effort starting from second iteration of the development process. In particular, junior and less experienced programmers may profit from such early estimates as they gain more confidence in their subjective assessment by comparing model forecasts with their own and actual effort data at the end of each iteration. Managers may benefit from having a more reliable tool to allocate resources, to verify if the project is kept on track and to make - if necessary - early adjustments to cost estimation or reschedule the project plan. This seems to be a crucial point in software engineering as in general, managers tend to be over-optimistic and over-confident in estimation and scheduling (Conrow & Shishido, 1997; Glass, 1998; Lee, 1993), and are normally reluctant to move from initial estimates and schedules when progress slips (McConnell, 1996). An estimate should be dynamic – as the project progresses more information becomes available – and therefore estimates more accurate (Ahituv *et al.*, 1999). And finally, customers may obtain more accurate information on how many requirements can be implemented within the next iteration: they may use such information for prioritizing and selecting requirements.

Furthermore, empirical studies like this contribute to the discussion on which type of prediction models is the best for agile development. In addition, we enrich the body of effort estimation models by proposing a new methodology for any kind of iterative process. Clearly, further investigation is required to ascertain whether the results we have obtained can be generalized to a larger class of XP-like and other agile projects.

13.2 EFFORT ESTIMATION MODELS: AN OVERVIEW

13.2.1 Global Prediction Models

Let us highlight the essence of traditional, global prediction models encountered in software engineering (Putnam, 1978; Boehm *et al.*, 2000; Briand & Wieczorek, 2000; Jørgensen & Shepperd, 2007). At the beginning of a software development project, we identify several meaningful predictor variables and collect their values. A list of predictor variables could involve size, design metrics, qualitative and quantitative development factors (including type of development environment, application domain, experience of developers, organizational structure, etc.). Most of the time the models are derived from historic data and used to predict development effort (say, point estimation or some probability distribution) for similar projects. There are crucial model development and utilization issues that have to be clearly underlined:

- The choice of the predictor variables. This task is highly demanding as at the beginning of the project we may not know which variables of the project could have a high impact on the assessment of the development effort.
- While we might be tempted to collect a lot of variables (in anticipation of a proper compensation for the shortcoming identified so far), the process could be time consuming, costly, and at the end lead to overly complicated models

whose development (say, estimation of parameters) could be quite complex and inefficient (Chen *et al.*, 2005).

In the construction of global models we rely on historic data or/and expert opinion. This requires that first one has to gain experience and collect data for at least one project and only afterwards she can construct the model and apply it to similar projects. This is not only a long-term process, but comes with some risk that given the unstable and highly non-stationary environment of software development, it may lead to models whose predictive capabilities are questionable. Moreover, software industry is moving into a direction where projects are not completed but proceeding with new updates and deliveries in response to market demand. In such scenario it is not obvious when to freeze the project for model building purposes.

Agile software development brings another problem to traditional effort prediction models. Predictor variables usually are not known at the beginning of a project, but become available at the beginning of each iteration as requirements change often and fast. Under these circumstances a long-term model of effort estimation that naturally relies on information available at the beginning of a project seems to be of limited applicability. However, one could still contemplate the use of the long-term, global cost estimation model and use it for reference purposes.

13.2.2 Incremental Prediction Models

The main idea of an incremental prediction model is that it is built after each iteration instead of at the end of a project. Thus, it is able to accommodate to any changes during development in a much smoother way than a global model. Moreover, we endow the incremental model with a dynamic character by using the estimates of effort reported in the previous iterations that are treated as an additional input. In this way, effort prediction does not only depend on the usual predictor variables but also on the past effort distribution itself, which may make a significant contribution for explaining future effort variation. The incremental model operates only for iterative effort prediction as it cannot be used to predict total development effort at the beginning of a project. The essence of the incremental model can be explained as follows:

- Model building: At the end of each iteration a new model is built using as input the predictor variables of that iteration and development effort of previous iterations. Thus, the main difference to the global model is that this model is dynamic in the sense that it depends on the phase of development it is built and past effort distribution.
- Iterative effort prediction: At the beginning of a new iteration predictor

variables are collected and fed together with past effort into the newly built incremental model. The output of the model produces an estimation of the cumulative development effort starting from iteration one to the end of this iteration.

When comparing incremental models versus global ones, let us stress the following essential differences:

- An incremental model is constantly adjusted during development and evolves with the project; therefore, it can much better accommodate to any changes in technology, requirements, personnel, tools, working environment, or other occurring during project evolution.
- The relative impact of different predictor metrics on development effort is likely to change during project evolution. An incremental model can select the best features for each single iteration; hence, it should give more accurate and reliable estimations.
- The incremental model is useful and applicable right from second iteration of development. There is no need for historic data and also no risk that the model is outdated. In particular, this is very valuable in highly volatile domains where it is unlikely to find stable and general models.
- Medium and small companies usually get development projects for very different business environments and domains. They often face the problem to have no expertise in the project's problems or solution domains. An incremental effort estimation model can help produce more reliable estimates and raise confidence in their personal judgments only after a few development iterations.

Clearly, with an incremental effort prediction model a company cannot estimate the total development effort at the beginning of a project. This may be an important issue for a company that is trying to decide whether they want to take on a given software project. However, in today's software industry companies often negotiate with customers which and how many features have to be developed for a given budget and period of time. In such scenarios an incremental model may help a software firm to get a reliable estimate of the number of features that can be implemented within one development iteration. A realistic estimate is important for a strong marketing strategy and for being at the same time competitive and keeping business terms.

13.2.3 Models of Effort Prediction

Given the two fundamental modes of incremental and global modeling, we contemplate several detailed architectures of the models considering various predictor variables and forms of mapping from these variables to the predicted development effort. In software engineering we can encounter many types of effort prediction models. We can recall here empirical models based on subjective judgment (Angelis *et al.*, 2001; Shepperd & Schofield, 1997), regression models (Miyazaki *et al.*, 1994), regression trees, neural networks (Srinivasan & Fisher, 1995), theory based models such as COCOMO II (Boehm *et al.*, 2000), so-called hybrid models (Trendowicz *et al.*, 2006), and more recently Bayesian nets (Pendharkar *et al.*, 2005). In this research, we consider only algorithmic models that can be effectively constructed (without human interaction) from quantitative data. Models based on Bayesian inference could also work well for iterative development environments as prior probabilities could be updated and adjusted as the project evolves (Pendharkar *et al.*, 2005); however, they require manual operation and usually call for a larger number of predictor variables (both quantitative and qualitative data). In agile environments manual collection of qualitative and quantitative data is difficult to realize, as such activities are not in line with a process that emphasizes: *individuals and interactions over processes and tools*[1]. Therefore, considering the constraints imposed by data collection in agile environments we restrict our analysis to two different families of prediction models, which are representative for common types of approaches in software engineering:

- Regression models that are easy to understand and develop; we can use them as a reference model (straw man) to compare with other, more advanced models. Note that most effort estimation methods considered in the past are based on regression models (Jørgensen & Shepperd, 2007).
- The use of neural networks.

As starting point we consider the oldest and most studied type of neural networks: a feed forward Multilayer Perceptron Neural Network. For network training we use a fast variant of the backpropagation algorithm, namely the Levenberg-Marquardt training method (Hagan & Menhaj, 1994). It works well if the network size – as in our case - is small to medium. Since we apply MLP's on small samples and use 5 input features a high number of layers and connections would allow the network to memorize data; this would yield an almost zero training error but a large cross-validation or generalization error (over fitting). Therefore, we start with the simplest MLP network with a single hidden layer of neurons with hyperbolic tangent activation function and a linear output neuron. Radial Basis Functions (RBF) provides a flexible way to generalize linear regression functions. RBF networks exhibit properties of universal approximation (Girosi & Poggio, 1990). An RFB network functions as follows: First, input data are mapped in a non-linear way using basis functions (we use Gaussians); then, the final response variable is built as a linear combination of the output of the basis functions with the network weight vector. RBF have only been recently used for effort estimation (Shin & Goel, 2000) and show some promising results. The difficulty with RBF models is the model selection process: RBF are completely specified by 3m parameters where m is the number of basis functions (we use also the terms receptive fields or neurons), which may be considerably high for fast fluctuating target functions. Usually a modeler has to specify the type and number of radial basis functions and the center and spread for each basis function. There is no mathematical theory that determines the topology of such network by using for example statistical properties of the data set to be modeled. We use the strategy proposed by (Chen *et al.*, 1991): initially the hidden layer has no neurons. The following steps are repeated until the network's mean squared error falls below an error goal or a prefixed maximum number of neurons have been added to the network:

- The network is simulated
- The input vector with the greatest error is found
- A receptive field is added with weights equal to that vector
- The linear layer weights are redesigned by solving a set of linear equations

The last model we analyze is the so-called General Regression Neural Network (GRNN), which has been proposed by Specht (1991). The principal advantages of GRNN over back-propagation networks are fast learning (the network does not require iterative adjustments of the parameters) and convergence to the optimal regression surface (even if the data sample is small and noisy). However, GRNN cannot converge to poor solutions responding to local minima of the error criterion, which may happen with iterative techniques such as back-propagation multilayer perception.

In general, the performance of MLP, RBF, and GRNN models depends highly on the chosen network architecture (number of layers, number of neurons, activation function, number of receptive fields, spread, etc.). While there is no general theory behind the structural optimization of the topology of the networks, they are developed as a result of some trial and error process. For each set of parameters, that specify the model, we compute the cross validation error. We keep the set that produces the lowest error and this topology of the network is deemed optimal. For the MLP we start with 2 neurons in the hidden layer and keep adding one neuron at a time until the leave-one-out cross validation error (LOOV-RMSE) stops decreasing. Its minimum value determines the optimum number of neurons to choose for the hidden layer. For RBF we do exactly the same: We start with one receptive field and add one at a time until the cross-validation error stops decreasing. We repeat this procedure for a range of spread parameters and keep the spread and number of receptive fields that return the absolute smallest cross-validation error. The same applies to GRNN: We minimize again the LOOV-RMSE by optimizing the spread parameter of the network.

13.3 COMPARATIVE ANALYSIS USING TWO CASE STUDIES

We use the two case studies described in Chapter 12 for instantiating both traditional and our proposed incremental effort estimation models and perform a comparative analysis between the two estimation methods and data sets. The two projects are denoted as project A and project B.

13.3.1 Selection of Predictors and Output Variables

Many different metrics have been proposed as effort predictors: The most common one is for sure software size (lines of code, function or feature points, number of requirement documents, etc.). COCOMO/COCOMO II, one of the most popular cost estimation models uses in addition to size a wide range of so called cost drivers (mostly technology and human factors). In this study we use the Chidamber and Kemerer (CK) set of object-oriented design metrics (Chidamber & Kemerer, 1994) for effort prediction.

The CK metrics have some interesting properties, which make them in particular attractive for the kind of prediction model we propose:

- They are widely accepted both by practitioners and researchers and validated by several previous studies (Basili *et al.*, 1996; Briand & Wüst, 2001).
- For the purpose of model building the CK metrics can be extracted automatically from source code.
- In agile development documentation, requirements elicitation or design plans are minimalist and only produced as far as they are really needed. Therefore, we cannot expect to collect a lot of data before starting an iteration that could be used for effort prediction. However, even in the most extreme case of agile development, XP, at the beginning of a new iteration there are some planning activities that produce at least some sort of design documents (CRC cards). These documents can be used to estimate fairly well the CK design metrics for the new iteration, which will be used as input variables for effort prediction.

We do not use all 6 CK metrics as predictors but exclude the NOC (number of children) and LCOM (lack of cohesion of methods) metrics. We excluded the NOC because in both projects its values were equal to 0 for almost all classes and hence this metric does not contribute significantly to the explanation of variation of development effort. Both projects do not use large inheritance hierarchies and classes are not primarily designed for reuse. Therefore, only few classes are sub-classed. As for LCOM several researchers have questioned its meaning and the way it is defined by Chidamber and Kemerer (Counsell *et al.*, 2002); the impact of LCOM on development effort and other metrics such as maintainability is little understood by today and therefore we decide to exclude it from this analysis.

As output variable we use the total coding effort per class in hours at any point in time, for example at the end of the project for the global model or at the end of each iteration for the incremental model. As said before in this context development effort is defined as coding effort only and other activities such as planning, designing, documenting are not included. For the projects under scrutiny – and in general for agile projects – this is not a serious limitation as all non-coding activities are reduced to a minimum and most of the actual development effort is indeed coding effort. Furthermore, for the analyzed projects we know that developers spent one day per week for planning activities while the rest of the time was used for actual coding (including unit testing).

For building a global model we extract the CK metrics from the final release of the software and use them to predict the total coding effort. For incremental models we have different choices for computing CK metrics and coding effort: For example, we could consider as input changes of CK metrics and coding effort per iteration or their cumulative values starting from beginning of development. Or – by blasting up the input space - we could even think of more complex architectures using changes of CK metrics of previous iteration(s) and their absolute values and so on. The only way to find out which architecture is most suitable is to try several of them and select the one, which optimizes a given performance function (in our case prediction accuracy). Moreover, as a general rule we follow the principle of parsimony (also known as Occam's Razor): If a more complex model explains data only slightly better than a simple one the researcher should favor the simple model.

Overall, we find that using the cumulative effort of past iterations and CK design metrics of the current iteration as input variables works best for incremental effort prediction. Such architecture uses all available data points (given the limited number of data this is an important requirement) as it uses cumulative values and not differences between iterations as input vectors. Moreover, it is stable and convergent in the sense that the training and cross validation errors show a decreasing trend over time.

Figure 1. Box plot of effort and predictor variables

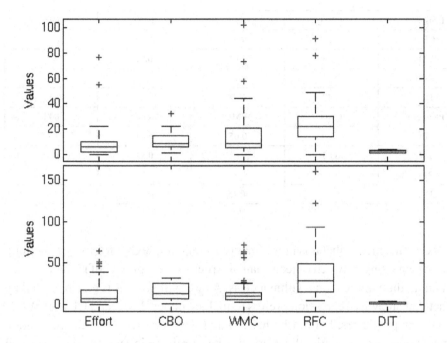

13.3.2 Peculiarities of Data

Figure 1 shows a box plot of the data sets collected with PROM (Sillitti *et al.*, 2003) for the two projcts. It is evident that both effort and predictor variables (in particular the WMC and RFC metrics) have outliers and/or are skewed. We do not assume that they have been introduced by measurement errors, but they could rather indicate that data are naturally clustered: For example, such clusters (representing different populations) could be defined by different parts of a software system or different developers. Unfortunately, our data samples are too small to investigate and derive models for single clusters. Such clustering may possibly improve estimation models and has to be addressed in a future study.

Table 1 shows the results of correlation analysis of features. As we can expect by the definition and computation of CK metrics some of them are highly correlated with each other (this observation is also confirmed by other researchers (Succi *et al.*, 2005)). Both the WMC and RFC metrics for example contain the number of methods defined in a class. Thus, it is likely that they will be correlated to some extent. It is interesting to note that RCF is strongly correlated with CBO (more than

Table 1. Correlation of predictor variables. Values higher than 0.5 are set in bold face.

Project A	CBO	WMC	RFC	DIT
CBO	1	**0.52**	**0.84**	0.47
WMC	0.52	1	**0.72**	-0.16
RFC	0.84	0.72	1	0.19
DIT	0.47	-0.16	0.19	1
Project B	CBO	WMC	RFC	DIT
CBO	1	0.05	**0.61**	**0.71**
WMC	0.05	1	**0.51**	-0.15
RFC	0.61	0.51	1	0.27
DIT	0.71	-0.15	0.27	1

to WMC). This means that it is more a measure for complexity in terms of coupling or message passing between objects than of structural complexity of method definition and method invocations within a class. As we will see this is also reflected by the fact that stepwise regression prefers to include either WMC and CBO or WMC and RFC as predictors, but not both CBO and RFC metrics. Overall, correlation analysis suggests that multicollinearity may be a problem in regression models that use the subset of CK metrics we employ as predictors in this study.

Multicollinearity may lead to high variance of regression coefficients, while outliers may bias them if using standard least square regression methods. We have to address both issues in regression analysis. We overcome these problems to some extent by using (a) techniques for reducing the dimension of input space and (b) applying robust regression techniques that are less sensitive towards outliers.

13.4 MODEL BUILDING AND PREDICTION

We want to emphasize that we first discuss models regarding their data fitting and generalization properties. After, we use them for predicting actual development effort for future iterations. In this study we use different data for model building and prediction. While many past studies use the same set of data for both purposes such approach may be questioned and give biased results: (a) It could yield over-optimistic estimates as data can be fitted to any degree of accuracy but lose completely generalization properties. (b) It does not reflect a real world scenario where models have to be built using past data and are used to predict unknown future data.

Moreover, we compare the prediction performance for different models and also for the two different projects.

13.4.1 Results for Model Building

13.4.1.1 Results for the Global Approach

Table 2 reports the root mean squared error (RMSE) obtained by leave-on-out cross-validation for the training and test data set. The 4th column reports the input variables used by the model, in particular the ones selected by stepwise regression, and the basic architecture and parameters of neural networks.

It is interesting to observe that any neural network *per se* is not better than simple regression. The MLP network for example performs worse than most regression models. However, the RBF network, which is able to capture better local properties of single data points than an MLP network works by far best for project A. For project B a GRNN network (which is a special kind of RBF network), which again handles good local distortions of data yields the best results.

In general linear models work much better for project A than for project B. For neural networks is not the case. An analysis of the distribution of data sets for both projects reveals that data distribution for project A satisfies better the assumptions for linear regression than the one of project B. This explains why linear regression works better on project A. Neural networks on the other hand do not require any particular assumptions of data distributions and therefore they work even if data are skewed and have a lot of outliers. It is interesting to observe that although the two projects are very similar (almost the same development environment and methodology, similar domain) nevertheless one has to be careful when applying models derived from one project to the other: While on a higher level the projects may look similar there are many hidden factors that are implicitly encoded in the collected data. Such factors can be the cause that in one case linear regression models work well while in the other do not. The lessons we learn from these comparative analysis of two projects are:

- Data collected for different projects may exhibit different properties even if the projects are very similar on a higher level (development environment, application domain, development methodology)
- Models that work well for one project do not necessarily work well for a similar project.
- In Agile development technology, requirements, personnel, and other factors change very fast. Therefore, it is almost impossible to apply models derived from one project to another.

- Models should be auto-adaptive and applied in the same context they have been derived from.

13.4.1.2 Results for the Incremental Approach

For the incremental model we have not that clear picture than for the global one: whereas for project A again RBF outperforms all other models, this not the case for project B. However, for project B still RBF and best regression models are very close, as their differences in the RMSE error do not exceed a value of 0.06. And as

Table 2. Regression and neural networks for the global approach

	Model	RMSE training	LOOV-RMSE test	Input variables
Regression models for project A	L	2.12±0.19	2.10±2.71	All
	S-L	2.16±0.16	1.76±2.43	CBO, WMC
	QR	3.27±0.64	3.32±9.05	All
	S-QR	2.94±0.29	1.64±2.48	WMC, RFC, CBO²
	R	2.74±0.25	1.71±2.89	All
	S-R	3.26±0.29	1.62±2.92	CBO, WMC
	RPCR	2.70±0.31	1.68±2.54	All
Regression models for project B	L	3.26±0.06	2.72±2.68	All
	S-L	3.27±0.06	2.58±2.57	WMC, RFC
	QR	3.44±0.29	3.99±6.53	All
	S-QR	3.33±0.12	2.97±3.60	WMC, RFC, WMC²
	R	3.63±0.20	3.40±5.47	All
	S-R	3.65±0.10	2.85±3.78	WMC, RFC
	RPCR	4.07±0.10	2.50±3.35	All
Neural networks - project A	MLP	1.28±0.81	3.09±4.89	All, 2-1 architecture
	RBF	0.74±0.03	1.26±1.10	All, spread=10, 12 receptive fields in hidden layer
	GRNN	2.25±0.10	2.19±3.96	All, spread=2
Neural network - project B	MLP	1.20±0.57	2.52±2.56	All, 4-1 architecture
	RBF	1.12±0.03	1.77±2.53	All, spread=1.8, 17 receptive fields in hidden layer
	GRNN	0.94±0.03	1.42±1.51	All, spread=0.4

Legend: L - ordinary multi-linear regression, S-L - stepwise, multi-linear regression, QR - quadratic robust regression, S-QR - stepwise quadratic robust regression, R - robust regression, S-R is stepwise robust regression, RPCR - robust principal component regression. MLP - multilayer perceptron neural network RBF - radial basis functions network. GRNN - general regression neural network.

for the global approach MLP performs by far worse than both RBF and regression models. For project B we find that past Effort and WMC are good predictors for development effort as they are selected as significant input features by almost all models (the last model uses only past effort as input feature).Overall, for incremental models we can make the following observations:

- Neural networks per se are not better than regression models.
- RBF and GRNN models seem to be very promising for effort prediction. This could be explained by the nature of software engineering data: RBF and GRNN networks are able to adapt well to single data points and thus deal better with outliers and skewed data sets than other models.
- Robust regression combined with a stepwise procedure is also a successful approach. Moreover, regression analysis suggests that past Effort is the single most efficient effort predictor.

Although the results for the RMSE error indicate that GRNN and RBF models are very promising for effort estimation they (as also regression models) have a relatively high variance; therefore, we are not able to infer statistically - for example using a Mann-Whitney test - that they are significantly better than regression models.

Incremental regression models for project B suggest that past Effort, RFC, and WMC are the most important predictors for development effort.

13.4.2 Results for Iterative Effort Prediction

In order to determine whether an incremental model is more efficient for effort prediction than a global one we choose the two best models for each category and use them for iterative effort prediction in a real world scenario. This means that we have to use the best global model of project A for predicting effort of project B and vice versa, since a global model is available only after project conclusion and thus cannot be used for real prediction for the same project. In practice one would use a global model to predict future projects that are similar to the one used for model building and/or calibration. Such scenario applies for the two case studies considered in this paper: They are similar in size, development environment and methodology, programming language/technology and tools used. On the other hand, an incremental model is based on data of previous iterations and can be used to predict effort of future iterations for the same project. Having said that, we use the following strategy for comparing incremental models with global ones.

For predicting effort of project A we use the best global model of project B, which is a GRNN network and compare it with the best incremental models of project A, RBF networks. Whereas for predicting effort of project B we use the

Table 3. Results for effort prediction per class for incremental and global model

	Prediction for iteration	Model	Average MRE	Median MRE	Median MER	PRED (0.25)	SD
Results for project A	3 (G)(**)	GRNN	1.29±1.96	61%	0.85	26%	4.29
	3 (I)	RBF	2.62±3.81	127%	-1.11	11%	3.15
	4 (G)	GRNN	1.20±1.76	61%	0.82	28%	5.55
	4 (I)	RBF	0.61±0.59	42%	0.66	21%	2.03
	5 (G)	GRNN	1.24±1.84	64%	0.83	23%	5.95
	5 (I)(**)	RBF	0.25±0.34	**14%**	**0.14**	73%	0.62
Results for project B	3 (G)	RBF	3.67±7.90	89%	0.74	15%	3.83
	3 (I)	S-QR	3.57±8.70	63%	0.56	19%	2.39
	4 (G)	RBF	3.56±7.64	89%	0.71	12%	8.91
	4 (I)(**)	R	1.21±1.80	60%	0.3	20%	2.1
	5 (G)	RBF	3.28±7.45	91%	0.46	15%	9.45
	5 (I)(**)	S-R	1.06±3.14	39%	**0.25**	31%	2.74

Legend: (G) - best global model and (I) best incremental model for the respective iteration. GRNN - general regression neural network, RBF - radial basis functions network, S-QR is stepwise quadratic robust regression, R robust regression, and S-R stepwise robust regression. (**) A Kruskal-Wallis test confirms that models flagged with (**) outperform the alternative model for the same iteration at 0.05 level of significance regarding the MRE value of single classes. MRE – Magnitude of relative error. MER – Magnitude of relative error to the estimate. PRED(0.25) - % of classes with a MRE less than 25%. SD – Standard deviation.

best global model of project A, an RBF network, and compare it with the best incremental models of project B, which are robust regression models. The results for predicting the coding effort per class using global and incremental models are reported in Table 3.

Overall, the results for predicting coding effort for a single class are rather fair for both types of approaches and not very helpful in practice. The prediction at a 25% level for example is high only for the last iteration of project A. For all but one cases the relative error is higher than 25%. However, if we compare the relative performance of global and incremental approach we find clear evidence of the superiority of an incremental model in particular in later iterations of development. Moreover, there is evidence that incremental models stabilize and converge as development goes on leading to more and more accurate predictions. The behavior of the global model is completely different as it shows a constant high error for all iterations. Overall, for project A an incremental model is better than a global one for iterations 4 and 5, while for project B the incremental model outperforms the global one for all iterations. Moreover, predictions for project A are in general more accurate than predictions for project B. This is even more evident for the global model. Again this sustains the claim that effort prediction models should be derived and used on

Table 4. Prediction of total effort per iteration with the use of the incremental and global models.

Iteration	Model	MRE Project A	MER Project A	Model	MRE Project B	MER Project B
3 (G)	GRNN	58%	1.40	RBF	40%	0.67
3 (I)	RBF	71%	2.41	S-QR	41%	0.29
4 (G)	GRNN	66%	1.98	RBF	88%	7.56
4 (I)	RBF	33%	0.49	R	25%	0.20
5 (G)	GRNN	66%	1.97	RBF	82%	4.71
5 (I)	RBF	6%	0.06	S-R	22%	0.18

Legend: (G) - best global model and (I) best incremental model for the respective iteration. GRNN - general regression neural network, RBF - radial basis functions network, S-QR - stepwise quadratic robust regression, R - robust regression, and S-R - stepwise robust regression.

the same project as it is the case for the proposed incremental models.

In Table 4, we present the results for predicting the total coding effort per iteration obtained summing up the coding effort for each single class.

Again the results emphasize that an incremental model produces (a) more accurate effort prediction and (b) stabilizes during development. For example, for iteration #4 a global model gives a relative error of 66% in project A and 88% in project B, while an incremental model drops the relative error to 33% respective 25%. Moreover, from iteration 4 onwards the relative error for incremental effort prediction falls under 25%, which is considered a good result in software effort estimation.Altogether we can state that:

- In general, incremental models outperform global ones for iterative effort prediction.
- The superiority of the incremental approach is even more manifest in later development iterations.
- The incremental approach gives very promising results for predicting the effort of last iterations of development.

Our findings that incremental models outperform global models could also be explained by the fact that the two projects have some subtle differences that are hidden in the data but are not evident in domain factors – and thus we are not aware of them. In fact if we use the global models for each project for predicting effort for the same project we find that the results are competitive with and in part even superior to incremental models. However, also in this case incremental models converge to more accurate predictions and outperform global models in particular in later development iterations. Our observation again sustains the claim of other researchers (Mohanty, 1981) that prediction models should be *local models* and in general work only for data used for building or calibrating them. In this light we may conclude that for highly volatile environments such as XP incremental models are the only way to develop prediction models that are of real practical use. Overall, the results enable us to answer our research hypothesis and we can state that for the projects under scrutiny incremental models are more suitable for iterative effort prediction than global models.

13.5 SUMMING UP

We have identified a number of reasons for which the suitability of the monolithic prediction models is limited when dealing with agile software development:

- Most companies using agile development are rather small (94% of software companies in US have less than 20 people (Fayad *et al.*, 2000)). Thus, it is very likely that they may not have historic data to build traditional effort prediction models.
- Agile projects change rapidly and it is difficult to anticipate that a model constructed with the use of data for one project would be valid for another project.
- In general, predictor variables may not be known at the start of the project but become available at the beginning of each iteration. Therefore, early estimation of total development effort is out of reach and should be replaced by an iterative estimation of development effort for the next future iteration.

Considering these arguments we developed an incremental, iteration-based prediction model. It has the following advantages over a monolithic model:

- There is no need for historic data.
- It fits naturally into iterative development cycles, as it evolves and accommodates to changes from one iteration to another.
- There is no risk that the model is outdated; this is in particular important for companies that accept projects in new application domains or with new technologies. In such cases models based on historic data may completely fall short.
- An incremental model gives early and more frequent feedback to developers and managers. A short feedback cycle is important to detect early aberrations

from preset targets. In such cases a company may investigate why predicted effort goals are not met or eventually re-calibrate the prediction model (MacDonell & Shepperd, 2003).

We applied the incremental approach to two agile, semi-industrial development projects and could evidence that it is superior to a global, monolithic prediction model, in particular for later iterations of development. For this first validation we use the Chidamber and Kemerer set of object-oriented design metrics as predictors and both regression models and neural networks for model realization. It remains to future experiments if the results hold also for other models and predictor variables.

Incremental models are stable and convergent in the sense that their cross-validation and prediction error decreases from iteration to iteration. They can be used right from the start of development and improve their accuracy throughout project evolution due to their iterative nature. Global models on the other hand are based on historic data; even in the best case if we assume that they are used in exactly the same project they have been derived from they still do not perform as good as incremental models; this is more evident the more iterations are completed as incremental models adapt themselves to project and product characteristics increasing their predictive performance and accuracy.

Nowadays intelligent data collection and analysis tools allow easy automation of the model building and prediction process. At the beginning of development iteration they could be integrated in a planning game where customers, developers, and managers develop a first objective and independent cost estimation.

13.6 REFERENCES

Ahituv, N., Zviran, M., & Glezer, C. (1999). Top management toolbox for managing corporate IT. *Communications of the ACM, 42*(4), 93–99. doi:10.1145/299157.299177

Albrecht, A. J., & Gaffney, J. E. (1983). Software function, source lines of code, and development effort prediction. *IEEE Transactions on Software Engineering, 9*(6), 639–648. doi:10.1109/TSE.1983.235271

Alshayeb, M., & Li, W. (2003). An empirical validation of object-oriented metrics in two different iterative software processes. *IEEE Transactions on Software Engineering, 29*(11), 1043–1048. doi:10.1109/TSE.2003.1245305

Angelis, L., Stamelos, I., & Morisio, M. (2001). Building a software cost estimation model based on categorical data. *7th International Symposium on Software Metrics*.

Basili, V. R., Briand, L., & Melo, W. L. (1996). A validation of object-oriented design metrics as quality indicators. *IEEE Transactions on Software Engineering*, *22*(10), 751–761. doi:10.1109/32.544352

Boehm, B. W. (1981). *Software engineering economics*. Prentice-Hall.

Boehm, B. W., Abts, C., & Chulani, S. (2000). Software development cost estimation approaches–a survey. *Annals of Software Engineering*.

Boehm, B. W., Clark, B., Horowitz, E., Madachy, R., Shelby, R., & Westland, C. (1995). Cost models for future software life cycle processes: COCOMO 2.0. *Annals of Software Engineering*.

Briand, L. C., & Wieczorek, I. (2000). *Resource estimation in software engineering* (Tech. Rep. No. ISERN-00-05). Germany: Fraunhofer Institute for Experimental Software Engineering.

Briand, L. C., & Wüst, J. (2001). Modeling development effort in object-oriented systems using design properties. *IEEE Transactions on Software Engineering*, *27*(11), 963–986. doi:10.1109/32.965338

Chen, S., Cowan, C. F. N., & Grant, P. M. (1991). Orthogonal least squares learning algorithm for radial basis function networks. *IEEE Transactions on Neural Networks*, *2*(2), 302–309. doi:10.1109/72.80341

Chen, Z., Menzies, T., & Port, D. (2005). Feature subset selection can improve software cost estimation. *1st International Workshop on Predictor Models in Software Engineering (PROMISE 2005)*.

Chidamber, S., & Kemerer, C. F. (1994). A metrics suite for object-oriented design. *IEEE Transactions on Software Engineering*, *20*(6), 476–493. doi:10.1109/32.295895

Conrow, E. H., & Shishido, P. S. (1997). Implementing risk management on software intensive projects. *IEEE Software*.

Counsell, S., Mendes, E., & Swift, S. (2002). Comprehension of object-oriented software cohesion: The empirical quagmire. *10th International Workshop on in Program Comprehension*.

Fayad, M. E., Laitinen, M., & Ward, R. P. (2000). Software engineering in the small. *Communications of the ACM*, *43*(3), 115-118. doi:10.1145/330534.330555

Girosi, F., & Poggio, T. (1990). Networks and the best approximation property. *Biological Cybernetics, 63*, 169–176. doi:10.1007/BF00195855

Glass, R. L. (1998). Short-term and long-term remedies for runaway projects. *Communications of the ACM, 41*(7), 13–15. doi:10.1145/278476.278480

Hagan, M. T., & Menhaj, M. (1994). Training feedforward networks with the Marquardt algorithm. *IEEE Transactions on Neural Networks, 5*(6), 989–993. doi:10.1109/72.329697

Johnson, P. M., & Disney, A. M. (1998). Investigating data quality problems in the PSP. *6th International Symposium on the Foundations of Software Engineering (SIGSOFT'98)*.

Johnson, P. M., Kou, H., Agustin, J., Chan, C., Moore, C., Miglani, J., et al. (2003). Beyond the personal software process: Metrics collection and analysis for the different disciplined. *25th International Conference on Software Engineering*.

Jørgensen, M., & Shepperd, M. (2007). A systematic review of software development cost estimation studies document actions. *IEEE Transactions on Software Engineering, 33*(1), 33–53. doi:10.1109/TSE.2007.256943

Layman, L., Williams, L., & Cunningham, L. (2004). Exploring extreme programming in context: An industrial case study. *Agile Development Conference*.

Lederer, A. L., & Prasad, J. (1995). Causes of inaccurate software development cost estimates. *Journal of Systems and Software, 31*(2), 125–134.doi:doi:10.1016/0164-1212(94)00092-2

Lee, H. (1993). A structured methodology for software development effort prediction using the analytic hierarchy process. *Journal of Systems and Software,21*.

MacDonell, S., & Shepperd, M. J. (2003). Using prior-phase effort records for re-estimation during software projects. *9th International Software Metrics Symposium (METRICS'03)*.

Mair, C., Shepperd, M., & Jørgensen, M. (2005). An analysis of data sets used to train and validate cost prediction systems. *1st International Workshop on Predictor Models in Software Engineering (PROMISE 2005)*.

McConnell, S. (1996). Avoiding classic mistakes. *IEEE Software*.

Menzies, T., Port, D., Chen, Z., Hihn, J., & Stukes, S. (2005). Validation methods for calibrating software effort models. *27th International Conference on Software Engineering*.

Miyazaki, Y., Terakado, M., Ozaki, K., & Nozaki, H. (1994). Robust regression for developing software estimation models. *Journal of Systems and Software, 27*(1), 3–16. doi:10.1016/0164-1212(94)90110-4

Mohanty, S. (1981). Software cost estimation: Present and future. *Software, Practice & Experience, 11*, 103–121. doi:10.1002/spe.4380110202

Moløkken-Østvold, K., Jørgensen, M., & Talinkan, S. S. (2004). A survey on software estimation in the Norwegian industry. *10ᵗʰ International Symposium on Software Metrics (METRICS'04)*.

Pendharkar, C. P. C., Subramanian, G. H., & Rodger, J. A. (2005). A probabilistic model for predicting software development effort. *IEEE Transactions on Software Engineering, 31*(7), 615–624. doi:10.1109/TSE.2005.75

Poppendieck, M., & Poppendieck, T. (2003). *Lean software development: An agile toolkit for software development managers*. Addison-Wesley Professional.

Putnam, L. H. A. (1978). A general empirical solution to the macro software sizing and estimation problem. *IEEE Transactions on Software Engineering, 4*(4), 345–381. doi:10.1109/TSE.1978.231521

Sauer, C., & Cuthbertson, C. (2003). *The state of IT project management in the UK 2002-2003*. Templeton College, University of Oxford.

Shepperd, M. C., & Schofield, C. (1997). Estimating software project effort using analogies. *IEEE Transactions on Software Engineering, 23*(11), 736–743. doi:10.1109/32.637387

Shin, M., & Goel, A. L. (2000). Empirical data modeling in software engineering using radial basis functions. *IEEE Transactions on Software Engineering, 26*(6), 567–576. doi:10.1109/32.852743

Sillitti, A., Janes, A., Succi, G., & Vernazza, T. (2003). Collecting, integrating, and analyzing software metrics and personal software process data. *29ᵗʰ EUROMICRO*.

Specht, D. F. (1991). A general regression neural network. *IEEE Transactions on Neural Networks, 2*(6), 568-576. doi:10.1109/72.97934

Srinivasan, K., & Fisher, D. (1995). Machine learning approaches to estimating software development effort. *IEEE Transactions on Software Engineering, 21*(2), 126–137. doi:10.1109/32.345828

Succi, G., Pedrycz, W., Djokic, S., Zuliani, P., & Russo, B. (2005). An empirical exploration of the distributions of the Chidamber and Kemerer object-oriented metrics suite. *Empirical Software Engineering, 10*(1), 81–104. doi:10.1023/B:EMSE.0000048324.12188.a2

Trendowicz, A., Heidrich, J., Münch, J., Ishigai, Y., Yokoyama, K., & Kikuchi, N. (2006). Development of a hybrid cost estimation model in an iterative manner. *28ᵗʰ International Conference on Software Engineering*.

ENDNOTE

[1] http://agilemanifesto.org/ (accessed on November 11, 2008)

Chapter 14
Discontinuous Use of Pair Programming

14.1 INTRODUCTION

Pair Programming (PP) has usually considered non effective for distributed teams, not working most of the time together (Williams *et al.*, 2000; Baheti et al., 2002). In this chapter we discuss the effectiveness of PP at transferring knowledge and skills among students that met only occasionally and worked mostly independently.

The effect of geographical distance between pair programmers has been already addressed by Baheti *et al.* (2002). They performed an experiment on a graduate class to assess whether it is feasible to use distributed PP to develop software. It turned out that distributed (i.e., geographically distant) pair programming teams can effectively develop software, that is, with productivity (in terms of LOC/hr) and code quality (in terms of grade awarded to the project developed) comparable to those of close-knit teams.

Kircher et al. (2001) identify the aspects of XP which require co-located programming teams. The authors analyze these aspects in the distributed development of software for collaborative productivity. They found that the effectiveness warranted by physical proximity could not be completely substituted by any communication tool, though various combinations turned out to be quite effective. However, their findings are based only on the personal opinions of the participants, the authors themselves, and no empirical evidence is provided.

DOI: 10.4018/978-1-59904-681-5.ch014

We report on the experience of a group of fifteen students doing a summer internship experience at the end of their first year of a first degree in Applied Computer Science at the Free University of Bolzano (Italy). For three months students worked either in companies or research centers the whole week but Friday afternoons, when they met altogether in a university laboratory. Here, they worked on a different project using PP. Our aim was to monitor the knowledge they acquired from such a structured context. Even if such an environment is not distributed in the genuine sense of the term, similar factors may affect the success of the project. Indeed problems with non-continuous use of the same software practices, difference of environments and requests and geographic distance can be equally experienced.

14.2 STRUCTURE OF THE EXPERIMENT

As mentioned, this research deals with a group of fifteen (volunteer) students doing a three-month summer internship.

Eleven students worked in local companies for all the working days but Friday afternoons, when all of them met in a university laboratory for four hours to share their experience. A group of four students worked for a research center of the Faculty – joining the others on Friday afternoons.

The environment was distributed in the sense that the students had the chance to work together only one afternoon per week, spending the rest of the week working in geographically distant places.

In the Friday afternoon meetings all the students had the possibility to share their knowledge and skills by developing software using PP. This work was completely independent from what they were doing over the rest of the week. In all the companies there were no special indications to use XP practices except for students working for the university lab, where XP was continuously adopted.

Altogether, the use of PP was non-continuous – only on Friday afternoons – and alternated with other coding styles.

At the end of their experience students answered to a questionnaire.

14.2.1 GQM of the Experiment

To properly structure the experiment, we use the well known Goal-Questions-Metrics (GQM) paradigm (Wohlin *et al.*, 2000) according to the guidelines of Succi *et al.* (2002):Goal:

- Monitoring skills acquired in using PP in order to investigate:
- Knowledge transfer

- Effectiveness of a non continuous PP practice - alternated with a different programming methodology
- Integration of XP skills learned at the university and practices acquired during an industrial internship

Questions:

- How much effective is the use of PP in transferring knowledge in a distributed environment?
- How much effective is PP in a non temporary continuous work alternated with other practices?
- How much effective is the use of PP in integrating university studies and applicative practices of a company of an industrial environment?

Metrics:

- Final questionnaire

14.2.2 Structure of the Questionnaire

The final questionnaire was developed according to standard questionnaire-writing styles. It consisted of three main parts: the first described the student's status – work experience and skills, the second dealt with the Internship experience and the third reported the students' opinion on the PP style. The questionnaire was structured by several multi-choice questions alternated with some rating and free-style questions. It covered topics listed in Table 1.

In the first three points of Table 1, the student's work experience in computer science is evaluated. It was measured by common questions on work experience and on some aspects of team working.

Points 4 to 9 of Table 1 describe the environment of the internship. Point 4 focuses on what of the project was known before the Internship experience, such as

Table 1. Main subjects of the questionnaire

Topics	
1. General work experience	7. Internship: Communication tools
2. Skills in Computer Science	8. Internship: PP Best Aspect
3. Skills in some PP features	9. Internship: Benefits
4. Internship: Project knowledge	10. Evaluation PP: Hardest Thing
5. Internship: Project structure	11. Evaluation PP: Non Effectiveness
6. Internship: Project support	12. Evaluation PP: Most Important Aspect

tools (Eclipse, NetBeans, etc.), languages (Java, C#, PHP, etc.) and approach to the problem – how to translate requirements into code.

To evaluate the students' degree of comprehension of the project, point 5, 6 and 7 asked students to describe the project – structure, and technical and human support – and the communication tools they used during the experience.

Points 8 and 9 measured the PP practice rooted in the students' experience, while points 10 to 12 asked students to give an opinion on the PP style independently from the project.

In Table 2 we reproduce the acronyms of the measures. Besides each acronym we put the reference number of Table 1. Points 8, 10 and 12 were in the form of free-style questions, so they are not included in Table 2.

14.2.3 Details on the Sample

In this section we characterize our sample by studying the answers to the first part of the questionnaire and the cross-correlations among them.

Fifteen students volunteered for this project. Eleven were full-time students with some previous work experience, while four were part-time students (with part-time jobs). In Table 3 we report the frequencies for the answers of the questionnaire regarding the students' previous skills and knowledge. The frequencies are based on a sample of size fourteen, as one questionnaire was not returned. Frequencies, Pearson's cross-correlation coefficients and p-significance (as usual, we consider $\alpha < 0.05$) are calculated using R, a well-known OS statistical tool.

We also note that the sample of the PPW variable has size five, that is, the number of students who answered *yes* to the Experience in Working in Pair (WPE) question.

From Table 3, we can infer that the majority of the students had a previous work experience (WE), a few of them in Computer Science (WECS). More than 70% had a good knowledge of the project they were going to start (TL, PA in Table 3). Some students (WPE 35.7%) had already practiced PP in the past, and most of them found it worth (PPW 80%). Students with work experience (WE) have more experience in teamwork (WTE) than working in pair (WPE).

The cross-correlations resulting from the first part of the questionnaire (Table 4) confirm the students' curricula. Again, we see that students' work experience is mainly in computer science. General team working has a good correlation with work experience.

From Table 4 we may infer that students who experienced a general work in pair, know and appreciate the PP practice in some of its aspects – Experience in working in pair sharing the Same Computer (PSC) and Experience in working on the Same Code (SC).

Table 2. Acronyms of measures

1-2	WS	Working student
	WE	Work experience
	WECS	Work experience in Computer Science
	WTE	Experience in working in team
	WPE	Experience in working in pair
	PPW	If WPE: Is pair programming worth?
3	PSC	Experience in working in pair sharing the same computer
	SC	Experience in working on the same code
	WD	Experience in work division
	SE	Experience in sharing experience
4	TL	Project Tools knowledge
	PA	Knowledge on how to translate requirements in code – Problem Approach
5	SP	Switched partner more than two times
6	CP	Customer's physical presence
	PS	Reference Instructor's technical support
7	T	Use of telephone
	NM	Use of NetMeeting
	IM	Use of instant messenger
	EM	Use of e-mail
9	LC	Increasing learning and comprehension
	CT	Increasing communication and team working
	TM	Increasing Time Management
	OE	Increasing Opportunity of experimentations
	SR	Increasing Self-Reliance
	PSST	Increasing Problem Solving and Strategy Thinking
11	SAFYC	The use of PP is not effective Soon After a First Year Course
	STE	The use of PP is not effective for a Short Experience
	BPEC	The use of PP is not effective if Both Partners are not Equally Competent
	PU	The use of PP is not effective if the Project is Unknown

Table 4 also shows that the four different aspects of PP are each other correlated. This might mean that students had a somehow homogeneous experience of PP (i.e., they did not practice just one aspect).

Table 3. Frequencies of the previous skills and knowledge of the sample

(%)	General working experience (1-2)					
	WS	**WE**	**WECS**	**WTE**	**WPE**	**PPW**
no	71.4%	14.3%	64.3%	42.9%	64.3%	20%
yes	28.6%	85.7%	35.7%	57.1%	35.7%	80%
n/a	0%	0%	0%	0%	0%	0%
(%)	PP aspects experience (3)				Project Knowledge (4)	
	PSC	**SC**	**WD**	**SE**	**TL**	**PA**
no	50%	57.1%	14.3%	28.6%	28.6%	21.4%
yes	35.7%	28.6%	71.4%	57.1%	71.4%	78.6%
n/a	14.3%	14.3%	14.3%	14.3%	0%	0%

Table 4. Correlations between different aspects of students' know how

	WTE	**WECS**	**CP**	**PSC**	**SC**	**WD**
WS		0.85 $p=0.000$				
WE	0.57 $p=0.032$					
PSC			0.60 $p=0.023$		0.92 $p=0.000$	
WD				0.77 $p=0.001$	0.74 $p=0.002$	
SE				0.69 $p=0.007$	0.64 $p=0.015$	0.88 $p=0.000$
WPE				0.65 $p=0.012$	0.53 $p=0.050$	

14.2.4 Details on the Environment

The companies selected for the internship were mainly local businesses. Some were software houses, others non-IT organizations with an EDP department. Students selected the companies on a First-In-First-Out basis.

To take full advantage of the internship, students were introduced to the project with several seminars related to the experience they were about to begin. Different subjects were presented: legal rights and duties, role of the unions, importance of, and techniques to communicate within corporate organizations, how to secure funds to create a start-up and so on. They were also introduced to team working by role play. They were taught time and stress management, how to support a talk and how to give priorities.

At the beginning of the internship, each company assigned a task to the student. Most of the time company assignments were part of a big project already started. Since the students had attended a course on Java during the previous semesters, all of them were not only able to use Java, but also to learn new languages and tools.

A company-internal reference person was selected to act as internal tutor of the student. Additionally, some selected members of the Faculty of Computer Science provided technical and social support to students and monitored the overall experience.

So, almost every week a member of the university staff visited the student in the company and reported on the student's situation. Reports were published on an internal web site, so each instructor could access them. Students and companies were aware of the dates of the visits in advance, so that the internal tutor could be present to the visit.

In the Friday afternoon meetings all the students gathered in a university laboratory and worked, using PP, on a project different from what they were working on in the rest of the week. Therefore, in such meetings all the students had the chance to communicate, to compare and to analyze their weekly experience, evidencing similarities and differences. In this way they had the possibility of increasing their skills by knowledge transfer.

An instructor and a *virtual customer*" i.e., a faculty member acting as the customer, were always present in the room.

The Friday afternoon project was divided into independent subprojects, each assigned to a group of four students experiencing PP. They periodically switched partners in the team.

In each of the four teams there was a member of the group who was experiencing PP the whole week.

14.3 RESULTS

We analyze the results in two parts. First, we study how communication tools were used. Second, we report on how PP was effective in transferring knowledge and skills among participants.

As usual, we only consider Pearson's correlation coefficients whose p-significance is less than 0.05.

14.3.1 Use of Communication Tools

The two tables below provide some understanding on the use of communication tools. The most used communication tool has been e-mail, but telephone and instant messenger were also adopted (Table 5).

The use of telephone is negatively correlated with the tools used for coding during the internship (Table 5). This means that students used telephone when they had troubles with the software tools. In the same way we may say that NetMeeting was used by students who initially knew little on how to approach the project. The use of Instant Messenger is negatively correlated with *Self-Reliance* (SR) (Table 6). These three facts might indicate that the more students think they have increased skills, the less they use synchronous communication tools.

On the other hand, *Use of E-Mail* (EM) has a good correlation with the initial ability in approaching the project (PA). From this we may instead infer that students with increased skills preferred to use asynchronous communication tools.

To summarize, the results of this part of the questionnaire indicate that students preferred synchronous, real-time communication tools when they knew little about coding tools or problem approach, otherwise, e-mail was the most used communication tool.

Table 5. Use of communication tools

(%)	Communication Tools (7)			
	T	NM	EM	IM
no	57.1%	85.7%	21.4%	57.1%
yes	42.9%	14.3%	78.6%	42.9%
n/a	0%	0%	0%	0%

Table 6. Cross correlations between use of communication tools and knowledge of the project

	Cross Correlation		
	TL	PA	SR
T	-0.73 p=0.003		
NM		-0.78 p=0.001	
EM		0.58 p=0.031	
IM			-0.58 p=0.031

14.3.2 Knowledge Transfer and Effectiveness of PP

We omit frequencies On Internship benefits and non effectiveness of PP, 80% of the students answered positively on each benefit listed in Table 7a (except for the last two items, for which slightly less than 50% gave a positive answer). This entails that students actually experienced a transfer of knowledge and skills. In Table 7b less than 50% of the students considered PP non effective whether the kind of project is unknown and even less considered PP unfeasible for a short time experience.

From Table 8, the two abilities *Increasing Learning and Comprehension* (LC) and *Increasing Problem Solving and Strategy Thinking* (PSST) are both correlated to each other and with *Switch partner more then two times* (SP). This might mean that switching partner more than two times during the Friday afternoon PP sessions had a good influence in increasing global comprehension of the project and maturity of the students.

Communication and Team working (CT) is positively related with the *Virtual Customer's physical Presence* (CP). From this we might infer that the on-site presence of the customer (one of the XP practices) influenced favorably the communication and teamwork skills of the students. This also suggests that PP should always be practiced with a strong presence of the customer.

The ability to manage time is highly and significantly negatively correlated with the non-effectiveness of a brief PP experience. By the frequency of the positive answers (72%) to *Increasing Time Management* (TM) we may infer that students think that PP helps to manage time better.

Table 7. Ranking internship benefits (a) and conditions for non-effectiveness of PP (b)

Benefits of Internship (a)	
Low → High	Communication (CT)
	Problem solving (PSST)
	Learning and comprehension (LC)
	Time management (TM)
	Self-reliance (SR)
	Opportunity to experiment (OE)
Conditions for Non-Effectiveness of PP (b)	
Low → High	Unknown project (PU)
	Experience soon after a first year course (SAFYC)
	Member of pair not equally competent (BPEC)
	Short experience (STE)

Table 8. Cross-correlations with internship benefits

	PSST	OE	SP	CP	EM	IM	STE
LC	0.78		0.59				
	p=0.001		P=0.026				
CT				0.68			
				p=0.008			
TM							-0.74
							p=0.002
SR						-0.58	
						p=0.031	
PSST		0.57	0.57				
		p=0.032	p=0.032				
OE					-0.55		
					p=0.042		

The last part of the questionnaire provided the students with the possibility of giving a personal opinion about PP independently from the project. In Table 9 we report the most significant cross-correlations between variables that we have extracted.

The correlation of *Considering the use of PP not effective soon after a first year course* (SAFYC) with *Considering the use of PP not effective for a short experience* STE and *Considering the use of PP not effective if both partners are not equally competent* (BPEC) confirm well known results on the XP practices.

By the students' answers to the free-style questions and by the individual meeting with a faculty member we inferred that at the end of the experience the students were conscious of the limitations and benefits of PP. In particular, conflict of personalities and difference in skills caused most of the problems in PP. The most common

Table 9. Cross-correlation - condition for non-effectiveness of PP

	SAFYC	STE	TM
SAFYC		0.64	
		p=0.014	
STE			-0.745
			p=0.002
BPEC	0.54		
	p=0.046		

answer to the best aspect of PP has been – as students said – "two minds working on the same code". This might mean that although PP attracts students, they realize that this coding style is really involving.

To summarize, we saw that the vast majority (80%) of the students benefited from the experience in four ways: *Learning and Comprehension* (LC), *Communication and Teamwork* (CT), *Time Management* (TM), and *Problem Solving and Strategy Thinking* (PSST). We saw from Table 9 that these four benefits are correlated with PP aspects, namely *Switched partner more than twice* (SP), *Virtual Customer Presence* (CP), and *Use of PP is not effective for a short experience* (STE). From this we may infer that the benefits which participants received came from experiencing PP.

14.4 SUMMING UP

We performed a first analysis of the experience of a summer internship program run on a group of fifteen students. The goal was to assess the transfer of knowledge and skills when using PP.

The peculiarity of this case study consisted in the kind of distributed environment and in a methodology approach in which PP was alternated with other programming styles. Most of the students worked in separate companies the whole week but Friday afternoons, when they met in a university laboratory to work on a different project using PP (there were no special indications to use PP when working for the companies).

Increased communication ability was the benefit that 92% of all the students felt to have gained. Also, the vast majority of students found their problem-solving, time management and learning abilities improved. These benefits are correlated with the practice of PP. Therefore, PP was effective at transferring knowledge and skills. We also found that the students' levels of self-reliance and project knowledge affect the use of communication tools: the more students become conscious of their abilities the less they use communication tools (and the more they think that meeting the partner once a week is enough).

Our results confirm previous empirical evidence about the benefits and the good resistance to distance hampering factors of PP. We gathered new empirical evidence which shows that PP keeps its effectiveness also when alternated with other coding styles. Our findings might be of help to people involved in the distributed development of software projects (e.g., OSS), as well as to educators for planning and running programming projects with teams composed of distance-learning students.

14.5 REFERENCES

Baheti, P., Williams, L., Gehringer, E., Stotts, D., & Smith, J. (2002). *Distributed pair programming empirical studies and supporting environments* (Tech. Rep. No. TR02-010). Department of Computer Science, University of North Carolina at Chapel Hill.

Kircher, M., Jain, P., Corsaro, A., & Levine, D. (2001). Distributed eXtreme programming. *XP 2001*.

Succi, G., Marchesi, M., Pedrycz, W., & Williams, L. (2002). Preliminary analysis of the effects of pair programming on job satisfaction. *XP 2002*.

Williams, L., Kessler, R., Cunningham, W., & Jeffries, R. (2000). Strengthening the case for pair programming. *IEEE Software*.

Wohlin, C., Runeson, P., Höst, M., Ohlsson, M. C., Regnell, B., & Wesslén, A. (2000). *Experimentation in software engineering: An introduction.* Kluwer Academic Publishers.

Chapter 15
Requirements Management

15.1 INTRODUCTION

Existing literature (Boehm, 1981; Brooks, 1987; Cook, 2002) and empirical studies (Basili & Perricone, 1984; Emam & Madhavji, 1995; Marshall & Rossman, 1989) emphasize the importance of the Requirement Engineering (RE) activities as these activities have a strong and positive correlation with the success of most software projects. Four of the ten main success factors deal with RE: user involvement, clear business objectives, minimized scope, and firm basic requirements.

RE can be broadly defined as the process of discovering, identifying, and documenting the actual customer needs (Nuseibeh & Easterbrook, 2000).

This chapter focuses on Requirements Management (RM), one of the main activities in the RE process. RM is about organizing the information and requirements gathered during the RE process and managing changes of these requirements (Grehag, 2001).

As AMs and OSD highlight, one of the most challenging aspects of RM is that the requirements gathered are seldom static. They are likely to change over time, during the project phases and during maintenance (Berry, 2002; Harker & Eason, 1992). Consequently, changes to requirements must be managed during the whole lifecycle of a product starting early in the elicitation phase (Lauesen, 2002).

DOI: 10.4018/978-1-59904-681-5.ch015

Managing changing requirements is a critical activity. In fact, requirements changes impact on costs and time. Consequently, they affect the uncertainty and risk of a project (Cook, 2002; Lubars *et al.*, 1993; Stark, 1998).

Furthermore, the level of requirements uncertainty and variability may affect the choice of the development approach to employ in a project (MacCormack & Verganti, 2003). Because of this, AMs have been proposed in order to deal with changing requirements. These methods should help companies deliver valuable software in situations with constant change and turbulence (Highsmith, 2002).

There are two main strategies to deal with changing requirements (Saiedian & Dale, 2000; Grehag, 2001):

1. **Defensive strategy:** Trying to reduce or avoid changes (e.g., using an effective requirements definition strategy).
2. **Reactive strategy:** Managing properly the changes that actually occur (e.g., including support to changes into the product or process adding flexibility).

We focuses on both the defensive and the reactive strategy. In order to understand how to implement a defensive strategy, we have analysed the factors that lead to change the requirements. In fact, addressing properly these factors allow companies to improve their requirements definition process and, consequently, reduce the amount of change requests. Furthermore, to understand how to manage inevitable requirements changes, we have investigated how software companies consider and deal with requirements variability.

To address these issues, an empirical investigation has been performed interviewing personnel of 35 software companies. The final findings of our survey highlight some potential areas to improve RE and some suggestions for RM.

15.2 BACKGROUND

15.2.1 Changing Requirements

To implement a defensive strategy, it is necessary to understand the factors that lead to changing requirements. Most of them originate from problems, difficulties, or constraints during the requirement definition process.

We have identified four main classes of potential problems during the requirements definition process:

1. Human cognitive constraints and lack of information/incomplete knowledge.
2. Difficulties or barriers in the communication process.
3. Emotional and relational problems or constraints.
4. Internal and external context of the project.

These problems can affect directly or indirectly the requirements variability during the project life cycle. This section describes briefly the following problems.

The first source of requirements problems deals with *information and knowledge*. In particular, it refers to both the problem of too much information and lack of information.

Too much information can results in difficulties in responding to requests for requirements. Asking users their requirements will not necessarily yield a complete and correct set of requirements. The possible human constraints are (Davis, 1982; March, 1998):

- **Short-term memory:** This may affect the number and type of requirements remembered by the customer
- **Human bias in selection and use of data:** There could be a significant bias toward requirements based on current procedure, currently available information, and recent events.
- **Bounded rationality:** Procedures for determining information requirements may apply bounded rationality.
- **Limited attention:** It may influence the number of issues on which both the customers and the analysts/developer can focus.

The lack of information can affect the ability of the customers to specify all their requests (especially at the beginning of the project) (Verganti, 1999). Moreover, knowledge limitations can affect the ability of the development team to understand the problem and the domain of the customer, or to use new technologies (Curtis *et al.*, 1988). The lack of information regarding the point of view of all the stakeholders of the projects may result in conflicts in the organization of the customer and inside the development team (May, 1998).

The second source of requirements problems emphasizes the role of *communication*. The success of the requirements definition process depends largely on the knowledge of the problems and domain of the customer. However, such knowledge ultimately depends on how people communicate and work together (Saiedian & Dale). RE is based on communication; it involves negotiation, discussion, and information sharing among all the stakeholders of the project (Byrd *et al.*, 1992). The main problems with communication during the requirements gathering activity are caused by:

- **Stakeholders' diversity:** The requirements gathering process involves key players belonging to different communities. All of them have different knowledge, experiences, abilities, and interests. Consequently, communication problems, conflicts, and misunderstandings among them are possible (Byrd *et al.*, 1992).
- **Stakeholders' language and communication channels:** Many misunderstandings regarding the requirements depend on the notations used in the specification and on the languages used by the different stakeholders. Moreover, stakeholders share knowledge using mainly one communication channel: documentation (Al-Rawas & Easterbrook, 1996).
- **Poor communication:** How project participants communicate can be just as important as what they communicate. Both the customer and the analyst/developer should listen actively to the other, avoid contradictions, rapid conclusions, assumptions, etc. (Saiedian & Dale).

The third source of problems during the requirement definition process focuses on *emotional* and *relational* aspects. RE is a human-intensity activity. Accordingly, RE needs to be sensitive to how people perceive and understand their environment, how people interact, and how the relationships in the workplace affect their actions and emotions (Gougen & Linde, 1993).The most dangerous and common emotions during the requirement gathering activity are:

- **Resistance:** Is a process taking place within a person that takes the form of opposition. For example, it can appear as opposition to new ideas, changes, or technological revolutions (Saiedian & Dale).
- **Fear or suspect:** Many users can be reluctant to tell enquiring analysts the way they actually work because the analyst is regarded as a representative of the authority (Land, 1982). This usually results in a defensive attitude that can cause incomplete requirements specification.

Software development requires collaboration among project stakeholders. Good relationships and communication among members of the development team reduce conflicts, misunderstandings, and promote knowledge sharing (Highsmith, 2002).

During the requirements gathering activity, collaboration between the customer and the analyst/developer usually results in a pleasant, relaxing, and friendly atmosphere. This behaviour encourages trust and mutual commitment. Because of this, the amount and the quality of the requirements gathered increase (Tan, 1992). Moreover, it can affect positively the customer involvement.

The last sources of requirements problems highlight the importance of the *internal* and *external context*. The internal context includes those factors that the project stakeholders can control and manage. The internal factors that can cause problems with the requirements are:

- **Type of project (complexity and duration):** In a complex project, (a) the human constraints (e.g., short-term memory, bounded rationality, limited attention, etc.) during the requirements definition process tend to be stronger; (b) it is more difficult to have all the necessary information and knowledge; (c) the number of project participants increase causing a greater need of communication and coordination; (d) misunderstandings and conflicts are more common. The most important factor affected by the duration of the project is the level of uncertainty (Naumann *et al.*, 1980).
- **Structure of the organizations involved in the project:** Companies with a strict separation among functions or departments tend to have communications barriers and collaboration problems. Moreover, the diversity among project stakeholders may result in misunderstandings and internal conflicts regarding requirements (Al-Rawas & Easterbrook, 1996). The decision making structure may affect the importance of different requirements as well as the person responsible for the requirements definition.

The external context involves those factors that the project participants cannot control. Thus, they can be managed only in a reactive way. These factors affect uniformly all the companies operating in a particular time period or environment and result often in changing requests (Harker & Eason, 1992; Land, 1982).

- **Technological progress:** The speed of the innovation process cause continuous and frequent changes in the tools and technology adopted by companies.
- **Market and business stability:** The economical changes force companies to modify frequently their business strategies and goals.
- **Stability of the political, institutional, and legal context:** These factors influence more the companies operating in some business areas such as software for public administrations, government, etc.

Although these factors affect seriously the stability of the requirements, they are not under the control of the project participants; consequently, we do not have investigated them in this survey.

15.2.2 Managing Changing Requirements

A proper understanding of the potential sources of changing requirements can result in a better requirements definition and in a reduction of the change requests during the product life cycle. However, there are changes that cannot be avoided or reduced. For instance, requirements changes caused by the increased understanding and experience of the stakeholders during the project. Accordingly, requirements management needs to find means for addressing these kinds of requirements (Harker & Eason, 1992).

One of the main reactive strategies to address requirements volatility is the implementation of flexible software solutions (Harker & Eason, 1992). This kind of solutions can handle changing requirements without excessive costs and time, but they require *anticipation capabilities* (i.e., the capabilities to anticipate information into the early phase of product development (Verganti, 1999). The specific mechanisms that allow anticipation of information and reduce uncertainty at the outset of a project are (Verganti, 1999):

- Systemic learning (i.e., the capability of building knowledge by transferring experience from previous similar projects).
- Teamwork and communication (i.e., the early involvement of all major actors).
- Supported proactive thinking (i.e., the use in the early phases of techniques such as prototyping).

Implementing products with modular architectures is a common way to obtain flexible solutions. The development team structures the system into modules in a way that each change does not affect the interface (Berry, 2002).

Another possible reactive strategy focuses more on the flexibility of the development process. Such flexibility can be achieved in the following ways:

- Overlapping development activities (Verganti, 1999)
- Adopting an incremental delivery or an iterative development process (Harker & Eason, 1992)
- Involving flexible resources in the product development process (Verganti, 1999)

15.3 SURVEY

15.3.1 Design of the Survey

The design of the survey follows the assumptions of Silverman (2000) and the principles of the GQM approach (Basili, 1992). We have chosen to perform a qualitative survey, using a semi-structured questionnaire as research methodology. Only projects that have a single customer, that is, customer-specific projects were considered (Lubars *et al.*, 1993).

Given the nominal nature of most variables, the characteristics of the questions, and the low number of data gathered, we have not used the existing non-parametric statistical tests (e.g., binomial test and chi-square test). The statistics used are mode, frequency count, and the relative frequency distribution (Siegel & Castellan, 1988).

The sample consisted of 35 managers of software companies located in different countries (Italy, Switzerland, Canada, and U.S.), and operating in different business areas (telecommunication, aerospace, defence, pharmaceutical, IT, etc.).

15.3.2 Questionnaire

Questionnaires are always subject to loss of information and lack of integrity of the collected data. A typical solution to these problems is the collection of massive number of questionnaires (Converse & Presser, 1986). The questionnaire is intended for managers of software companies, whose time and availability is usually very limited. From the very beginning, we have expected a low number of respondents. Therefore, there has been a compelling need to perfect the structure of the questionnaire and the way to administer it, in order to minimize the number of losses of valuable information. The final form of the questionnaire has been achieved after several drafts:

- First the soundness of each question and of the questionnaire as a whole has been carefully checked, according to the principles of Marbach (1996).
- Then, a first draft of the questionnaire has been administered to a group of volunteering students, and their feedback has been collected and used to produce a second draft.
- Finally, the second draft of the questionnaire has then been administered to 3 companies, and their feedback has been collected and used to produce the final draft.

The questionnaire collection has been a very careful activity according to the principles of Marbach (1996):

- The questionnaire has been sent by e-mail.
- Personal or phone interview has been performed.
- The results of the interview have then been put in text, and the interviewee has been asked for a final check.
- Only upon a positive feedback from the interviewee, the questionnaire has been considered accepted.

The questionnaire has been done using psychological criteria according to Converse and Presser (1986):

- The questions have been ordered from general topics to ones that are more specific.
- The data about interviewee (age, gender, etc.) have been asked in the last section to avoid encroaching upon the privacy.
- Oriented questions, that could cause distorted and obvious answers, have been avoided.

The questionnaire includes three main parts. The first describes the companies and the main features of the requirement gathering approach used by such companies. The second investigates the impact of the factors identified in the background section on:

- Initial requirements
- Relationship between the customer and the development team
- Relationship among project stakeholders of the same organization

Finally, the third part evaluates the importance of the changing requirements and how companies address this problem.

15.4 RESULTS

15.4.1 General Description of the Companies

The average age of the interviewees is forty, nearly all (83%) are males and most of them (71%) are manager or R&D directors. Moreover, 77% of the respondents have a university degree, and 71% worked in the company for less than ten years.

According to the data, half of the companies have less than fifty employees, and almost half of them have been founded before the nineties.As regard to the requirement gathering approach of the companies, the results show that:

- **When.** The requirements are gathered: only during the early phases (14%), mostly during the early phases (44%), and constantly during all the phases (42%).
- **Who.** The requirements gathering process is usually carried out by the analyst (61%), the project manager (53%), the developers (36%).
- **How.** The main requirement gathering techniques are: conventional techniques such as interviews and questionnaires (69%), group techniques such as focus groups (58%), and techniques based on simulation or models of the system such as use cases and prototyping (56%). Furthermore, 42% of the companies use tools in the requirements management process. Most of them use these tools to support or document the communication with the customers (73%) or to assist the requirement traceability process (63%).

15.4.2 Factors Leading to Changing Requirements

We have evaluated how companies consider the requirements in terms of completeness and correctness. As results show, most companies are not satisfied with the customer ability to provide a complete and clear list of requirements, at the beginning of the process (Figure 1).

The reasons for the poor requirements are showed in Figure 2. Most of the companies consider the lack of clear business goals in the customer's organization the main problem. A large part of them emphasizes the importance of information and knowledge during the requirements elicitation phase.

Regarding the relationship between the customer and the development team, most of the companies are not much satisfied; only 5% of them are really satisfied (Figure 3).

The dissatisfaction with the customer's relationship is mainly due to: **(a)** communication problems caused by the subjects diversity, **(b)** lack of customer involvement in the project (Figure 4).

Concerning the relationships among the project stakeholders, only 11% of the companies experience often conflicts during the requirements definition process. Most of them (62%) declare to experience such conflicts rarely.

The majority of the conflicts during the requirement definition process (53%) are caused by problems among representatives of different functions (Figure 5).

Figure 1. Satisfaction with the requirements

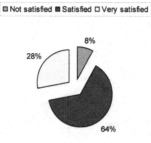

Figure 2. Causes of the poor requirements

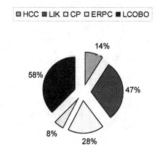

Figure 3. Satisfaction with the customer's relationship

Figure 4. Factors affecting the relationship between the customer and the development team

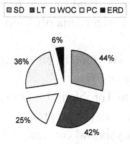

Figure 5. Most difficult relationships

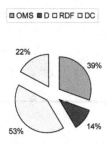

Figure 6. Reasons for the conflicts during the requirements definition process

For instance, between the marketing representatives and the technical people or between the developers and the testers.

The main reason for the conflicts among stakeholders is the structure and culture of the organizations involved in the project, followed by the diversity of the stakeholders, and by the complexity of the projects (Figure 6).

15.4.3 Changing Requirements

We have evaluated how companies consider and deal with changing requirements. A large part of companies experience requirements variability often or sometimes. Only in few companies (3%), requirements are stable for the entire project (Figure 7).

We have investigated the main kind of requirements changes (Figure 8). The results show that companies experience mainly scope changes (33%) and additions (32%).

Changing requirements impact mostly on the contractual aspects and on the quality of the architecture (Figure 9).

In order to solve the contractual problem, 17% of the companies usually renegotiate the contract. Several companies (25%) prefer to solve the contractual problem through an accurate initial analysis and contracts with special clauses for changes

Figure 7. Frequency of changes in requirements

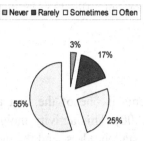

Figure 8. Main problems with requirements

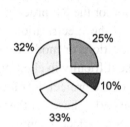

Figure 9. Effects of changing requirements

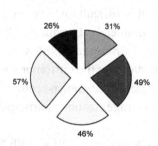

Figure 10. Main solutions for changing requirements

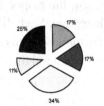

requests (Figure 10). To solve the problem of the quality of the architecture, most of the companies (34%) implement a flexible architecture.

15.5 DISCUSSION

The elicitation of requirements is one of the first activities in the RE process (Nuseibeh & Easterbrook, 2000). This activity includes the identification of the system boundaries, the main stakeholders, and the goals of the system. It is often the case that customers find it difficult to articulate clearly and completely their requirements at the beginning of the project (Gougen & Linde, 1993; Nuseibeh & Easterbrook, 2000).

According to the results of this survey and of other similar surveys (May, 1998), poor requirements are a problem for the RE process (Figure 1). They can affect the completeness and correctness of the specifications. Consequently, they can cause changes requests in terms of additions or modification of the requirements during the project life cycle. Due to the difficulty in eliciting a complete and correct list of requirements at the beginning of the project, just few companies (14%) can gather all the requirements only in the early phases of the project.

The organization of the customer affects strongly its ability to specify the requirements (Figure 2). For instance, the volatility of the market in which the customer operates may result in unclear and changing business goals, thus requirements. Another important factor is the lack of knowledge about the application domain or the problem. At the beginning of the project, it is difficult for the customer to anticipate all the information needed for specifying completely its requests. Other studies have highlighted the importance of this problem [Curtis *et al.*, 1988; Gougen & Linde, 1993).

The be successful in understanding the customer and in meeting his real needs, the development team should define customer-centered strategies and adopt communication techniques that encourage customer participation and knowledge sharing (Saiedian & Dale, 2000).

The results gathered show a low satisfaction with the customer's relationship (Figure 3).

Most of the companies (44%) experiences relational and communication problems caused by the diversity between the members of the development team and the customer (Figure 4). In particular, the respondents emphasize the diversity in terms of domain knowledge and language. Such differences may result in developers' misunderstandings about the customer's needs or domain-specific assumptions. Moreover, the customers may not understand the technical issues. As a result, they may underestimate the effort required to implement a feature or a change request (Saiedian & Dale, 2000).

Respondents complain that their customers are not sufficiently involved in the project (42%). Because of this, their relationship is mainly based on written documents and there is a lack of direct interaction with the customer. Consequently, more requirements misunderstandings are possible. Other studies have pointed out the importance of the customer involvement for the success of the projects (Lubars *et al.*, 1993).

Several companies (25%) experiences problems related to the choice of the customer representative in the requirement gathering process. In some organizations, the requirements are specified by intermediaries due to the internal structure (decision making structure) or to the lack of time of the people interested in the application. This behavior can result in incomplete or wrong requirements, requirements that do not match the real user's needs. This problem has been highlighted also by the study of Curtis *et al.* (1988).

RE involves a lot of negotiation, discussion, and information sharing (Byrd, Cossik, & Zmund 1992). During the requirements definition process different stakeholders with different interests, needs, and goals should agree on a list of requirements. Such process can result in conflicts among participants.

In contrast with the study of May (1998), stakeholder conflicts do not seem to be a frequent event. Moreover, companies experience problems mainly among functions representatives (Figure 5). The internal factors (e.g., the structure of the company and the type of the project) are the main reasons for the conflicts during the requirement definition process (Figure 6).

Most of the companies organize teams by functions or roles. Every team has well-defined and specific tasks to accomplish, and teams interact mainly through documents. As a result, differences among functions representatives can arise and communication barriers could be created causing conflicts (Al-Rawas & Easterbrook, 1996). Usually, a complex project involves a large number of stakeholders. As the number of people increase, communication, negotiation, and agreement about requirements are more difficult. Because of this, conflicts are possible. Another important reason for the conflicts during the requirements definition process is the diversity among project stakeholders (Figure 6). Diversity can inhibit communication, cause misunderstandings, and lead to conflicts.

The importance of changing requirements has been highlighted by most of the companies (Figure 7). Due to this, a large part of them (42%) has to gather constantly the requirements, during all the phases and not only at the beginning of the project. Several studies have emphasized the importance of changing requirements in software projects (Curtis *et al.*, 1988; Lubars *et al.*, 1993). The most common forms of requirements change are scope changes, followed by additions (Figure 8). This does not match with the results of another similar survey (Stark, 1998). In fact, this survey pointed out additions, followed by deletion, and finally scope changes as the most common requirements changes.

Changing requirements result often in additional costs and time. Because of this, some of the clauses of the original contract are not more applicable or valid. This situation cause often conflicts and discussions with the customer. According to the data, most of the companies (25%) solve the problem trying to anticipate all the potential requirements changes through a detailed initial analysis (Figure 10). In this way, it is possible to write a flexible contract with special clauses that regulate the implementation of changes requests. This solution requires good anticipation abilities (Verganti, 1999). In contexts with high uncertainty, it is not possible to anticipate the requirements changes at the beginning of the process. Consequently, 17% of the companies solve the contractual problem through a renegotiation of the clauses of the original contract (Figure 10).

The graph of Belady-Lehman (Berry, 2002) shows clearly what happens to the software structure when a program undergoes continual changes. The software structure can be complicated to the point that it is very hard to add or change something without affecting negatively others parts or adding bugs. In order to solve this problem, most of the companies (34%) implement flexible solutions (Figure 10). In this way, change requests can be implemented without additional costs and time. From the experience of similar projects, companies may predict the unstable parts of a system and encapsulate them in a specific and loosely coupled module. This solution can be adopted only in predictable environments and in well-known domains.

Data gathered shows other solutions to changing requirements. Some companies (11%) highlight the importance of a greater involvement of the customers and a more frequent communication with them. This solution allows the development team to understand better the customers' needs and to define more precisely their requirements (May, 1998). To overcome changing requirements, several companies (17%) adopt a flexible process. They deliver the application incrementally, allowing the customers to test it in their domain. Consequently, the development team retrieve important feedback for the next releases (Harker & Eason, 1992). The use of tools for facilitating the requirements traceability can be another way to deal with changing requirements. The development team can control the effects of changing requirements on the different parts of the product.

15.6 SUMMING UP

The analysis of the factors that lead to changing requirements highlights some potential areas to improve RE, reduce requirements variability, and improve customer satisfaction. In particular, companies should:

- Consider the internal organization of the customer's company during the requirements definition process. In particular, the actual business goals have to be clearly defined.
- Be aware of the initial customer's uncertainty and the lack of information and knowledge about the problem, the application domain, and the potential solutions.
- Overcome the communication problems caused by the diversity between the analysts/developers and the customers in terms of knowledge and language.
- Enhance the customer interest in the project in order to achieve a greater involvement and collaboration.
- Interact with the customer's representative that knows better the problem and the application domain.
- Reduce the internal communication barriers among project stakeholders.
- Consider the internal context factors such as the organization structure and the project size.

It is interesting to notice the small emphasis that companies place on the emotional problems and on the human cognitive constraints.

Regarding the requirements changes that cannot be avoided or reduced, the survey has highlighted two kinds of potential solutions. The former can be applied in situations with low requirements uncertainty and high domain knowledge. In these situations companies should:

- Implement flexible solutions with the help of the experience of previous similar projects.
- Write contracts with special clauses for requirements changes.
- Define and follow a formal change request procedure.
- Introduce a requirements traceability process.

The latter can be applied in situations in which the level of existing uncertainty does not allow the development team to anticipate or predict information. In these situations companies should:

- Renegotiate the contract with the customer if the changes can affect significantly the costs and time of the project.
- Deliver incrementally the application in order to obtain feedback from the customer at every release.
- Communicate more frequently with the customer in order to gather information constantly.

The research study described was based on the idea that it is critical to understand factors leading to changing requirements in order to improve RE and RM. A central contributor to this understanding is the exploration of the main problems and constraints in the requirements definition process. Moreover, the study has emphasized the role of uncertainty in the RM process. In fact, companies decide how to deal with changing requirements on the basis of the existing uncertainty and their anticipation abilities.

15.7 REFERENCES

Al-Rawas, A., & Easterbrook, S. (1996). Communication problems in requirements engineering: A field study. *1ˢᵗ Westminster Conference on Professional Awareness in Software Engineering*.

Basili, V. R. (1992). *Software modeling and measurement: The goal/question/ metric paradigm* (Tech. Rep. No. CS-TR-2956). Department of Computer Science, University of Maryland.

Basili, V. R., & Perricone, B. (1984). Software errors and complexity: An empirical investigation. *Communications of the ACM, 27*(1), 42-52. doi:10.1145/69605.2085

Berry, D. M. (2002). The inevitable pain of software development: Why there is no silver bullet. *Innovation of software and systems engineering in the future*.

Boehm, B. (1981). *Software engineering economics*. Prentice-hall.

Brooks, F. P. (1987). No silver bullet: Essence and accidents of software engineering. *IEEE Computer, 20*(4).

Byrd, T. A., Cossik, K. C., & Zmund, R. W. (1992). A synthesis research on requirements analysis and knowledge acquisition techniques, *MIS Quarterly*.

Converse, J. M., & Presser, S. (1986). *Survey questions: Handcrafting the standardized questionnaire*. Sage.

Cook, D. A. (2002). Requirements risks can drown software projects. *Crosstalk*.

Curtis, B., Krasner, H., & Iscoe, N. (1988). A field study of the software design process for large systems. *Communications of the ACM, 31*(11), 1268-1287. doi:10.1145/50087.50089

Davis, G. B. (1982). Strategies for information requirements determination. *IBM Systems Journal, 21*(1).

Emam, K., & Madhavji, N. H. (1995). Measuring the success of requirements engineering processes. *2nd IEEE Symposium on Requirements Engineering*.

Gougen, J. A., & Linde, C. (1993). Techniques for requirements elicitation. *IEEE International Conference on Requirements Engineering*.

Grehag, A. (2001). Requirements management in a life cycle perspective–a position paper. *7th International Workshop on Requirements Engineering: Foundation for Software Quality*.

Harker, S. D. P., & Eason, K. D. (1992). The change and evolution of requirements as a challenge to the practice of software engineering. *IEEE Computer*.

Highsmith, J. (2002). *Agile software development ecosystem*. Addison-Wesley Professional.

Land, F. (1982). Adapting to changing user requirements. *Information & Management, 5*.

Lauesen, S. (2002). *Software requirements styles and techniques*. Addison-Wesley Professional.

Lubars, M., Potts, C., & Richter, C. (1993). A review of the state of practice in requirements modeling. *IEEE Computer*.

MacCormack, A., & Verganti, R. (2003). Managing the sources of uncertainty: Matching process and context in software development. *Journal of Product Innovation Management, 20*.

Marbach, G. (1996). *Le ricerche di mercato*. Utet.

March, J. G. (1998). Theories of choice and making decisions. *Society, 20*.

Marshall, C., & Rossman, G. B. (1989). *Designing qualitative research*. Sage Publications.

May, L. J. (1998). Major causes of software project failures. *The Journal of Defense Software Engineering*.

Naumann, J. D., Davis, G. B., & McKeen, J. D. (1980). Determining information requirements: A contingency method for selection of a requirements assurance strategy. *Journal of Systems and Software*, 1.

Nuseibeh, B., & Easterbrook, S. (2000). Requirements engineering: A roadmap. *IEEE Computer*.

Saiedian, H., & Dale, R. (2000). Requirements engineering: Making the connection between the software developer and the customer. *Information and Software Technology*, 42.

Siegel, S., & Castellan, N. J. (1988). *Nonparametric statistics*. McGraw-Hill.

Silverman, D. (2000). *Doing qualitative research*. Sage Publications.

Stark, G. (1998). An examination of the effects of requirements changes on software releases. *Crosstalk*.

Tan, M. (1992). The effects of verbal and nonverbal behaviors on mutual understanding: An empirical study. *Communication of ACM*.

Verganti, R. (1999). Planned flexibility: Linking anticipation and reaction in product development projects. *Journal of Product Innovation Management, 16*(4), 363-376. doi:10.1016/S0737-6782(98)00067-8

Chapter 16
Project Management

16.1 INTRODUCTION

Surveys covering over 8000 projects indicate that the major sources of software project failure lie less with shortfalls in formal methods skills and more with shortfalls in skills to deal with stakeholder value propositions (Johnson, 1999). Five of the top six reasons of failure do not deal with programming languages, development environment or hardware choices, but are related to communications among developers and customers (Boehm, 2002). Moreover, the updated Standish Group study, conducted in 2000, identified 10 software success factors. The second factor is user involvement and the third is experienced project manager. This means that most projects fail because of people and project management issues rather than technical issues (Thomsett, 1993). Several recent studies (Philips, 1998) indicate that project managers are learning how to become more successful at IT project management. To improve the software success, more highly skilled project managers are using improved management processes.

The aim of this chapter is the investigation of the main problems in software development and the adopted solutions from the point of view of managers. We have performed a pre-experimental design based on 21 interviews with software managers. We adopt the Petroski's views (Petroski, 1982): analyze the causes of failures can do more to advance knowledge than all the successes in the word.

DOI: 10.4018/978-1-59904-681-5.ch016

Our goal is to find out differences and analogies in software management techniques derived by the adoption of AMs and their effectiveness in the improvement of the software production.

16.2 THE STRUCTURE OF THE INVESTIGATION

16.2.1 Goals, Questions and Metrics of the Research

We want to determine how project management is approach dealing both with of people (developers and clients) and with the process (planning and organization).

We use the well-known GQM model by Basili (1992) to determine the overall structure of the study. Here below there are the details.Goals:Monitoring what a Project Manager considers important to develop better processes, organize teams more effectively and deal with problems faster.

Perspectives:

- Main problems in a software development process and main solutions adopted for improving the situation
- Evaluate the software process planning
- Estimate the relationship with the customer
- Assess the real knowledge and use of AMs focusing on their benefits and disadvantages

Context:

- Managers in local and international software companies

Questions:

- Which is the biggest problem in software development? How have you tried to address it?
- How much effective is planning and organizing the software process?
- How much effective is the relationship with the customer to improve the final satisfaction?
- How much effective is the use of AMs in addressing main software problems?

Metrics:

- Telephone questionnaire

16.2.2 Design of the Experimentation

Our research can be classified as a pre-experimental design, according to classification of Cambell and Stanley (1966), in particular it is a statistic group comparison.

We have selected two different groups: managers using AMs and managers not using them. The adoption of AMs is the experimental variable, the effects of which have been measured. Interviewees have been selected among managers involved in the funded projects in our research center[1]. Both groups have answered a questionnaire (questionnaire is the process of observation).

The pre-experimental design has two limits. The former deals with the selection: differences between the two groups could be affected by how the two groups have been recruited. The involvement in the projects could have influenced managers. The latter limit is the mortality, which is when differences in groups are due to the lack of answers to the questionnaire. This limit does not affect our data collection because all the selected managers have filled in the questionnaire.

16.2.3 Questionnaire

Questionnaires are always subject to loss of information and lack of integrity of the collected data. A typical solution to these problems is the collection of massive number of questionnaires (Converse & Presser, 1986).

The questionnaire is intended for managers of software companies, whose time and availability is usually very limited. From the very beginning, we have expected a low number of respondents. Therefore, there has been a compelling need to perfect the structure of the questionnaire and the way to administer it, in order to minimize the number of losses of valuable information. The final form of the questionnaire has been achieved after several drafts:

- First the soundness of each question and of the questionnaire as a whole has been carefully checked, according to the principles of Marbach (1996).
- Then, a first draft of the questionnaire has been administered to a group of volunteering students, and their feedback has been collected and used to produce a second draft.
- Finally, the second draft of the questionnaire has then been administered to 6 companies, and their feedback has been collected and used to produce the final draft.

The questionnaire collection has been a very careful activity according to the principles of Marbach (1996):

- Potential respondents have been selected among the companies involved in some projects or have some relationships with our research center.
- The questionnaire has been sent by e-mail.
- One of the authors of this paper has then run a phone or a personal interview.
- The results of the interview have then been put in text, and the interviewee has been asked for a final check.
- Only upon a positive feedback from the interviewee, the questionnaire has been considered accepted.

The questionnaire has been done using psychological criteria according to Converse and Presser (1986):

- The questions have been ordered from general topics to ones that are more specific.
- The data about interviewee (age, gender, etc.) have been asked in the last section to avoid encroaching upon the privacy.
- Oriented questions, that could cause distorted and obvious answers, have been avoided.

According to principles of Marbach, critical aspects of the questionnaire that could invalidate or reduce the efficiency of the results have been carefully analyzed:

- The questionnaire is quite long (26 questions) but the interview has been organized in a lively way in order to avoid the decrease of the attention.
- The use of open questions could cause misunderstandings. For this reason, the correctness of the answers, transcribed by the interviewer, were checked by the interviewee.
- The use of multiple choice questions could provide answers not very valuable when the interviewee does not know precisely the topics. This problem does not affect our research because the interviewees were managers with a deep technical knowledge.

The questionnaire consists of four parts: the first analyzes the interviewee's status, main problems in software development and the adopted solutions; the second deals with the planning and the organization of the software development process; the third evaluates the relationship with the customer; finally, the fourth assesses the knowledge, the real use of AMs and the vantages or the disadvantages of their use.

It includes several multi choice questions alternated with some open questions. The topics covered in the questionnaire are listed in Table 1.

Here we list the acronyms of measures which have a significant correlation (Table 2). Besides each acronym we put the reference number of Table 1.

Table 1. Main topics of the questionnaire

ID	Topic
1	Firm's general information
2	Main software problems
3	Planning and organization of the software development process
4	Relationship with customers
5	Planning and feasibility of a project
6	Developer's characteristics
7	Agile Methods
8	Firm and interviewee's personal data

Table 2. Measures acronyms

Topic ID	Acronym	Meaning
1	CCR	Changes in the customer's requirements
1	CAT	Changes in the adopted technologies
1	MC	Major competition
1	MLT	Major legal ties
1-2-3-4-5	O	Other
1-2	THE	High turnover of employees
2	DDSFT	Difficulties to deliver the software with all functions in time
2	LQS	Lack of qualified staff
2	HC	High competition
2	RC	Relationship with client
2	EDC	Excessive documentation of code
2	DMRD	Difficulties in managing relationships with developers
4	RMUF	Requirements of too many unnecessary functions

16.2.4 Statistical Evaluation

An objective set of decision criteria is required to state whether a hypothesis is verified or not using a specific set of data. Such objective procedure usually involves several steps.According to statistical techniques (Siegel & Castellan, 1988), we proceed as follows:

- *Null hypothesis (H_0)*. The null hypothesis is: there are no differences between the two groups from the point of view of the management approach. The alternative hypothesis (research hypothesis) predicts differences between the two groups.
- *Statistical test*. We do not know exactly the nature of the population distribution. The statistical test, which is appropriate to verify our hypothesis, is the non-parametric statistical test.
- *Significance level*. In advance we decide to use $\alpha = 0.05$ as our level of significance.
- *Sample size*. The sample size consists of 21 software managers

We structure the results in tables showing the frequencies, percentage and the Sperman's correlation coefficient and p-significance.

The numeric computation of the statistical indexes has been performed using R^2.

16.2.5 Structure of the Sample

The twenty-one interviewees are project managers in software companies.

There are 20 males and one female: it is a quasi-homogeneous distribution. The Gini's index is 0.09.

Nineteen managers have a university degree; two managers have a school-leaving certificate and the average age of interviewees is forty. This means that the interviewees have a deep knowledge and experience about project management.

Seventeen companies have been created after the eighties, more than 80%. There are fifteen selected companies in Italy, five in the U.S. and one in Switzerland.

The sectors of the firms are different: consulting, service software, software development, and so on. The majority of them have a high number of employees, only four of them that have less than ten employees.

16.3 RESULTS

All the companies interviewed have been exposed to changes in their software production process.

The motivations are clear: 43% because of changes in the customers' requirements, 48% because of changes in the adopted technologies and 9% because of failure with the prior software development process (Table 3).

According to 15 managers, delivering software with all functions in time is the main problem in software development (Table 4). There is no significant correlation between the main problem in software development and the adoption of AMs in the software process. A survey, made by the Standish Group on 8000 projects in the 1999, shows the same result: only 26% of the development projects were completed on time, on budget and with all the functions originally specified.

The selected managers have adopted different solutions for the delivery of software with all functions in time: use of new methodologies such as XP and Scrum (5 managers), improvement of productivity process thanks to Project Managements culture and techniques (5 managers), focus on people (clients and developers)

Table 3. Motivations for changes in the software development

Motivation for changes	Frequency	Percentage
CCR	9	43%
CAT	10	48%
MC	0	0%
MLT	0	0%
HTE	0	0%
O	2	9%

Table 4. Main software problems

Main software problems	Frequency	Percentage
DDSFT	15	71.5%
LQS	2	9.5%
HC	0	0%
RC	2	9.5%
EDC	0	0%
DMRD	0	0%
THE	0	0%
Others	2	9.5%

through an improvement of communication and knowledge transfer (small realize, good communication between clients and developers, etc.).

The majority of managers are focus on process and people in order to improve the performance of the company, according to the results of Thomsett (1993).

Important things depend on customers and suppliers in a particular marketplace. Thinking about business, costumers, marketplace, process, etc., does not come easy to programmers and programmers turned into project managers.

This means that the Project Management has a fundamental role in the solution of software problems.

It is interesting how common planning and organization tools, such as Gantt's chart and Pert's chart, are used to improve the software development process (Table 5).

Most of managers (85.7%) would like to improve the process planning even if more than the 60% of managers are sufficiently satisfied with it (Table 6 and Table 7).

Satisfaction with the planning of projects has a good correlation with satisfaction with client's relationship. Anyway, the significant correlation is due to the use of AMs in the selected companies (Table 8).

Table 5. Planning and organization of software development process

Planning Tools	Frequency	Percentage
Gantt's chart	15	71.4%
Pert's chart	9	42.9%
Critical Path Method	4	19%
Others	6	28.6%

Table 6. Improvement of process planning

Improvement of process planning	Frequency	Percentage
Yes	18	85.7%
No	3	14.3%

Table 7. Satisfaction with the planning of projects

Satisfaction with project planning	Frequency	Percentage
Not at all	2	9.5%
Not much	1	4.8%
Sufficiently	13	6.9%
Very much	5	23.8%

Table 8. Correlation between satisfactory with planning and satisfactory with client's relationship

	Adoption of AMs		Non adoption of AMs	
	SWP	SWC	SWP	SWC
SWP		0.647 p= 0.002		0.285 p= 0.457
SWC	0.647 p= 0.002		0.285 p= 0.457	

For the managers that are using AMs, an improvement in the software development planning produces also an improvement in the satisfaction with client's relationship.

This result is in accordance to the principles of the AMs (Beck, 1999). AMs highlight the importance of planning and organization in projects. Planning is a stable dialog between clients and developers. To build a good planning, a deep and constant feedback from clients is essential. Improving planning and improving relationships with customers are strictly related due to the direct and continuous communication required.

In our research, high individual ability is the least ability considered by managers using AMs.

The adoption of AMs is correlated with the importance attributed to teamwork (Table 9). The importance of developer's high individual ability is negatively correlated with the adoption of AMs and with the importance of teamwork (Table 9). The strategy of inspected AMs managers is: preference of developers who can work in team instead of developers with high individual ability.

These results are in accordance to Schumpeter's principles (1911): innovations are new combinations of existing knowledge and incremental learning. The sharing of knowledge facilitates the transfer of knowledge within a group and it makes easier the development of new ideas. These results are also in accordance to the principles of AMs (Beck, 1999), and Thomsett (1993).

Table 9. Developer's characteristics

	Adoption of AM	High individual ability	Good time work
Adoption of AM		- 0.471 p= 0.031	0.46 p= 0.036
High individual Ability	- 0.471 p= 0.031		- 0.612 p= 0.003
Good time work	0.46 p= 0.036	- 0.612 p= 0.003	

AMs consider teamwork, in particular the practice of pair programming, essential in software development in order to improve the communication and the transfer of knowledge within the organization.

Interviewed managers have adopted several solutions to improve the three developers' characteristics included in the questionnaire. Continuous training contributed to improve individual abilities; teamwork ability and motivation improved through regular communication and involvement in projects.

We have also analyzed the different approaches adopted in the relationship with customers. There is a negative correlation between the practice of customer on site and the use of limited contracts (Table 10). The correlation is significant only for AMs managers. In AMs, the understating of what the customer really wants requires a constant participation of customers in the projects. This participation implies interactions between customers and developers and allows quick changes in the software product. The definition of limited contracts with predefined functions and time cannot be used by AMs managers.

The main problems in the relationships with customers are clear: variable requirements during the process (71.4%) and requests to deliver the final product too quickly (47.6%) (Table 11). The adopted solutions are different and are not correlated with the adoption of AMs.

The last part of the questionnaire deals with the knowledge and the adoption of AMs in the companies. Table 12 shows the most significant frequencies and correlations.

About 90% of selected managers know AMs and 57% are adopting them (Table 12). It means that AMs are a well-known phenomenon and their adoption is quite remarkable (Charette, 2003).

The main causes of non-adoption of AMs are: superficial knowledge of the topic, resistance inside the company and from customers, big or geographically separated development teams. These results are in accordance to the limits of XP pointed out by Beck (1999).

Table 10. Correlation between client on site and limited contracts

	Adoption of AMs		Non adoption of AMs	
	Client on site	Limited contracts	Client on site	Limited contracts
Client on site		- 0.683 p= 0.014		- 0.632 p = 0.074
Limited contracts	- 0.683 p= 0.014		- 0.632 p = 0.074	

Table 11. Relationship with clients

Main problems with clients	Frequency	Percentage
Variable requirements during the process	15	71.4%
Requests to deliver the final product too quickly	10	47.6%
Unsatisfied customers	2	9.5%
Requirements of too many unnecessary functions	7	33.3%
Other	4	19%

Table 12. Knowledge and adoption of agile methods

AMs		Frequencies	Percentage
Have you ever heard about AM?	Yes	19	90.5%
	No	2	9.5%
Are you adopting AM?	Yes	12	57.1%
	No	9	42.9%

There is a homogeneous distribution between the knowledge of AMs and the knowledge of XP, as shown in Table 13, but managers adopting AMs also know SCRUM.

Main problems with software development and main problems addressed with the adoption of AMs are correlated. This means that the adoption of AMs has been a good solution for the main software problems. In particular, all managers adopting AMs have evidenced as the main software development problem the delivery of all functionalities in time.

Benefits derived by the introduction of AMs are the following: improvements in the software quality, in requirements management, in customer satisfaction and team satisfaction.

Table 13. Correlation with agile methods

AMs	XP	SCRUM	Main problems with software development
Have you ever heard about AM?	1.000 $p = 0.000$		
Are you adopting XP?		0.556 $p = 0.013$	
Main problems solved adopting AM			0.724 $p = 0.014$

The main problems derived by the introduction of AMs are: lack of an ex-ante evaluation of costs and the troubles resulting by the introduction of new concepts (pair programming, test first, customer on site, etc.). The real difficulty seems to be a cultural problem: people (customers and developers) are not able to accept drastic changes in the traditional environment.

16.4 SUMMING UP

This chapter is a first analysis of the differences and the analogies derived by the adoption of AMs in twenty-one selected software companies from the point of view of project management. Our statistical research shows some interesting results.

Most of mangers indicated as the main software problem the delivery of software with all functionalities in time. This result is unrelated with the adoption of AMs and it has been confirmed by several studies.

Methods used to improve software are different but most of the managers adopt solutions focused on people and process. Anyway, an important conclusion of our work is that the managers using AMs focus more on people (customers and developers) and on the process (planning and organization) rather than managers not adopting AMs. Agile Methods focus on people in a number of different ways, this orientation is also confirmed in our collected data.

The correlation between the satisfaction with planning and the satisfaction with customer shows a deep attention for the development of a constant interaction between the development team and the customers. This approach generates a constant learning, knowledge creation and knowledge sharing through a direct and continuous communication and incremental development.

The correlation between the adoption of AMs and the preference for teamwork among developers is another good strategy based on people. Teamwork is useful to improve knowledge transfer, communication and coordination within an organization. Knowledge sharing within a group makes easier its transfer and the development of new ideas.

The customer on site practice is negatively correlated with the use of limited contracts. According to the principles of AMs, a constant relationship with the customer provides feedback useful to allow quick changes. In AMs projects, flexibility is absolutely needed and it rejects the use of limited contracts.

The main problems with software development and the main problems solved with the adoption of AMs are correlated. This might mean that the adoption of AMs has been a good solution for delivering functionality customers quickly (Highsmith & Cockburn, 2001).

Several results we have obtained in this chapter confirming previous experiences and deductions (Highsmith & Cockburn, 2001; Schwaber & Beedle, 2001). The adoption of AMs has a significant impact in practices and values of managers because they have to focus on people and process more than the others managers do.

The use of AMs seams to provide a contribution to the improvement of the software development process.

The analysis presented in this chapter is a quite preliminary one and further investigation is required.

16.5 REFERENCES

Basili, V. R. (1992). *Software modeling and measurement: The goal/question/ metric paradigm* (Tech. Rep. No. CS-TR-2956). Department of Computer Science, University of Maryland.

Beck, K. (1999). *Extreme programming explained.* Addison-Wesley Professional.

Boehm, B. (2002). Six reasons for software project failure. *IEEE Software.*

Cambell, D. T., & Stanley, J. C. (1966). *Experimental and quasi-experimental designs for research.* Houghton Mifflin Company.

Charette, R. (2003). The decision is in: Agile vs. heavy methodologies. *Cutter IT Journal, 2*(19).

Converse, J. M., & Presser, S. (1986). *Survey questions: Handcrafting the standardized questionnaire.* Sage.

Highsmith, J., & Cockburn, A. (2001). Agile software development: The business of innovation. *IEEE Computer.*

Johnson, J. (1999). Turning chaos into success. *Software Magazine.*

Marbach, G. (1996). *Le ricerche di mercato.* Utet.

Petroski, H. (1992). *To engineer is human: The role of failure in successful design.* Vintage Books of Random House.

Philips, D. (1998). *The software project manager's handbook principles that work at work.* IEEE Computer Society Press.

Schumpeter, J. (1911). *The theory of economic development.* Harvard University Press.

Schwaber, K., & Beedle, M. (2001). *Agile software development with scrum*. Prentice Hall.

Siegel, S., & Castellan, N. J. (1988). *Nonparametric statistics for behavioral sciences*. McGraw-Hill.

Thomsett, R. (1993). *Third wave project management upper Saddle River*. Yourdon Press.

ENDNOTES

[1]   http://www.case.unibz.it/ (accessed on November 11, 2008)
[2]   http://www.r-project.org/ (accessed on November 11, 2008)

Section 4
Industrial Adoption and Tools for Agile Development

Chapter 17
Open Source Assessment Methodologies

Barbara Russo
Free University of Bozen-Balzano, Italy

Marco Scotto
Free University of Bozen-Balzano, Italy

Alberto Sillitti
Free University of Bozen-Balzano, Italy

Giancarlo Succi
Free University of Bozen-Balzano, Italy

Etiel Petrinja
Free University of Bozen-Balzano, Italy

17.1 INTRODUCTION

The evaluation of software is a critical task for corporations that are planning to use OSS components. The amount of OSS available is vast and often its quality is not appropriate to adoption for real business processes. Therefore, companies have to analyze the available solutions and chose the software that meets their functional needs and quality standards. Different Capability Maturity Models (CMM) for software assessment exist, however OSS is characterized by specific features that are not appropriately handled in standard software assessment methodologies.

Project success and the software quality are a multidimensional construct and the variety of different measures to assess its quality is rich and varies from one method-

DOI: 10.4018/978-1-59904-681-5.ch017

ology to the other. However, there are some characteristics of OSS that are inserted in different methodologies. The most often considered characteristics are:

- The number of developers working on the OSS,
- The number of downloads of the software,
- The developer's satisfaction,
- The level of activity on the project,
- The time between consequent releases,
- The time to close bugs and
- The reputation in the community.

These characteristics are added to the characteristics already measured in close-source software. Since the code is available to everybody it can be reviewed and assessed by using traditional methodologies that measure the level of understanding, completeness, conciseness, portability, consistency, maintainability, testability, usability, reliability, structuredness and efficiency. These assessments can be done by everybody who is interested in the quality of the OSS.

Different OS assessment methodologies have been proposed to help users analyze and estimate the quality of software products and the related production processes. The most popular methodologies available to the OSS community are the following:

- Open Source Maturity Model (OSMM) from Cap Gemini (Duijnhouwer & Widdows, 2003)
- Open Source Maturity Model (OSMM) from Navica (Golden, 2005)
- Methodology of Qualification and Selection of Open Source software (QSOS) (Atos-Origin, 2006)
- Open Business Readiness Rating (OpenBRR) (Wasserman *et al.*, 2005)

All the four assessment methodologies listed are oriented mainly toward the analyses and evaluation of OS products. Such methodologies consider some aspects of the OSD process and try to include these elements inside the overall assessment procedure.

17.2 OPEN SOURCE MATURITY MODEL (OSMM) FROM CAP GEMINI

The Open Source Maturity Model (OSMM) provides a systematic approach for evaluating and implementing OS products within a commercial environment. It describes how an OS product should be assessed to ensure that it meets all the IT requirements that the company requires. The OSMM accomplishes this by linking an effective FLOSS product analyses and a review of the company and its IT issues. The OSMM enables to:

- Determine the maturity of an OS product,
- Assess a OS product's match to the business requirements and
- Compare OS products with commercial alternatives.

The OSMM approach makes a distinction between product indicators that are units of measure describing how the product was developed, and how it is accepted by the community; and between application indicators that measure relevant aspects of the product within a specific context (aspects like maintenance, training facility, connectivity, etc.). Application indicators cannot be measured using the Capgemini's OSMM without gating information provided by the customers and possible future users of the OS products.

Capgemini's OSMM defines four product indicators groups; each of these four groups contains a number of basic indicators. The four groups are:

- Product focuses on the internals of the product.
- Integration measures the integration of the analyzed software with other components.
- Use measures the everyday support to users.
- Acceptance group assess how the product is perceived inside the community.

Application indicators introduce into the assessment the specificity of the final user of the OSS. Basically, it analyzes present and future needs of each user. The measures inserted in the OSMM assessment are: usability, interfacing, performance, reliability, security, proven technology, vendor independence, platform independence, support, reporting, administration, advice, training, staffing, and implementation.

For some indicators the data is recorded in three different periods of time. The second record is done 6 months later than the first and the third is done two years later. This procedure shows the trend of change of some indicators that can represent better the development in time of the analyzed software. When all the scores are collected and written down, they are combined to the final score that indicates the suitability of the product for the given demands. Determining one single score allows an easy comparison between different OS products.

Scores range from 1 to 5. If an indicator is not applicable for the assessed product, the score is set to 3. This value is a threshold that does not affect the outcome of the whole assessment. Scores bellow 3 represents scores that cut-off OS products from further selections. The procedure in the OSMM is composed of 7 consecutive steps that are:

- **Step 1:** Product research and rough selection of appropriate solutions.
- **Step 2:** Scoring the product by using the product indicators.
- **Step 3:** Scoring by using application indicators.
- **Step 4:** Interviewing the customer on the importance of specific application indicators.
- **Step 5:** Scoring of the application indicators together with the customer.
- **Step 6:** Determining score cards for product and final selection of the right product for the specific customer.
- **Step 7:** The final evaluation of the OS product.

Capgemini is a private company that developed OSMM to improve its offer of OS assessments services. Therefore, the method has a non-free license and it requires an authorized distribution. Few metrics, that cannot be measured and calculated deterministically, are assessed by more than one person inside the company. This way it is guaranteed an objective score of the analyzed software product.

17.3 OPEN SOURCE MATURITY MODEL (OSMM) FROM NAVICA

The Navica's OSMM is an assessment method that provides a formal set of assessment criteria. The Barton Group report describes the OSMM as a tool that provide additional information to pragmatic software adopters. If the software's early adopters do not need additional products that are delivered along the software, the pragmatic adopters, that represent 85% of users, demand additional tools, descriptions, assessments, robust support and documentation. Proprietary software usually contains many of these additional products. On the contrary, OS developers, especially in the beginning phases do not provide these additional products. Navica's OSMM offers the assessment of OS code and of additional products and it also represents one of the additional products that help pragmatic users to adopt OSS.

The OSMM assesses the FLOSS product's maturity in three phases.

17.3.1 Phase 1: Assess Element Maturity

The first phase basically identifies key product elements and assesses their maturity level. Key elements are critical for a proper implementation of the OSS. These key elements are: product software, support, documentation, training, product integrations and professional service. Key elements are assessed according to a four step procedure.

- **Step 1:** Define Requirements allows the assessment of the OSS from specific needs of the user.
- **Step 2:** Locate Resources provides addresses and links to all kind of resources that support the adoption of the analyzed OSS. Forums provide a rich source of information about additional products that describe the analyzed products.
- **Step 3:** Assess maturity is the key step where users have to determine each element on the maturity continuum.
- **Step 4:** Assign maturity score to each element. The score range is from 0 to 10 points and it represents how well the element needs the user's requirements.

Maturity scores allow the comparison of different OS products. Since there are singular scores for each element and one general score for the whole product it is visible if maybe in general the software is good but one element score is low. Therefore, it provides also an indication for an improvement of one or more singular parts of the assessed software.

17.3.2 Phase 2: Assign Weighting Factors

Navica's OSMM includes in its assessment procedure also additional products not just the software code. Therefore it provides a score list for: Software (4), Support (2), Documentation (1), Training (1), Integration (1) and Professional service (1). The numbers in the brackets are the default values proposed by the OSMM. Their sum is 10. Users can change default values according to their specific needs, however the sum has to be always 10. The software code value by default is 4 and it represents the importance of the code part of the product; however other elements bring to the overall assessment additional positive or negative points.

17.3.3 Phase 3: Calculate the Product's Overall Maturity Score

After the assessment of each element's score in the first phase and weighting factors in the second phase, the scores and factors are summed to give an overall product maturity score that ranges between 1 and 100.

17.4 METHODOLOGY OF QUALIFICATION AND SELECTION OF OPEN SOURCE SOFTWARE (QSOS)

The QSOS method helps to differentiate OSS from the technical and functional point of view. Additionally, it provides a framework that allows the set up of an efficient risk management process. The method supports software qualification by integrating OS characteristics and it allows software comparison according to formalized need requirements of weighted criteria. The QSOS method was developed by Atos-Origin, an IT service provider company as a tool for its support and technological survey services. The assessment process is divided in four interdependent steps. The four steps are:

Step 1: Definition

The step provides definitions of various elements typology that are used later in the assessment process. It supports the definition of software families, types of licenses on which the OS products are offered to users and the types of the communities that are developing and supporting the assessed software products.

Step 2: Evaluation

The objective of this step is to carry out the evaluation of the software. The results of the step are a collection of identity card of the assessed software and a detailed evaluation sheet by scoring criteria split on three axes:

- Functional coverage,
- Risks from the user's perspective and
- Risks from the service provider's perspective.

Software identity cards contain just factual data that is not scored; these data however helps in the scoring process that is described in the evaluation sheet. OSS identity cards contain general information about the software, existing services that support the use of the assessed software, information about functional and technical aspects and a synthesis section.

The scoring is inserted into the evaluation sheet and it describes and analyzes in detail evaluations brought by new releases of the software. All criteria are scored from 0 to 2. As an example we can take the functional coverage of the OSS; the scores are the following:

- Score 0: The functionality is not covered,
- Score 1: The functionality is just partially covered
- Score 2: The functionality is completely covered.

The central criteria are split into five categories that are: the intrinsic durability (maturity, adoption, development durability, etc.), industrialized solution (services, documentation, quality assurance, etc.), integration, technical adaptability (modularity, by-products) and strategy (license, copyright owners, roadmap, etc.). The QSOS method supports the iteration of the scoring procedure and the user can score just the five main categories or he can score also their sub criteria and therefore obtain a finer score granularity.

Step 3: Qualification

Once the evaluation step is finished the user has to define filters translating his specific needs and constraints related to the OSS. This step introduces into the assessment procedure the whole context in which the selected OSS will have to function properly. A first level of filtering can be done using just identity cards and a detailed filter can be done by using the functional grid defined in the second step.

Step 4: Selection

The last step is used to identify the software that best fits user's requirements or it can be used to compare different software products belonging to the same family. The QSOS method supports a strict selection process and a loose selection process.

The QSOS method supports an iterative process where some of the steps can be repeated in order to refine the assessment results. Atos-Origin developed a tool (O3S – Open Source Selection Software) that implements the proposed method and helps users to analyze and compare OS products according to roles present inside the method.

17.5 OPEN BUSINESS READINESS RATING (OPENBRR)

The Business Readiness Rating (BRR) method goes a step further than the before proposed methods and proposes an assessment that is open and flexible but at the same time standardized. Therefore it allows a better systematic implementation and as a result a transparent assessment of OSS and as well of close-source software. The authors of the method are the SpikeSource centre (Centre for Open Source Investigation at Carnegie Mellon West) and the Intel corporation. They emphasise the importance of an open and standard method for acceleration in the adoption of OSS and the trustworthy in its components. A standardized assessment model would allow sharing assessment results and the comparison of different software products. Authors think that four crucial requirements have to be addressed for a good software rating model:

1. The model has to highlight every prominent characteristic of the product. It must provide a complete overview of all positive and also negative characteristics.
2. It must be easy to understand the assessment process and the produced scores system. The terminology has to be user friendly.
3. The model has to be flexible and it must adapt to rapid changes inside the IT sector. The openness of the BRR method allows it extension without serious problems.
4. The model must be consistent across different target uses. Consistency of the model allows the comparison of diverse software products from different domains.

Authors of the BRR model wish to provide a more detailed evaluation data and scoring to assess the software's business readiness in comparison with the already available methods. They aim to provide a scientific model that contains a clear mapping from evaluation data to scoring and to the final rating of the software. The assessment process of the BRR method includes four phases:

Phase 1: The initial filtering

In the first phase users can roughly filter the software products according to quantitative and qualitative characteristics. The characteristics can be the licensing/legal situation of the software, whether the software is standardized or not, if the software was included inside largely adopted packages, what is its implementation language and others.

Phase 2: Target usage assessment

This phase contains two sub tasks that are the category weighting and the metrics weighting. The former is intended to list twelve categories (functionality, usability, quality, security, performance, scalability, architecture, support, documentation, adoption, community, and professionalism) from the most important to less important and selecting just the first seven categories for further assessment. In the second subtask, the user has to rank the metric within each category and assign a percentage of importance totalling 100% over all the metrics within one category.

Phase 3: Data collection and processing

The user collects data for each metric in each category and calculates the applied weighting for each metric.

Phase 4: Data translation

By using category ratings and weighting factors it is possible to calculate the Business Readiness Rating score that can be published on appropriate web boards and used by other potential adopters of specific OSS products.

17.6 REFERENCES

Atos-Origin. (2006). *Method for qualification and selection of open source software (QSOS)*. Retrieved on November 11, 2008, from http://www.qsos.org/download/qsos-1.6-en.pdf

Duijnhouwer, F. W., & Widdows, C. (2003). *Open source maturity model*. Cap Gemini.

Golden, B. (2005). *Making open source ready for the enterprise: The open source maturity model*. Navica.

Wasserman, A., Pal, M., & Chan, C. (2005). The business readiness rating model: An evaluation framework for open source. Retrieved on November 11, 2008, from http://www.openbrr.org/ff

Chapter 18
Adoption of Open Source Processes in Large Enterprises

Barbara Russo
Free University of Bozen-Balzano, Italy

Marco Scotto
Free University of Bozen-Balzano, Italy

Alberto Sillitti
Free University of Bozen-Balzano, Italy

Giancarlo Succi
Free University of Bozen-Balzano, Italy

Etiel Petrinja
Free University of Bolzano, Italy

18.1 INTRODUCTION

This chapter summarizes the results of a questionnaire submitted to 50 companies and focusing on their usage of OSS. The people interviewed are project managers.

DOI: 10.4018/978-1-59904-681-5.ch018

18.2 THE STUDY
18.2.1 Trust

What are the elements (practices, tools, techniques, etc.) in the process of OSD that allow you to trust the quality of the final product?

Some interviewee distinguished between internal OSS development and external OSS to be adopted by the company. The answers were mainly interested on the importance of the quality of the source code and the final product first, and only then the interviewee expected additional quality issues. The quality of the OS product is based on its utility to the company and on a list of other criteria. The most often mentioned elements that assure the quality of an OS product are (Figure 1):

- A quality software development process
- The availability and a prompt implementation of the roadmap
- Explicative documentation and possibly some examples of the use
- The product has to be tested appropriately by developers and other users (a large user base)
- Some companies prefer a third party assessment (a major certification authority) of the product and sometimes also of the process that was followed for the development of the final product; however, this assessment may be also performed or replaced by previous use experiences of trusted partners like providers, or even competitors.
- The community developing the product has to use version control systems, bug tracking, mailing lists and other OS development tools in order to permit a clear assessment of their development process.
- The community has to be still active on the improvement of the product and promptly responsive to user's questions
- The license of the product must be in accordance with the use that the company needs it for.

OS product must provide all functionalities that the company needs and these functionalities must have a good quality level. Some interviewee answered that an additional quality criteria for OS products is the list of (important) companies that support and sponsor the development of the OS product.

Figure 1. Trust elements

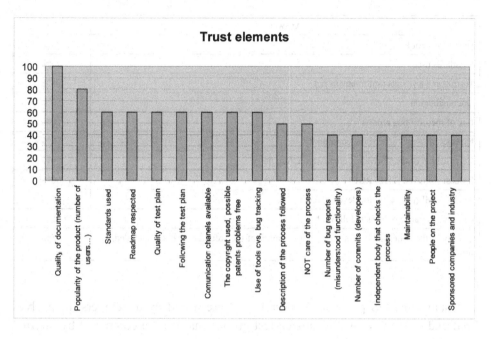

18.2.2 Quality Assurance

What are the aspects for verifying quality of the product you use or/and produce?

The companies interviewed use different criteria to develop and test internal OSS and external OSS to be adopted by the company. The majority prefers to test OS products following a combination of automatic and manual tools and the OSS to be used and adopted has to provide necessary functions. Since there is not yet a well established methodology for assessing OS products neither OS development processes, the companies, either assess it according to non-OS methodologies or they apply hybrid methodologies that take in consideration some additional specific aspects of OSS. The size of the user community is one of the important aspects; the response time from the community to specific requirements is another important aspect. However, it is expected that OS developers follow industrial standards for data formats and user interaction. Additionally, it is desired that the standards used for developing OS are open and largely used (Table 1).

Who tests the product?

Table 1. Aspects for verifying the quality of OSS

Answer	%
User satisfaction	75%
Standards used	75%
Testing and test suits (automatic or not)	75%
Documentation	50%
Use of metrics: bug reports	50%
Number of users - size of the community	50%
Certification of the software's quality by a third party	50%
Process followed (ITIL, RUP)	50%
NOT CMMI (too heavy for development)	25%
Quality assurance process is followed	25%
Quality of the code, stability, security and usability of the software, features included, the time frame	25%

Usually the OS products to be released are tested by developers themselves first, and then often by specialized test groups that can be composed by internal people from the company, by the component integrator, by the module's owner or by committers from the OS community. From the interviews, it seems that there is not a specific person or group of persons that conduct tester on OS products; therefore the tests are performed by different stakeholders. This is aligned with the usual process inside the OS communities, where everyone using the software may do tests and communicate results to the community that can improve future releases of the software (Table 2).

Which manually test methods are used? (internal/user testing)

Table 2. Who tests the product

Answer	%
The developers inside the company	80%
The community	60%
Project owner, manager	40%
Selected users test the software	40%
A separate team	40%
Customers	20%
Quality assurance team	20%
Integrators team	20%

Manual tests of OS products in the companies interviewed do not follow any specific methodology; nevertheless this is quite a common practice to assess the quality of OS products. Manual tests are carried out for testing specific functionalities in OS products or in the form of walkthroughs through the source code of OSS. The variety of testing methodologies is rich either the companies want to use OS products or they are developing OSS and they have to release it to the public.

Which automated testing techniques are used?

The interviewed companies use a variety of automated testing tools for testing external OSS to be adopted and to testing their own OS products; from in-house developed software, to external OS solutions as OpenSTA, JUnit, JMeter, Macro-Scheduler, TestZilla, to commercial solutions that provide static and dynamic code analyses, detailed performance and features tests.

How often, how much, and what do you test?

Tests of OSS are very frequent; often some tests are done for every smallest change of the code usually by automatic tests. More thorough tests are conducted when there is a code merging, before new major version releases, when users (or in some occasions customers) report some bugs or some new functionality is inserted into the software. Usually tests are done according to a test plan and according to the schedule of new releases. Some of the tests interviewed companies perform are: complete tests, delta tests and tests of whole collections of software modules.

Are new releases scheduled?

Usually new OS releases are scheduled in advance and they follow a roadmap. However not all the companies stick to a release plan; it depends on the formality of their software development process and on the importance of each OS project. Some companies have also different levels of releases. Some releases provide OSS that was tested intensively and the expected number of bugs is therefore smaller than in minor software releases.

How regularly are releases rolled out?

New OSS releases depend on the type of the new software. Some releases are distributed weekly, but most are rolled out every two or three months. However some companies roll out new, bigger and major, releases once per year therefore moving away from the very frequent releases that are a common place in OS development.

From the answers it was clear that new releases inside the companies that use and produce OS are a bit rarer than the releases in the OS communities. This depends on the software development process that inside the companies is usually much more formal and rigid than in the OS communities and that cannot allow for more regular and frequent releases.

Is it planed in which release which features will be added?

The companies we interviewed usually plan in advance which features will be added to the OS product and in which release. They have a time plan (usually a roadmap) for new features and they try to stick to that plan. However, in some occasions and for some type of projects, not all features are planned in advance.

Is it planed in which release which bugs will be solved?

The resolving of known bugs is usually also planned in advance and often they are solved before a major new software release. Exist the practice to solve the new detected bug as soon as possible, and only if this is not possible immediately, interviewed companies schedule a date to which the specific bug will be solved.

How is the work managed in the time of delivering a new release?

Companies act differently before new releases; some intensify the work by working more hours and even during the weekends, on contrary other shift slightly the release date. It depends on the size of the company and on the formality of their software development process. However, all the companies interviewed try to maintain a high quality level of their software. Companies following a more rigid and elaborate software development process define exact quality gates and stop the addition of new features to the product weeks before a new release; doing so they can concentrate on the solution of detected bugs and do not insert potentially new bugs inside the product.

18.2.3 General Questions

Which OSS tools are used within the company?

The companies use mainly OSS for developing other OSS. The variety of software products is substantial. The most common products used by companies are: application servers (middleware), development frameworks, operating systems (open and closed source), groupware software, project management software, Eclipse, OO,

Maven, Ant, Jamon, Hibernate, ServiceMix, Cimero, Drools, Linux, Apache Web Server, Tomcat, mySQL, PostgreSQL, Struts, JBoss, Jonas, Subversion, Bugzilla, ThalesForge, Firefox, OpenLDAP, ObjectWeb components, Cyrus, OpenLDAP, postfix, LemonLDAP, PHP, amanvis, ocs invertory, nageos, debian, redhat, mozilla, thunderbird, gimp, ubuntu (for desktops), 7zip, ethereal, and others.

Proprietary products are used only when there are no OS solutions available. Some specific problems the companies encounter maybe were not yet solved or inserted inside an OS product. Therefore interviewed companies have to buy and use proprietary software.

If there is a commercial alternative available, why do you choose OSS?

The most important reason for the companies we interviewed is still the price of the license (Table 3). Nevertheless this criterion is not the only one. Often the answers mentioned the quality of OSS in comparison with closed source software as an important criterion, the time spend by the community to answer to problems that users have, and they use OSS because it is more rich and innovative than proprietary solutions. Some interviewee answered: to promote European software industry. The availability of the source code permits to resolve specific problems that companies have therefore improving the usability of the available software solutions. Commercial alternatives are much more rigid on software changes and they do not permit specific customizations.

Is an OSS product usually used/developed/modified/customized in a single location within the company or at several locations?

The companies usually customize, use and develop OSS in a distributed environment with more locations all over the world. Some companies also use worldwide communities that provide some solutions to specific software problems.

Table 3. Why do you choose OSS

Answer	%
Cost of license	100%
Quality	70%
Easier install	70%
Community	70%
License used, ROI, adaptability, standards used	30%
To promote EU industry	30%

When and where did the project start? Had the project already roots/backgrounds (outside of the company), that the company improved?

Companies often improve specific projects that have already started outside companies by the community on internet. However some components of the projects have started inside the company and have merged with outside components. The OS projects in the companies we interviewed were in the majority of cases not more than three years old and they were still alive and being developed.

How long does it last (approximately)?

The projects are still not finished. OS projects usually tend to live longer than commercial solutions. Sometimes the development process can slow down but the source code is still available on the Internet to everybody and therefore after a dormant period of time new developers can pick up the code and continue the work started years before.

18.2.4 Roles and Responsibilities

How many people were/are working in the project?

OS projects are developed by groups that contain from 2 up to 40 core developers and up to 100 and in some cases even 1000 part time contributors. The companies also take advantage from their OS communities if they are already formed and large enough. Successful community OS projects usually have much more contributors, but OS projects started by companies are hybrid entities that are influenced by some company's rules and processes and by some Internet OS community's rules. The number of developers involved in a specific OS project is strongly related to the size and complexity of the OS project.

How much is the turnover? (annual rate of people getting into/leaving the project)

The turnover is approximately 10% in all the companies we have interviewed however it depends on the size and time spent on the OS project. Bigger projects tend to have a more consistent turnover of developers and people that work on them.

Please determine the participants of the project (users, developers, committers, PMC (Project Management Committee) members, etc.) Do they have the standard roles?

The number and type of stakeholders involved in OS projects depend on the size and also on the type of the project. Smaller projects have a propensity to have les participants. On the contrary, complex OS projects are developed by simple users, by developers, committers, they are leaded by PMC members and often there are other participants as quality managers, integrator managers, product manager, project manager, many testers and others. In more formalized processes, the participants usually have standard roles.

PMC members typically decide what to implement, they choose the technology and also the architecture. They have to define the roadmap and select the features that will be implemented in each release.

Other participants are involved in the development process with various roles. Often different groups of users overlap in many processes; however, developers are mainly involved in the code implementation, on contrary users and ordinary contributors are involved mainly as testers and bug reporters.

Please determine which responsibilities the developer, committer, PMC member, etc. have.

The responsibilities in OS projects inside the interviewed companies are consistent with the onion model of OSSD. PMC members usually propose the project, the architecture the roadmap and the features to implement; they, together with few other developers, have the permission to change the code. Other users and committers may check the code and report for discovered bugs.

Please determine their number.

OS projects in the companies we interviewed have a limited number of internal participants. They have usually between 2 to 6 PMC members, up to 10 internal developers and committers and 1 to 2 project owners that are usually also project leaders. The number of external participants varies considerably between different projects.

Please determine how can one become a developer, committer, PMC member!

Regular users can become developers and committers by contributing, first, simple bug reports and new code proposals and extending their contribution over time. After a constant amount of good quality code has been sent to the project, the user can ask the project owner to become a committer. Long period committers can become part of the PMC group. In some companies the PMC group is composed only by individuals internal to the company, however more developed and complex

OS projects have also external PMC members. Some companies require external committers to sign an agreement with the company.

Is there any community within or outside of the company to make decisions?

The OS projects in the companies we interviewed are leaded mainly just by individuals inside the company. Only in some cases the external community is permitted to decide on some issues for OS projects. This happens only for specific projects that count intensively on external commits.

How are decision processes arranged?

The decisions are processed differently in different kind of projects; sometimes is the whole community that decides how to develop a feature by voting, sometimes is the project leader that decides what to implement and how to change the architecture. In this case usually the project board periodically controls the decisions taken by the project leader.

How do you decide about code modification, giving rights, package releases, etc? (voting, responsibilities, etc.)

Code modifications are sometimes discussed first on forums by the community and only then the decisions are taken by the developers and the PMC members, in some companies the decisions are taken directly by the project leader sometimes with the support from the PMC board. We have become aware of the fact that some OS projects we have survived are more community oriented and therefore they interact strongly with the community on public forums, on contrary others prefer to maintain a company centred OS project and therefore maintain all the important decisions inside the company.

18.2.5 Architecture Definition

How is the technical architecture of the project managed? Is it planed before, incremental?

The majority of the projects (80%) have an incremental design process for the architecture. However some companies in their OS projects prefer to define exactly the nucleus of the new OSS at the beginning and allow incremental design of not central modules in a second time. This nucleus definition in some projects relays on traditional software development patterns and is not very OS oriented. Therefore we have observed that some companies are still in a hybrid period where they are moving to OSSD but they use still some traditional approaches for part of the software development process. Design of the technical architecture is an important part of the software development process and in some projects it is still kept inside the companies.

What are the most important technical requirements?

Technical requirements for OS projects tend to be aligned with the most important and widespread (open) standards (Table 4). Modularization of the architecture is also one of the most important requests for OS projects. Some companies stress the importance of a modular architecture to avoid some *copy left* problems that can influence other close source software of the company. Other requirements are defined from the necessities of customers and partly by the OS community. Some additional requirements for OS projects that were mentioned during the interviews are: accessibility, Multilanguage, interoperability with different systems, easy to use, safe and working, hardware support, *freshness* of the solution and others.

Which technologies are used?

New OS projects rely strongly on the Java technology and on the whole family of Java solutions that are: the Java language itself, Java EE, J2EE, JSP, servlets, portlets, and similar initiatives (Table 5). The majority of the companies we interviewed base their development on these technologies. However there are other important

Table 4. Important technical aspects

Answer	%
Standards used	40%
Modularization	40%
Other	20%

Table 5. Technologies used

Answer	%
Java	75%
Perl	50%
UML	50%
Other	25%

technologies as the technologies supporting UML and RUP; other programming languages as PHP, Perl, and JavaScript; OS and close source database solutions such as MySQL and PostgreSQL; and network technologies as HTTP, SSH, wikis, XSL, XML, and others. An important new technology is also the Service Oriented Architecture (SOA) technology that nevertheless is still quite new, it is already built-in inside some OS projects.

18.2.6 Development Techniques and Practices

Which development methodology do you use? Can you describe it? (if it is not standard)

The software development methodology used in the companies we have interviewed varies considerably; Companies use many different methodologies; some very classical ones as the waterfall model, specially for safety critical modules, others modified RUP methodologies with some sporadic use of UML tools, to SCRUM and XP methods to other variations of evolutionary methodologies and sometimes also some internal methodologies developed by companies themselves. Some methodologies, or part of them, are imposed by internal standards of the company others are imposed by the technology that is used and some again are required by clients. Therefore we did not noticed a specific methodology that is more used inside the interviewed companies, nevertheless traditional methodologies as the waterfall model was sad to be used in only few companies and also just for some critical modules.

Companies use different practices during the software development process as: continuous code reviews, peer review, unit testing, load testing, continuous and often autonomous code integration and build (Table 6). Some companies use prototype practices and build on the next releases by solving bugs found by users in already delivered prototypes.

Requirements are usually still collected from clients and customers and integrated with internal company requirements; but especially in OS projects companies col-

Table 6. Development technologies

Answer	%
Code reviews	60%
Unit tests	60%
Continuous integration	40%
Prototyping	20%

lect requirements also from public mailing list, forums and wikis. Sometimes they use data from tools as Jira, bug trackers and other source of information for new features of the projects.

Coding standards used by companies depend mainly by the programming language used and sometimes also by the developers involved in some projects (Table 7).

How is the maintenance of the existing code worked out?

Developers of OSS usually maintain the source code by themselves. Only after a defined period of time this maintenance can pass to a specialized group inside the company. Sometimes there are individuals inside the development team that are appointed to maintain the code or fix the bugs. Some interviewed companies analyze the developed source code and find out its maintainability that can help them decide how to maintain the code (Table 8).

18.2.7 Tools Used

On which operating system is the project implemented? Is it running on other operating systems? If yes, on which one(s)?

Companies use different operating systems, however the most quoted for OS development is Linux. Nevertheless some companies together with Linux use also the Windows operating system and sometimes also Solaris.

Table 7. Coding standards used

Answer	%
Javadoc, OASIS, Java EE conventions	60%
Do not use specific code conventions	40%

Table 8. Who does the maintenance

Answer	%
Developers maintain the code themselves (for a limited period).	60%
Specific internal groups do the maintenance.	40%
External groups	20%

Which programming language is used for the implementation? On which platform?

The mostly used programming language is Java and all its derivatives; C++ is also quite popular. However the companies use a rich set of other languages as: C, Python, PHP, Perl, some specific proprietary domain languages, JavaScript, Microsoft developed languages and others (Figure 2).

The platforms on which projects are developed are usually the same as the operating system: Linux, sometimes Windows and Solaris and quite often the Java platform as development platform (Figure 3).

The programming language and/or the platform on which the OS projects are developed influence considerably the whole development process. Languages and technologies can define development methodologies and considerably the efficiency of the development process. The use of Java and Linux confirm our expectations related to the language and the platform used by OS communities and OSSD.

Which development tools are used in the project? Do you use any tool developed in house? Do you make these tools available to others?

Eclipse is the most frequently used development tool inside the interviewed companies. Some use also Emacs for software development that is not based on the

Figure 2. Languages used

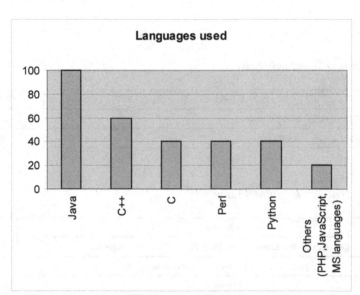

Figure 3. Operating system used

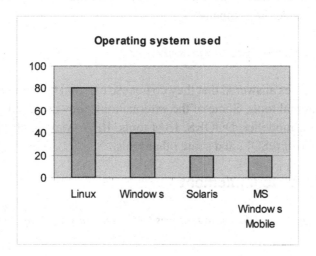

java language. Other tools that are used by interviewed companies are: vi, Visual Studio, ClearCase, Visual Source Safe, Doors, Calibre, and others (Table 9).

Do you use any tool developed in house?

Interviewed companies (60%) usually use external tools; some of them are OS and others are proprietary. Only a limited number of OS projects (40%) are somehow supported by tools developed inside the companies, for example some tools to test the newly developed software and some tools to generate usage scenarios. Since the interviewed companies are in early phases of OS development (nevertheless some try to enter the OS community for more than five years now) they do not have many self developed OS products to use for new products development. Probably in few years they will continue to use software they are developing now.

Do you make these tools available to others?

Table 9. Tools used

Answer	%
Eclipse	80%
Emacs	40%
Others (Visual studio, Vi, Primavera, MS Project, ClearCase, Visual Sourc Safe, Doors, Caliber, Requisite Pro)	20%

Some companies make the developed tools available as OS, some make them available only inside the company.

Do you use other OS or commercial software?

Some companies answered that they do not use external OSS and half answered they do use external tools. Some of the external tools they use are: UML modeller (Rose), database modeller, DOORS, IBM tools, BEA, Maven, checkstyle, SVN, Jira, MySQL, PostgreSQL, and some other tools.

18.2.8 Features to Implement

Who makes suggestions for new features? (Is there any mailing list/newsgroups for doing this?)

The users or the customers are the main source of new features requests. OS projects have often mailing list and forums that are available to users. Usually, suggestions can come from everybody; however, in some cases, the suggestions from important customers of the company have the priority before other suggestions. Since companies develop software as their main activity and it is usually an important source of revenue, they have to listen to requests from customers. However, the suggestions come often from developers alone and from persons inside the company (Table 10).

Who is deciding about new features?

In the interviewed companies the decision about which new features will be included in OSS is usually carried out by the project manager or leader and sometimes by the whole PMC or the whole core development team. In many cases, the customers as well can decide which features will be included in new distributions and which not ().Table 11

Table 10. Who suggests new features

Answer	%
Clients of the company Users The community	80% 80% 80%
The administration of the project Developers	40% 40%
Technical direction	20%

Who has to implement the new features?

The new features are usually implemented by developers from the companies we have interviewed. Sometimes, these implementations are done in part also by external developers, either committers or just developers that have produced a service or software that is included in the new OS product. In some companies, the work tasks are distributed hierarchically by the core team or the manager of the project, on the contrary in other companies developers decide alone who will develop which feature.

Is there a time plan for implementing the features?

There is always a time plan for the implementation of new features (80% always; 20% always however just for some parts of the project). The plan is usually associated with the road map of the project. Some companies plan new features and releases in such a way that coincide with major events during the year (Christmas, CEBIT fair, other important fairs, etc).

Which feature should be implemented first? (ranking of features by priorities)

Usually there is a priority list for some features; the priorities of specific features depend on various criteria as:

- Architectural plan to be followed
- Major bugs detected to be solved
- Customer's wishes
- Technical point of view
- Market point of view
- Contributor's of source code opinions

Prioritized are features that have a higher impact on other features (Table 12).

Table 11. Who decides what to implement

Answer	%
Coordinators of the project	60%
Clients of the company Managers of the informatics sector. An internal group of developers The PMC	20% 20% 20% 20%

Table 12. Priority of specific features

Answer	%
The most requested features	75%
Features requested by clients Market point of view	50% 50%
Major bugs to be solved Technical requirements Features impacting other features	25% 25% 25%

How priorities are assigned?

Usually, the project manager decides which features have the priority; in some occasions after he has talked with the customers. However, often there are technical and architectural motivations for some features to be implemented before others. Usually, the features that are requested by more users are prioritized; complex features are left for the time when the simplest features are already implemented. However, it strongly depends on the type of the project. Therefore, it is difficult to trace a single line of prioritization of features in the companies we have interviewed.

18.2.9 Documentation and Bug Management

Do you have documentation of the project?

The main part of OS projects has some kind of documentation. More complex projects have separate documentation for:

- Users,
- Developers and
- Administrators.

Often, there are also wikis and readme files. However, the amount of documentation depends on the resources available for each OS project (time, payments, contributors).

Who writes the documentation? Where? (in the implementation, in a separate documentation, etc.)

In most of the companies, the documentation is usually written by the developers themselves. Everyone has the responsibility to prepare part of the documentation that explains their contribution to the project. Often, the documentation is already included inside the code with javadoc comments for example. More structured projects and larger companies tend to have specific employees that are appointed to write the documentation. More complex and structured projects have different kind of documentation as a: user guide, installation guide, manuals, developers guide, wiki, architecture guide, project plan, release notes, requirement specifications, product documentation, design, architectures, test specifications and others. Sometimes, some contributions to the documentation come from users, mostly internal in the company.

Does the project have a roadmap?

The interviewee answered that almost every OS project has a roadmap that helps them to check if they are on time with the scheduled development. It also provides an indication on what has already been developed and what is going to be developed in the near future.

Is it useful for the developers?

The majority of the interviewees agree that the roadmap is useful for the developers and for the OS project as a whole.

Which tools are used for bug-tracking? If there are several in use, which tool has the highest priority?

The issue/bug-tracking tools used most often are Bugzilla and Jira. However, the number of different issue/bug-trackers is large. Other tools are: Mantis, SourceForge, ClearCase, ClearQuest, ThalesForge, Trac, and other internal tools. Sometimes, bugs are reported in a form of paper reports (called technical facts). Quite often, bug reports arrive from customers and end users. Some customers prefer to use specific issue/bug-tracking tools; therefore, these tools (sometimes commercial) are also used inside the interviewed companies (Figure 4).

Are the issue/bug-tracking tools specialized for different persons (users, developers, etc), or do they use the same tool for reporting bugs?

Usually, all the stakeholders use the same issue/bug-tracker, only rarely in some specific projects they may use more than one tool.

How many bug reports do you get?

Figure 4. Bug/issue-tracking tools used

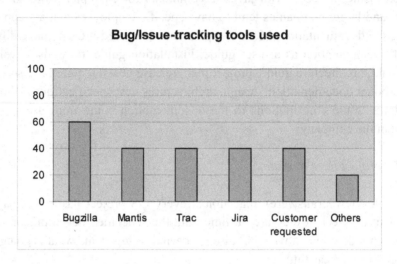

The number of bug reports varies considerably in the different projects and mainly in different interviewed companies. Usually, around 1 to 2 per day, where there are also included some new wishes from the users or customers. In the most long lasting projects, the total number of bug reports can arrive to 6 thousand reports. It seems that the number of bugs is strongly correlated with the size of the community that uses the software. In companies that do not have large user community but only few customers, the number of bug reports is considerably lower than in pure OS projects with well developed user communities.

Can the bug-tracking tool be used for other purposes too? (eg., making suggestions, looking for tasks to resolve them, etc.)

The bug tracking tool is often used also as a communication channel for expressing wishes, new features requests, fixing priorities, creating subtasks, assigning responsibilities, reporting problems with the process and other issues communicated by the customers or users to the developers and companies developing the OS product. However, some companies try to keep separate bug reports and other issues by using mailing lists for the latter.

How long does it take to solve a bug? How are priorities assigned?

The time needed to solve a bug goes from 2 days up to few months. It depends on the severity of the bug and on the effects that it can have on other parts of the software. Some bugs that can create security problems or data loss problems can be solved also in few hours. All bug reporting tools have a feature that permits to define the severity of the reported bug. Therefore users and developers can suggest which bugs have to be solved first.

Accordingly the priorities are assigned by the users that report the bugs, by the developers that reproduce the bug and check which bug has the priority, by the management of the project and sometimes by a group of developers that are appointed to solve bugs. Sometimes also the clients can suggest which bugs are more critical for their business and therefore which have to be solved first and which one can wait longer.

18.2.10 Version Control and People Management

Which version control system is used for the project?

Interviewed companies usually use Subversion as the version control system. Some companies use also other systems as the oldest concurrent versioning system (CVS) and systems as: GIT, PVCS, and ClearCase.

Is this tool freely available for everybody (user, company, etc.)?

Usually, the tools are available to everybody. However, sometimes the use is limited just to project members or even just to internal personnel of the company.

Who has access to the version control system?

The interviewed companies usually permit everybody to read the content of the version control system. However, the write permission is limited just to developers or only to the owner of the module or some core developers. The permission rules depend on the type of the project. Inside complex projects the permissions are strongly restricted.

Who and how can get more rights and which ones?

Committers and developers can get more rights. It depends on the quality of the committed code and the decision of the module's owner or team manager. The committers that want more permission have to ask for them by themselves.

Who can be the owner of a module?

Some projects do not have module owners. However, the majority of structured projects have module owners. These persons have to be able to manage the whole development regarding the specified module. Therefore the community decides on the base of the quality and amount of the code already committed by a single developer if he is responsible and skilled enough to be the owner of a module.

How are the tasks assigned? Can one choose what to implement?

In some cases, developers can chose what they want to implement. But most usually the project owner or the project leader assigns the tasks to each developer. In some projects, the general tasks are assigned by a technical committee and more local tasks are self assigned by developers. Some companies, that we have interviewed, have a more formal and hierarchical structure and, therefore, also the tasks assignment is carried on by specific teams and team managers. Companies developing OSS are still quite far from the OS communities; some tasks distribution is quite rigid and sometimes developers do not work exactly on what they really like, therefore these projects lose an important advantage that OS development process offers.

18.2.11 Business Model

Are developers employees?

In the companies we have interviewed, the developers are usually employee of the companies. However, some developers and committers are part of the OS community supporting the project and they are not employed in the company.

Which advantages/disadvantages/benefits has the developer for contributing?

The developers contributing to the project has aces to some additional software that is usually available only commercially. Some contributors collaborate inside the project also just to improve a part of the product they are using and that they need it for their job.

What is the goal of the project?

The answers we got are different, because the companies develop more than one OS project each and, therefore, the goals also vary broadly. Some of the goals that we got as answers are: to automate repetitive tasks, to provide new tools for building, testing and evaluating quality assurance of Linux distributions, to build a platform for communicating company and product information to the customer, to easy the access to Linux, to provide a Java EE infrastructure, but as well as to improve the reputation of OS infrastructure. Therefore, nevertheless the goals of the companies are business oriented some are also altruistic, oriented toward a further advance of the entire OS community.

Does the company sell this product? Are there any additional services to the product that can be sold (e.g., courses, support, extensions, etc)? If yes, which one(s)?

Some companies do not sell anything connected with developed OS projects; others do sell services like support, update notifications, downloads, training, support at start-up, subscription (they provide a certain level of services: support for a problem in a specified time), projects related to the available infrastructure; courses; requested extensions to the OS infrastructure and others. Companies we interviewed are in the starting phases of OSD, therefore, they have already offered some additional services connected to the OS products they develop but these services are still being improved. OSD is only a marginal development effort for some of the companies we interviewed therefore they do not expect big revenues from this business in the near future.

Chapter 19
Trust Elements in Open Source

Barbara Russo
Free University of Bozen-Balzano, Italy

Marco Scotto
Free University of Bozen-Balzano, Italy

Alberto Sillitti
Free University of Bozen-Balzano, Italy

Giancarlo Succi
Free University of Bozen-Balzano, Italy

Etiel Petrinja
Free University of Bolzano, Italy

19.1 INTRODUCTION

The quality of a software development process is based on a large spectrum of various elements that must be identified and assessed. The majority of elements can be measured quantitatively and possibly using an automatic process. Some elements, however, are rather subjective and depend strongly on different opinions of people using or evaluating the software development process. An automatic measurement approach is difficult to achieve (for example by on-line questionnaires or surveys inserted inside software products or software development tools). The foundation for all assessments is a set of elements that will be at a certain point of development or use measured and evaluated. This chapter provides a rationale for identifying elements that we call trustworthy elements (TWE), the process for their identifica-

DOI: 10.4018/978-1-59904-681-5.ch019

tion, sources for the identification of key trustworthy elements and at the end a list of the most important trustworthy elements identified.

Many just slightly different definitions about trustworthiness and trustworthy related concepts can be found on the web and in the literature. We present here just the most relevant definitions to our own understanding of the concept of a trustworthy element that is used inside this deliverable. Some of the definitions found on the web and in the literature are the following:

- Merriam-Webster's on-line dictionary defines the concept of trustworthy as *something being worthy of confidence; dependable; a trustworthy guide, trustworthy information.*

Other definitions found on the web and in the literature are:

- *Taking responsibility for one's conduct and obligations; trustworthy public servants[1].*
- *"Trustworthiness is keeping one's word and being worthy of others' confidence: sound in principles, full of integrity, reliable and dependable"* Ken Buist.
- The National Security Agency (NSA) defines a trusted system or component as one *whose failure can break the security policy,* and a trustworthy system or component as one *that will not fail.* (Wikipedia)
- The Committee on Information Systems Trustworthiness' publication, Trust in Cyberspace, defines a trustworthy computing system as one which: *Does what people expect it to do – and not something else – despite environmental disruption, human user and operator errors, and attacks by hostile parties. Design and implementation errors must be avoided, eliminated or somehow tolerated. It is not sufficient to address only some of these dimensions, nor is it sufficient simply to assemble components are themselves trustworthy. Trustworthiness is holistic and multidimensional. (Wikipedia)*

Our definition of trustworthiness and of the trustworthy element are closer to Wordnet's definition, since it depends on the personal beliefs or generic trust that people, users of OS systems and all the stakeholders, share about a specific software development process. We use the term element for describing all the components and aspects influencing the development and functioning of a software system.

Therefore, we define the trustworthy element as a specific factor or aspect of the software development process, or of product results that indirectly influence the perception of the trustworthiness of the OS development process, that influences the belief and trust of the stakeholders in the overall quality of the software development process used inside OS projects.

This chapter focuses on the elements assuring trustworthiness of the OS development process, which, in turn, should guarantee a high quality final product. Often, users of OSS are mainly interested in the quality of the final product, e.g., the source code they can inspect, the functionalities they can test or the final graphical user interface of the OS product. However, there is a large number of advanced OSS users that do not want just to use the product but are interested in its further development and evolution or integration with other software products. Such users (developers, integrators, software bundles distributors, etc.) are strongly interested in the development process used to produce the OS product. Usually, their further development is based on the already existent development processes or it can be started only using support material such as documentation, mailing list archives, roadmap specifications, testing documentation, or other results of a good development process.

Trust is basically related to users' belief that something is of high quality; the trustworthiness is intrinsically related to the object. A trustworthy object has a characteristic that talks about its quality. Therefore, trustworthy elements are aspects of an object (in our case of the development process) that guarantee its quality related to some well defined quality criteria and assessed by measurable quantities. For instance, if we can identify several quantitative measurements suitable for characterizing the current status and the evolution over time of the number of bugs submitted to the project, as well as the ratio of new, fixed and pendent bugs, we will be able to quantify the trustworthiness of the software development process regarding this aspect.

Based on the guiding elements, we have just described (trustworthy elements, quality criteria, and measurable quantities), we have designed the research using the Goal Question Metric (GQM) methodology (Mashiko & Basili, 1997) that takes in consideration those elements. Additionally, the GQM methodology allows its users to define key goals; that in our case helps to improve the quality and the trustworthiness of the OS development process. The trustworthy elements are the foundation for the goals we have defined. The goals defined offer an improvement guidelines for trustworthy elements identified.

Product quality and trustworthiness are tightly connected to the trustworthiness level of the software development process itself, since this is a consequence derived from the fact that software products are the outcomes of the development process. Their trustworthiness is also affected by the quality of the development process and vice versa.

Trustworthy elements are strongly linked to software quality criteria. These vary considerably and many different classifications of quality criteria exist.

Many classifications contain product quality criteria, such as: conformance to requirements, scalability, correctness, completeness, absence of bugs, fault-tolerance, extensibility, maintainability, and documentation.

Another kind of quality criteria are related only to the source code, such as: readability, low complexity, and low resource consumption.

Some of the factors presented above are strongly dependent on the development process followed. We can extract from different quality criteria classification twelve key software quality factors:

1. Understandability,
2. Completeness,
3. Conciseness,
4. Portability,
5. Consistency,
6. Maintainability,
7. Testability,
8. Usability,
9. Reliability,
10. Structure,
11. Efficiency, and
12. Security.

Such quality factors are perceived as important by people interviewed and surveyed during our research.

19.2 Trustworthy Elements

The software development process provides several factors and indicators suitable to assess its level of trustworthiness from a quantitative and qualitative point of views. The primary indicators are the extent to which trust is incorporated in the development process and the level of process maturity. Specific features include:

- Definition of trust requirements, considering the current and expected threat, network, and host environments;
- Definition of functional requirements and acceptance criteria;
- Use of coding standards;
- Tests and reviews for compliance with trust requirements;
- Background checks on employees and code development and testing processes, ensuring that certain good coding and design practices are respected

through the whole development process;
- Restrictions on developer write-access to production source code and systems, and monitoring developer access to development systems (all of these should be accomplished by using a good Source Code Management system).

Process maturity is an important indicator because mature processes result in a more controlled development of source code and of the final end-user-ready product.Some generic trustworthy elements can be identified in the OS development process. We can classify such elements in the following areas:

- **Trust:** Identifies a set of elements of the development process that allow trusting the final quality of the OS project. More specifically, the goal is to find critical aspects when adopting or inserting OSS components in their products. The trust rating of a certain development process could be computed as the combination of ratings obtained for every trustworthy elements that fall in this area. *Completeness, reliability,* and *security* are important quality factors in this area. On one hand, integrators will then be able to choose the appropriate combination of trustworthy elements that are relevant for their own area of interest. On the other hand, OS communities may publish their results from their own ratings, which can be checked by system integrators at any time. Therefore, this scenario could establish a common evaluation framework in which system integrators could define specific requests to OS development companies and communities, clearly defining which trustworthy elements are the most relevant for their own purposes, as well as the minimum ratings they expect from publishers of OS products to fulfill these requirements. Moreover, OS communities could then establish their own internal development processes, setting for every case the trust rating objective they would like to accomplish.
- **Quality assurance:** This area includes a set of trustworthy elements suitable for establishing quality metrics and review processes, that could be undertaken by OS publishers or by recognized third party entities, to ensure the quality of the whole development process from an objective point of view. *Understandability, consistency,* and *maintainability* are quality factors influencing this area.
- **Testing:** To ensure that OS products have an adequate quality, some testing methods should be put in practice. For instance, any testing methods to detect correctness of developed features and to ensure that these features fit users' needs. Release cycles and methodologies should also be taken into account, focusing on the existence of timing patterns, pre-release versions (alpha, beta, etc.) and the type of release planning (time-driven or feature-driven). *Understandability, conciseness, completeness, maintainability, testability,*

and structure can be important quality factors in this area.

- **General elements:** General trustworthy elements related to OS projects as a whole, e.g., previous background of selected projects, starting date, initial developers/community/company/groups. All these aspects can contribute to the credibility of the development process (e.g., a project that is active for a long time is more reliable then a newly proposed one). *Portability, usability, and efficiency* are key quality factors in this area.

- **Roles and responsibilities:** Identifying different roles within the community can help to classify gathered data to quantify the grade of success achieved in trustworthy elements. The existence of formal decision processes (e.g., voting processes) and the distribution of responsibilities among the people involved in the project can also provide valuable information to infer the quality of the development process.

- **Portability and architecture definition:** The careful selection of a software architecture may produce products with better quality, and it should also help to establish a good quality production process. It is obvious that *portability* is an important quality factor affected by trustworthy elements identified in this area, while efficiency may be also influenced.

- **Development techniques and practices:** A coherent and structured system to distribute different tasks among the project participants can definitely improve the quality of the development process. This has a direct impact over the *maintainability* and *structure* of the software through the development process.

- **Tools:** There are several well-known tools and platforms offering a convenient all-in-one solution to help the start, evolution, management, and maintenance of OS projects. Virtually any of the quality factors already identified may be affected by the type of development tools selected in the project.

- **Decision process to implement new features:** We need to identify the decision process (if any) used to make decisions about new features to be added to an OS project. New features could potentially affect the quality of the final product, and thus, how these decisions are taken significantly affect the quality and trustworthiness of the development process. Again, the decision-making process in software development projects has a direct impact in virtually any quality factors we may consider.

- **Documentation and issue/bug management:** This is another important point for the overall quality of the production process. The documentation should exist and be clear and consistent. The presence of a system for issue/bug management aims at monitoring the quality of the development process. Documentation and bug tracking tools have both a high impact on *maintainability* that, according to some studies, requires about 80% of the total effort

(Conger, 1994).

- **Version control and human resources management:** Several factors affect the quality of the process regarding the control, inclusion, and identification of new code to be included in future versions. Source Code Management (SCM) systems are a fundamental point in this area. It is also important to know how developers of OS projects select the tasks they to undertake, as in many communities nobody is explicitly forced to do any task. Once again, trustworthy elements included in this section have a strong influence over any quality factors shaping the software development process.

- **Business models and work-flows:** A careful study of developers motivations, along with the analysis of the economical background (communities, companies, groups, foundations, institutions, etc.) supporting the project are important to properly assess the quality of the process. The presence of a homogeneous and structured work-flow, encompassing the whole developing structure facilitates the management and control of the overall development process. *Consistency* is the most relevant quality factor affected by these elements.

19.3 TRUSTWORTHY ELEMENTS IN COMPANIES

This section presents a summary of the most relevant trustworthy elements identified in the interviews we carried out with members of European companies adopting OSS. Summarizing the trustworthy elements identified by companies, interviewees made a distinction between internal OSS development projects, controlled by the company, and external OSS projects to be adopted by the company. The main concern exhibited by all of them was to ensure the quality of the final product. That is, any metric trying to evaluate the quality of the OS development process should be directly oriented to guarantee the quality of the code developed and then assure the quality of the process itself. Some critical elements recurrently identified in the interviews were presenting clear connections with the factors previously described:

- Feedback from user experiences.
- Use of SCM (Source Code Management) platforms, to control the workflow of the development process.
- Following and enforcing a test plan, in order to systematically check new features and remove bugs.
- Using/adhering to well-known open standards (for representing data, exchanging data, storing data, programming styles and languages, etc.).
- Implementing a complete quality assurance plan, analyzing potential risks that may arise within the development.

○   Use a roadmap and release schedule to monitor the development process of the final product.

○   There should be a complete and detailed documentation, including some examples of use of the software.

○   Developing community should use management tools like version control systems, bug tracking, mailing lists, and other tools to ensure that it is possible to implement a clearly defined assessment policy of the development process.

○   OS products should have been released under a license suitable for the company purposes.

○   Additional aspects like the size of the community, their response time to specific requests, the use of open, standardized, and well-known formats for user interaction and data representation.

It is very interesting to notice that all the interviewees agree about the absence of a specific methodology or strategy to quantify the quality of the OSS product and also to analyze the trustworthiness of the development process. In many cases, an hybrid approach is adopted, using existing methodologies with the addition of further metrics to take into account OS projects peculiarities.

•   Testing methods usually include both automatic and manual checks. Testers are usually developers themselves, in the first place and then specialized groups composed by other members of the company, components integrators, modules manager or committers from the community.

•   Suggestions for new features come from any user, without any special privilege or role in the community. Suggestions from important customers have priority. So, an interesting element to ensure trustworthiness in the development process is to set up a system for the management of new features requests, approve them, and link them to the development roadmap.

•   Finally, bug-tracking systems are also identified as a major source of quality for the final product, and thus, constitute another element of trustworthiness for the development process.

19.4 REFERENCES

Conger, S. A. (1994). *The new software engineering*. International Thomson Publishing.

Mashiko, Y., & Basili, V. R. (1997). Using the GQM paradigm to investigate influential factors for software process improvement. *Journal of Systems and Software, 36*(1), 17-32. doi:10.1016/0164-1212(95)00194-8

QualiPSo. (2008). Trust and quality in open source systems. Retrieved on November 11, 2008, from http://www.qualipso.org/

ENDNOTE

[1]   http://wordnet.princeton.edu (accessed on November 11, 2008)

Chapter 20
Overview of Open Source Tools for Agile Development

20.1 INTRODUCTION

Tools support is extremely important in Agile development. As described in the previous chapters, the Agile development is based on the identification and the subsequent reduction of activities that do not provide value to the customer and the ability to change the code without including new and undetected bugs in the code. Tools are an important step towards such objectives and Agile development relies on them to:

- Automate as much as possible activities such as testing, building, etc.
- Support the development enhancing the communication among team members, simplifying the modification to the source code, etc.

1. Specific tools designed to support to some Agile practices
2. General-purpose tools that are adopted to support Agile development but not developed for this specific purpose.
3. Tools to measure the code and extract useful information

DOI: 10.4018/978-1-59904-681-5.ch020

In this section, we are going to present a set of tools belonging to both these categories, in particular: automated build tools, continuous integration, version control, issue tracking, synchronous and asynchronous communication, project management, testing, tools to support specific Agile practices, and measurement tools.

Table 1. Summary of the tools

Category	Tool name	URL[1]
Version control tools	CVS	http://www.nongnu.org/cvs/
	Subversion	http://subversion.tigris.org/
Automated build tools	Apache Ant	http://ant.apache.org/
	Krysalis Centipede	http://krysalis.sourceforge.net/centipede/
	Apache Maven	http://maven.apache.org/
Continuous integration tools	CruiseControl	http://sourceforge.net/projects/cruisecontrol/
	Anthill OS	http://www.anthillpro.com/html/products/anthillos/
	Rephlux	http://rephlux.sourceforge.net/
Issue tracking tools	Bugzilla	http://www.bugzilla.org/
	Scarab	http://scarab.tigris.org/
Synchronous and asynchronous communication tools	MailMan	http://www.gnu.org/software/mailman/mailman.html
	Jabber	http://www.jabber.org/
	Wiki	http://www.wiki.org/
	Twiki	http://twiki.org/
Project management tools	XPlanner	http://www.xplanner.org/
	XPWeb	http://xpweb.sourceforge.net/
	XP StoryStudio	http://www.xpstorystudio.com/
Testing tools	Cactus	http://jakarta.apache.org/cactus/
	JUnit	http://www.junit.org/
	NUnit	http://www.nunit.org/
	SwingUnit	https://swingunit.dev.java.net/
Tools to support specific Agile practices	Sangam	http://sangam.sourceforge.net/
	FitNesse	http://fitnesse.org/
	TightVNC	http://www.tightvnc.com/
	Refactoring Browser	http://st-www.cs.uiuc.edu/users/brant/Refactory/
	Transmogrify	http://transmogrify.sourceforge.net/
	jMock	http://www.jmock.org/
Measurement tools	NCover	http://ncover.sourceforge.net/
	JBlanket	http://csdl.ics.hawaii.edu/Tools/JBlanket/

This section includes a high level overview of these tools and the links to their home pages to retrieve more information and download them. The Table 1 summarizes the tools presented.

Since new tools are available every day, online resources are always the best source of information on this topic. There are a number of web sites listing Open Source Agile tools including the following:

- http://www.agile-tools.net/ (accessed on November 11, 2008)
- http://www.xpsd.org/cgi-bin/wiki?AgileTools (accessed on November 11, 2008)

20.2 VERSION CONTROL TOOLS
20.2.1 CVS

The Concurrent Versions System (CVS) is an OS version control system that keeps track of all work and all changes in a set of files, typically the implementation of a software project, and allows several, potentially geographically distributed developers to collaborate. It was invented and developed by Dick Grune in the '80s. CVS has become popular in the OSS environment and is released under the GNU General Public License.

CVS uses a client-server architecture: a server stores the current version of the project and its history, and clients connect to the server to check out a complete copy of the project, work on this copy and then later check in their changes. Typically, the client and server connect over a LAN or over the Internet, but client and server may both run on the same machine if CVS has the task of keeping track of the version history of a project with only local developers. The server software normally runs on Unix (although at least the CVSNT server supports various flavors of Windows and Unix), while CVS clients may run on any major operating system platforms. Several developers may work on the same project concurrently, each one editing files within their own working copy of the project, and checking in their modifications to the server. To avoid people interfering to each other, the server only accepts changes made to the most recent version of a file. Therefore, developers are expected to keep their working copy up-to-date by incorporating other people changes on a regular basis. This task is mostly handled automatically by the CVS client, requiring manual intervention only when a conflict arises between a checked-in modification and the yet-unchecked local version of a file. If the check-in operation succeeds, then the version numbers of all files involved automatically increment, and the CVS server writes a user-supplied description line, the date and the author's name to its log files. CVS can also run external, user-specified log processing scripts following each commit. These scripts are installed by an entry in CVS loginfo file, which can trigger email notification or convert the log data into a web-based format.

Clients can also compare versions, request a complete history of changes, or check out a historical snapshot of the project as of a given date or as of a revision number. Many OS projects allow anonymous read access, a feature that was pioneered by OpenBSD. This means that clients may check out and compare versions with either a blank or simple published password (e.g., *anoncvs*); only the check-in operation requires a personal account and password in these scenarios.

Clients can also use the *update* command to bring their local copies up-to-date with the newest version on the server. This eliminates the need for repeated downloading of the whole project.

CVS can also maintain different *branches* of a project. For instance, a released version of the software project may form one branch, used for bug fixes, while a version under current development, with major changes and new features, forms a separate branch. CVS uses delta compression for efficient storage of different versions of the same file. The implementation favors files with many lines (usually text files); in extreme cases individual copies of each version are stored rather than a delta.CVS has a number of limitations (most of them solved in Subversion):

- Moving or renaming of files and directories are not versioned. It was implemented this way because in the past *refactoring* was avoided in development processes. More recently the thinking has changed and *refactoring* can be managed by an administrator as it is required. If you develop in Oracle Forms, Cobol, Fortran, or even C++, the CVS reasoning is quite commonly accepted; if you develop with Java or using AMs, then the CVS reasoning may seem counterintuitive.
- No versioning of symbolic links. Symbolic links stored in a version control system can be a security risk. Someone can create a symbolic link *index.htm* to */etc/passwd* and store it in the repository; when the code is exported to a web server, the web site now has a copy of the system security file available for public inspection. A developer may prefer the convenience and accept the responsibility to decide what is safe to version and what is not; a project manager or auditor may prefer to reduce the risk by using build scripts that require certain privileges and conscious intervention to execute.
- Limited support for Unicode text files and non-ASCII filenames. Unix systems run in UTF-8 and so CVS on Unix handles UTF-8 filenames and files natively. If you only work on Unix systems then this response seems reasonable. However, when you work on Windows it may not.
- No atomic commit.

Over time, developers have the need to change the CVS code significantly to add new features, refactor the code, and improve developer productivity. CVS replacement projects include OpenCVS[2] and Subversion. URL: http://www.nongnu.org/cvs/

20.2.2 Subversion

Subversion (SVN) is a version control system initiated in 2000 by CollabNet Inc. It allows users to keep track of changes made to any type of electronic data, typically source code, web pages, or design documents. Subversion is currently a popular alternative to CVS, particularly among OS projects. Projects using Subversion include the Apache Software Foundation, KDE, GNOME, Free Pascal, GCC, Python, Ruby, Sakai, Samba, and Mono. SourceForge.net and Tigris.org also provide Subversion hosting for their OS projects, Google Code and BountySource systems use it exclusively. Subversion is also finding adoption in the corporate world. Subversion is released under the Apache License. The main features of Subversion are:

- Commits are true atomic operations. Interrupted commit operations do not cause repository inconsistency or corruption.
- Renamed/copied/moved/removed files retain full revision history.
- Directories, renames, and file metadata are versioned. Entire directory trees can be moved around and/or copied very quickly, and retain full revision history.
- Versioning of symbolic links.
- Native support for binary files, with space-efficient binary-diff storage.
- Apache HTTP server as network server, WebDAV/DeltaV for protocol. There is also an independent server process that uses a custom protocol over TCP/IP.
- Branching and tagging are cheap operations, independent of file size.
- Natively client/server, layered library design.
- Client/server protocol sends diffs in both directions.
- Costs are proportional to change size, not data size.
- Parsable output, including XML log output.
- Open Source licensed — "CollabNet/Tigris.org Apache-style license"
- Internationalized program messages.
- File locking for unmergeable files ("reserved checkouts").
- Path-based authorization for svnserve.
- PHP, Python, Ruby, Perl, and Java language bindings.
- Full MIME support - the MIME Type of each file can be viewed or changed, with the software knowing which MIME types can have their differences from previous versions shown.

20.3 AUTOMATED BUILD TOOLS
20.3.1 Apache Ant

Ant is a Java tool for build automation similar to well-known and popular tools such as make but providing a set of new and useful functionalities including:

- **Operating system independence:** Build automation tools such as make, gnumake, and nmake are operating system dependant since they are based on functionalities offered by the underlying operating system. On the contrary, Ant performs the different activities through Java classes that execute the tasks that the user specifies through XML files.
- **Extensibility:** Ant offers several pre-defined tasks but creating new ones is very easy extending the already existing classes. Ant tasks are implemented as Java objects; therefore, all the developed extensions can be used in any operating system.
- **Easy configuration:** The configuration through an XML file is much easier than make.

Ant is an Open Source tool that is integrated in several development environments such as Eclipse.

Usage in Agile development: the tool is essential to automate the building process. This allows developers to automate many activities required during the integration and the automated execution of tests. URL: http://ant.apache.org/

20.3.2 Krysalis Centipede

Krysalis Centipede is an Open Source build automation tool based on Ant. It has been developed to simplify and extend the usage of Ant, focusing on:

- **Usage simplicity:** Users should only start a script.
- **Extensibility:** Usage and installation of the extension is automated.
- **Flexibility:** The system supports a wide range of operations that can be configured by the advanced users.

The system is extensible through auto-installing modules. Some of the already available modules are:

- **Changelog:** Creates a log of the modification in HTML or XML format;
- **Forrest:** Automated generation of the web site of the project, automated generation of the documentation, integration of the output of other modules in the documentation;

- **Jalopy:** Automated restyle of the layout of the Java source code of an entire project using a specific layout standard;
- **Java:** Automates the compilation of the source code, the generation of the jar files, the creation of the binary distribution and/or the source code in a zip file, the generation of the javadoc documents;
- **Junit:** Executes the JUnit tests and creates a report about the status of the tests;
- **Release:** Creates a release, generates and sends by e-mail the announcement of the release.

Usage in Agile development: the same as Ant but with the enhanced features provided. URL: http://krysalis.sourceforge.net/centipede/

20.3.3 Apache Maven

Maven is an integrated system for project management able to take care of the build, the reporting, and the documentation of a Java project. The main goal of the system is to allow developers to understand the state of a development. To do that, Maven tries to perform the following:

- **Make the build process easy:** Even if it does not eliminate the need to know about the underlying mechanisms, it provides a lot of shielding from the details.
- **Provide a uniform build system:** It builds a project using its object model (POM) and a set of shared plug-ins. Since it provides a uniform build system, it is easy to manage many projects.
- **Provide quality project information:** It provides several project information that are extracted from the POM and from the source code including: change log document created directly from source control, cross referenced sources, mailing lists, dependency list, unit test reports (including coverage).
- **Provide guidelines for best practices development:** It collects data to support the development of best practices and makes it easy to guide a project in that direction. For example, specification, execution, and reporting of unit tests are part of the normal build cycle. Unit testing best practices were used as guidelines:
  - o Keep the test source code in a separate, but parallel source tree
  - o Use test case naming conventions to locate and execute tests
  - o Have test cases setup their environment and do not rely on customizing the build for test preparation

- ○ Moreover, the system aims at assisting the project workflow through release management and issue tracking.
- **Allow transparent migration to new features:** It provides an easy way for clients to update their installations so that they can take advantage of any changes. Therefore, the installation of new or updated plug-ins from third parties is trivial.

Usage in Agile development: the tool allows developers to focus on the code and not in how to automate the build. Since it provides a uniform interface, building several projects at the same time becomes easy and do not require the usage of different tools for different purposes. URL: http://maven.apache.org/

20.4 CONTINUOUS INTEGRATION TOOLS
20.4.1 CruiseControl

CruiseControl is an Open Source tool aiming at supporting the continuous integration process. The tool allows the entire automation of the building process of a project compiling it and executing all the tests several times a day. The results of the process are sent automatically to the developers. In this way, developers can integrate daily their work reducing the integration problems.

CruiseControl is extensible through Java plugins. Some of the plugins provided allow the email notification, the integration with Ant, the integration with version contro tools such as CVS, Subversion, VSS, etc.

CruiseControl is executed as a system demon that periodically verifies if the source code has been modified, builds the system if required, creates a log file, and notifies the status of the building process. The schedule of such activities is user-defined and the configuration is done through an XML file.

There is another version of the system called CruiseControl.NET specific for the management of projects developed using the Microsoft .NET framework.

Usage in Agile development: the tool performs continuous build of the developed system and provides detailed reports to the developers if there are problems. It can be configured to build the system several times a day, therefore it is highly effective to implement continuous integration and locate problems as soon as they appear in the code. URL: http://sourceforge.net/projects/cruisecontrol/

20.4.2 Anthill OS

Anthill is a tool for automating the building process based on Ant. It focuses on simplifying the building process in environments in which there are several developers in charge of different modules of the final product. The system is able to build several projects at the same time, it can be configured through a web page, its setup is extremely easy, and can generate detailed reports about building errors.

Usage in Agile development: the same as CruiseControl but with the enhanced features provided. URL: http://www.anthillpro.com/html/products/anthillos/

20.4.3 Rephlux

Rephlux is a system able to support continuous integration specific for projects developed in PHP. The system is based on the same concepts of CruiseControl and provides most of its functionalities adapted to PHP. Compared to CruiseControl, the system has some limitations such as: only Linux support, only CVS support, the generated reports contain only a limited set of information and are provided only through the RSS format, etc.

Usage in Agile development: the same as CruiseControl but for PHP projects. URL: http://rephlux.sourceforge.net/

20.5 ISSUE TRACKING TOOLS
20.5.1 Bugzilla

Bugzilla is a tool able to help developers to keep track of bugs and collect them in a centralized repository. It has been developed in Perl, therefore it can run on every platform supported by this language, but the official version is only for Linux. Commercial bug tracking tools are very expensive, therefore Bugzilla has become very popular (also because it was developed to track bugs in the Mozilla browser project).The main features of Bugzilla are:

- Tracking of the dependences of the bugs
- Generation of bug reports
- back-end based on a database
- API for the interaction with the email, XML, console, and HTTP
- Integration with version control systems such as CVS

Usage in Agile development: list bugs and develop test to locate them is required to implement a high quality product. Bugs traced can include unit test to locate the exact piece of code affected and plan the fix. URL: http://www.bugzilla.org/

20.5.2 Scarab

Scarab is a very flexible issue tracking system. The main features are the following:

- Data entry, query, report, notifications, collaborative comments collection, tracking of the issues dependences
- Import and export of the configuration through an XML file
- Modular design to support the development of new functionalities
- Configuration through a web page
- Adaptable look and feel
- Support the integration with other systems

Usage in Agile development: the same as Bugzilla but with the enhanced features provided. URL: http://scarab.tigris.org/

20.6 SYNCHRONOUS AND ASYNCHRONOUS COMMUNICATION TOOLS
20.6.1 MailMan

MailMan is a system for managing mailing lists. The administrator of a list can manage all the access rights of the users, the dispatching of the emails, the management of the archives, etc. MailMan integrated several functionalities such as: mail-to-news gateways, anti-spam filters, and email administration.

Usage in Agile development: effective communication is important in Agile development. Mailing lists are an effective way to provide information to all and only the team member that are involved in a specific topic avoiding to forget someone or to overload people not interested in a specific subject. URL: http://www.gnu.org/software/mailman/mailman.html

20.6.2 Jabber

Jabber is an open communication protocol based on XML. It has been developed to exchange messages over the Internet in real time. Compared to other proprietary protocols used in other tools (e.g., ICQ, Yahoo, MSN, etc.), Jabber provides several advantages:

- **Open protocol:** The Jabber communication protocol is open, therefore anyone can implement applications based on that. There are several implementations of the server, client, and development libraries.

- **Extensible:** The protocol can be easily extended to satisfy specific requirements.
- **Decentralized:** Anyone can install a private Jabber server.
- **Secure:** A Jabber server can be detached from the Jabber network to support only users in a specific organization and support secure communication protocols.

Usage in Agile development: even if most of the Agile practices are designed to work with co-localized teams, in many organization this is impossible. Therefore, tools for an effective synchronous communications are required. URL: http://www.jabber.org/

20.6.3 Wiki

A Wiki is a system for the development of web documents in a collaborative way. All the users can modify the existing pages or create new ones. Inside a Wiki, from every page it is possible to access an HTML web editor to modify the content of the page. The scripting language used is a simplified version of HTML.

Usage in Agile development: this tool is useful to share knowledge among the team members such as coding conventions, planning documents, user stories, outcomes on daily meetings, documentation, etc. URL: http://www.wiki.org/

20.6.4 TWiki

TWiki is a structured Wiki which combine the benefits of a traditional Wiki and a database application. The result is a collaborative database environment where knowledge can be shared freely and where structure can be added as needed.

TWiki is an enterprise collaboration platform and knowledge management system. Users can create web applications without knowing any traditional development. The system is used to create web applications in an easy and fast way. Such applications include: document management systems, knowledge bases, groupware tools, etc. All the content can be created collaboratively by the users through a web browser. Moreover, developers can extend the functionality of the system through specific plug-ins. TWiki support the information flow within an organization, allows distributed teams to work together, and eliminates the bottleneck caused by a single person that has to update the online content. The main features of the system are:

- **Browser support:** Pages can be created and modified using any web browser.
- **Text formatting:** Simple text formatting rules.

- **Multiple groups:** Pages are grouped into collections to create separate collaboration groups.
- **Search:** Full text search with regular expressions.
- **E-mail notification:** Users can subscribe to receive emails when something changes in a page.
- **Structured content:** The information can be classified to create simple workflow systems.
- **Version control:** All the changes to pages are tracked. Therefore, it is possible to access previous versions of a page highlighting the differences.
- **Extensible:** The system can be extended through plug-ins. Some available plug-ins are:
  - **ActionTrackerPlugin:** Keeps track of action items in meeting minutes and notify assignees by e-mail.
  - **CalendarPlugin:** Shows a calendar with highlighted events.
  - **ChartPlugin:** Creates charts to visualize TWiki tables.
  - **DatabasePlugin:** Allows to access data in a database.
  - **HeadlinesPlugin:** Allows to access RSS news feeds.
  - **SlideShowPlugin:** Transform pages into web-based presentations.
  - **XpTrackerPlugin:** Tracks Extreme Programming (XP) projects.

Usage in Agile development: the system provides an effective way to develop project-specific document management systems tailored to the specific approach used by a development team. Moreover the The XpTrackerPlugin plug-in provides a basic support for managing XP project. URL: http://twiki.org/

20.7 PROJECT MANAGEMENT TOOLS
20.7.1 XPlanner

XPlanner is a tool for planning and track the evolution of an XP project through a compete set of web pages. It is different compared to traditional project management tools because it is able to support the specific aspects of the XP methodology providing ad hoc tools. In particular, the most interesting functionalities are:

- Iteration-based planning
- Digital user stories management
- Tracking of iterations and user stories
- Tracking of the activities and automated generation of reports
- Support for the estimation

Usage in Agile development: it is designed to support XP development. URL: http://www.xplanner.org/

20.7.2 XPWeb

XPWeb is a web-based tool for managing XP projects. It includes features to support both XP-specific practices and XP adaptation of usual software development practices such as planning, printing statistic reports, and metaphors.

Usage in Agile development: it is designed to help developers to manage XP projects. URL: http://xpweb.sourceforge.net/

20.7.3 XP StoryStudio

XP StoryStudio is a project-management system to support the development of software projects adopting the XP method. The development of the tool started inside Egg Plc to support the development of their internal Agile projects and it leverages on the experience the company has in the area.

Usage in Agile development: it is designed to support XP development. URL: http://www.xpstorystudio.com/

20.8 TESTING TOOLS
20.8.1 Cactus

Cactus is a tool for automating server-side Java code. The system is based on JUnit with several extensions to simplify the development and the automated execution of server-side tests for Java classes such as servlets, EJBs, etc.

Usage in Agile development: it is used to create automated unit tests for server-side components. This allows developers to create automated tests for most of the features developed and use Test-Driven Development. URL: http://jakarta.apache.org/cactus/

20.8.2 JUnit

JUnit is a tool for automating unit tests. The system was designed to support Java development but its success pushed for its adaptation to several other languages. The system provides a simple way to develop and execute automated tests.

Usage in Agile development: it is used to create automated unit tests. This allows developers to create automated tests for most of the features developed and use Test-Driven Development. URL: http://www.junit.org/

20.8.3 NUnit

NUnit is a unit-testing framework for all .NET languages. It has been ported from JUnit and it is written entirely in C#. The system has been completely redesigned to take advantage of the .NET language features such as custom attributes and other reflection capabilities. NUnit brings xUnit to all .NET languages.

Usage in Agile development: it is used to create automated unit tests. This allows developers to create automated tests for most of the features developed and use Test-Driven Development. URL: http://www.nunit.org/

20.8.4 SwingUnit

SwingUnit is a unit test automation tool for Java Swing application. It works in combination with JUnit to create and run unit tests that involve GUI elements. The tool bases the execution on the meta-data associated to Swing graphical elements and not on the pixel position information. In this way, the developed tests can be executed in a more robust way and are not affected by elements such as screen resolution or the position of a window.

Usage in Agile development: it simplifies the development of automated unit tests that involve GUI elements. URL: https://swingunit.dev.java.net/

20.9 TOOLS TO SUPPORT SPECIFIC AGILE PRACTICES
20.9.1 Sangam

Sangam is an Eclipse plug-in that allows non co-localized developers to apply the pair programming technique. Sangam allows developers to communicate, write code together, perform modifications to the source code, perform refactoring, and execute the code in a shared environment. The main features provided by Sangam are:

- Code development in a collaborative and interactive way
- Synchronized debugging
- Integrated messaging system

Usage in Agile development: if co-localized pair programming is not possible and developers need to work in pairs, this tool helps them to overcome distance and simulate the pair programming experience. However, there are several limitations compared to a real pair programming practice. URL: http://sangam.sourceforge.net/

20.9.2 FitNesse

FitNesse is a tool for enhancing collaboration in software development focused on acceptance testing. FitNesse is designed to enable customers, testers, and developers to exchange information about what their software should do and to automatically compare to what it actually does. It compares customers' expectations to the actual implementation of the system. FitNesse is a lightweight, open-source framework that makes it easy for software teams to:

- Define acceptance tests in a collaborative way
- Run those tests and see the results

Usage in Agile development: the management of acceptance test is a basic requirement to implement any Agile Method. URL: http://fitnesse.org/

20.9.3 TightVNC

TightVNC is a remote control tool derived from VNC. The tool allows seeing the desktop of a remote machine and controlling it through a local mouse and keyboard. The main features are:

- **File transfer:** The user can upload files from a local machine to the TightVNC Server and download files from the server.
- **Support for video mirror driver:** TightVNC Server can use DFMirage mirror driver to detect screen updates and grab pixel data improving performances.
- **Scaling of the remote desktop:** The user can view the remote desktop in whole on a screen of smaller size or can zoom in the picture to see the remote screen in more details.
- **Web browser access:** It includes a Java viewer that can be accessed via any Java-enabled browser.

Usage in Agile development: the tool is useful to support distributed pair programming. Even if it is not a complete solution, the usage of this system in conjunction with other tools such as voice communication tools can provide a sufficient support to the practice. URL: http://www.tightvnc.com/

20.9.4 Refactoring Browser

This is the original refactoring tool and it is still one of the most full-featured. The tool supports only the Smalltalk language. Several refactorings are possible and they are organized in three categories:

1. **Class based refactorings:** They operate on classes, instance variables, and class variables.
   a. **Create subclass:** It allows you to add a new class into an existing hierarchy.
   b. **Rename:** It renames a class and updates every reference to it.
   c. **Safe remove:** It removes the class if there are no references to it in the code.
   d. **Add instance/class variable:** It adds a variable to the class.
   e. **Rename instance/class variable:** It renames a variable and all references to it.
   f. **Remove instance/class variable:** It removes a variable if it is not referenced.
   g. **Push down instance/class variable:** It moves the definition of a variable from the current class to the subclasses that use the variable.
   h. **Pull up instance/class variable:** It move the definition of a variable from a subclass of the current class into the current class.
   i. **Create instance/class variable accessors:** It creates getter and setter methods for a variable.
   j. **Abstract instance/class variable:** It runs the create accessors refactoring and converts all direct calls to the variable to calls of the accessor methods.
   k. **Protect/Concrete instance variable:** It converts all the call to accessor of a variable to a direct access to the variable.
2. Method based refactorings: they operate on methods and local variables.
   a. **Move to component:** It moves a method to another class.
   b. **Rename:** It renames all references to the method.
   c. **Safe remove:** It removes the method if there are no references to it in the code.
   d. **Add parameter:** It allows adding a parameter to the method and to all the method calls.
   e. **Push up:** It pushes up a method into its superclass.
   f. **Push down:** It pushes down a method into all subclasses that do not implement the method.

3. Code based refactorings: They operate on individual statements and are available through a context sensitive menus.
    a. **Extract method:** It extracts the selected code as a separate method.
    b. **Inline temporary:** It removes the assignment of a variable and replaces all the references with the right hand side of the assignment.
    c. **Convert to instance variable:** It converts a temporary into an instance variable.
    d. **Remove parameter:** It removes an unused parameter from all the calls of the method.
    e. **Inline parameter:** It transforms a parameter of a method into a value inside the method.
    f. **Rename temporary:** It renames a temporary variable.
    g. **Move to inner scope:** It moves the definition of a temporary variable into the tightest scope that contains the variable and its references.

Usage in Agile development: refactoring is one of the key practices of XP to keep the quality of the code high and avoid the degradation caused by modification and addition of requirements. URL: http://st-www.cs.uiuc.edu/users/brant/Refactory/

20.9.5 Transmogrify

Transmogrify is a Java code analysis and manipulation tool. The main goal of the tool is supporting refactoring. It can perform the following refactorings:

*   Rename Symbol
*   Extract Method
*   Replace Temp With Query
*   Inline Temp
*   Pull up field

Usage in Agile development: even if the tool is limited compared to the Refactory Browser, it is able to support developers in some important activities. However, it becomes nearly useless if the development is done using IDEs such as Eclipse or JBuilder that provide many more functionalities. URL: http://transmogrify. sourceforge.net/

20.9.6 JMock

jMock is a library that implements the idea of mock objects (http://www.mockobjects. com/) to support test-driven development of Java applications. Mock objects help the developer to design and test the interactions between the objects in a program even when some of them are still not developed. The elements that do not exist are simulated by mock objects.

jMock simplify the definition of mock objects and provides support to the specification of the interactions among objects.

Usage in Agile development: mock objects simplify the development of unit tests and allow developers to concentrate on the piece of code they are developing making easier the testing of the application even if the entire system is not yet developed. URL: http://www.jmock.org/

20.10 MEASURING TOOLS
20.10.1 NCover

NCover analyzes the source code and reports the percentage of branches that have been taken throughout the course of the automated testing. It does that instrumenting the source code at each branch. The system allows developers to identify:

- Code areas that need additional testing.
- Dead code (code that is never executed).
- Dead files not included in the build but still in the version control system.

- An automated build process.
- Automated tests.
- A continuous integration process to regularly build and run tests before analyzing the code coverage.

Usage in Agile development: understanding the coverage level is required to find out if the tests are really effective or not. The test first approach is not effective if there are significant parts of the code that are not tested. This tool allows developers to increase the effectiveness of the test ones the code has been developed.URL: http://ncover.sourceforge.net/

20.10.2 JBlanket

JBlanket is a method coverage tool for Java code. It instruments the byte code to trace the methods invocations during the execution of JUnit tests. The tool stores this trace into XML files and calculates the method coverage dividing the number of methods invoked during testing by the total number of methods. JBlanket is designed to provide automate support for test quality assurance according to Agile development practices. The goal of the tool is to provide coverage criteria that make it possible to achieve 100% coverage, throughout the development process. More rigorous forms of coverage, such as statement, branch, or loop coverage require too much testing resources to maintain 100% coverage in an Agile context. To make 100% coverage practical in an Agile context, the approach is to measure coverage only at the method level and make exceptions in specific cases where the cost of creating and maintaining test cases is not appropriate (e.g., getter and setting methods are usually one line long and do not require any testing).

Usage in Agile development: understanding the coverage level is required to find out if the tests are really effective or not. The test first approach is not effective if there are significant parts of the code that are not tested. This tool allows developers to increase the effectiveness of the test ones the code has been developed. URL: http://csdl.ics.hawaii.edu/Tools/JBlanket/

ENDNOTES

[1]   All the URLs have been accessed on November 11, 2008.

[2]   http://www.opencvs.org/ (Accessed on November, 11th)

Conclusions

This book has presented Agile Methods and Open Source identifying similarities, differences, and complementarities.

These two areas are very active and are evolving fast. For these reasons we expect that the influence of each other will increase in the future.

In or analysis, we have considered several aspects of the two areas including the founding principles, the technical details, and the organizational problems. Moreover, a number of case studies have been included to provide evidences of the effectiveness of specific approaches. However, in most of the cases, the implementation of such techniques is not straightforward and several difficulties emerge in their implementation in different kinds of environments.

Section 1 has compared AMs and OSSD focusing on their theoretical background and evolution from their beginning. We have highlighted that even if they have evolved from different communities and the basic values are expressed in different ways, the aims, the objectives, and the actual practices are not so different and they overlap in many cases. This investigation is just a first attempt in identifying relationships between AMs and OSSD. In particular, more investigation is required in the actual implementation of the Agile and OS models inside organizations (both communities and companies) and in the definition of a set of strategies to help them in the integration of such development approaches with the culture already existing in the organization. Such investigations should analyze not only the development teams but also the entire structure of the organization considering their specific environment and the related business models as well.

Section 2 has described the adoption of some Agile practices (and processes) in the development of OSS. Our investigation has considered some of the most common practices (e.g., test first and code ownership) and has evidenced that such Agile practices are also used in OSSD. However, there are several others that have been introduced in Section 1 and can be investigated. An interesting further research could be the investigation of such practices in different contexts such as in communities and in companies, analyzing not only the adoption of the practices but also the differences in their adoption if the two contexts.

Section 3 has presented a framework for conducting experiments and a set of experimental analysis related to the application in different contexts of some common development practices such as pair programming, requirements management, and project management in Agile and non-Agile environments. Such analyses have highlighted differences and commonalities in the application of the practices in the considered environments. These analyses are just a first set of experimental evaluations in real industrial settings; further investigations are required to enlarge both the practices analyzed and the application environments.

Section 4 focused on the industrial adoption presenting assessment methodologies, main adoption issues that companies face, and an overview of the available tools to support the adoption of the practices. According to the surveys carried on, trust is a key issue for the adoption of OSS and it relates to several aspects of the product itself and the development process used to build it. The data presented come from European companies (large, SMEs, and Public Administrations) and large well-known OS communities. The investigation could be extended including different areas, including more companies, and compare the different approaches different kinds of companies have. Moreover, a set of guidelines for the implementation of the assessment and the exploitation of OSS could be developed to help companies in such activities.

Summarizing, AMs and OSSD are deeply connected through the aims, the objectives, and the vision over the art of software development. They acknowledge that to produce good software you do not need just the right tools or process but you also need good people. There is a lot of research to carry on in this area, in particular for helping companies in the adoption of the methodologies and the specific practices that need to be customized to satisfy the needs of specific companies.

We hope that the analysis we have carried out will help the reader to better understand Agile and Open Source and push him to a further investigation of the topics.

Glossary

Glossary of the main abbreviations used in this book:

AM: Agile Method
FSF: Free Software Foundation
GPL: General Public License
OS: Open Source
OSD: Open Source Development
OSS: Open Source Software
OSSD: Open Source Software Development
PMC: Project Management Committee
TDD: Test Driven Development
XP: eXtreme Programming

About the Authors

Barbara Russo, PhD is associate Professor at the Faculty of Computer Science of the Free University of Bolzano-Bozen, Italy. She has a PhD in mathematics of the University of Trento (Italy). She was visiting researcher at the Max-Plank Institut für Mathematik in Bonn and The University of Liverpool. Professor Russo has experience in the coordination and development of European, national, and local research projects. She has been reviewer for various conferences on the sector and journals. She is local coordinator of the European Master in Software Engineering (in 2006 awarded as the Erasums Mundus top quality program) and the BSc program for working students in applied computer science (in 2006 awarded as national best project of collaboration with the industrial sector by the foundation Giuseppina Mai of the National Industrial Association). Her research interests are in the field of empirical software engineering and software measurement. Her competences concern statistical modelling of software data and software measurement with focus on Open Source Software development and Agile Methods.

Marco Scotto, PhD, PEng is a software architect at i4C s.r.l., an Italian company that delivers business intelligence solutions for the utilities market. He is focused on development of forecasting solutions for the gas market. His interests are extreme programming, agile methods, open source software, softwarer metrics, and J2EE applications. Previously, he worked as consultant at TXT Polymedia, a software vendor and integrator, specialized in media & channel integration. From 2005 to 2008, he was assistant professor at Free University of Bolzano-Bozen. In 2006, he received a PhD in electronic and computer engineering from University of Genova. He is author of more than 30 papers published in international conferences and journals.

Alberto Sillitti, PhD, PEng is assistant professor at the Faculty of Computer Science of the Free University of Bolzano-Bozen, Italy. He holds a PhD in electrical and computer engineering received from the University of Genoa (Italy) in 2005. He is involved in several EU funded projects related to Agile Methods and Open Source Software in which he applies non-invasive measurement approaches. He has served as member of the program committee of several international conferences and as program chair of OSS 2007 in Limerick (Ireland). His research areas include agile methods, open source development, software engineering, non-invasive measurement, web services. He is author of more than 80 papers published in international conferences and journals.

Giancarlo Succi, PhD, PEng is professor of software engineering and Director of the Center for Applied Software Engineering at the Faculty of Computer Science of the Free University of Bolzano-Bozen, Italy. His research areas include Agile Methods, Open Source Development, empirical software engineering, software product lines, software reuse, software engineering over the Internet. He is author of more than 150 papers published in international conferences and journals.

***

Raimund Moser, PhD is currently working as patent examiner at the European Patent Office in The Hague (The Netherlands). Before that, he was assistant professor in software engineering at the Faculty of Computer Science of the Free University of Bolzano-Bozen, Italy. He received an MSc in physics from University of Innsbruck, Austria, in 2000, and a PhD in electrical and computer engineering at the University of Genova, Italy, in 2007. His main research interests include experimental software engineering, software metrics, modeling software development processes, and agile software development methods. He was involved in several research projects on software quality and process measurement with particular emphasis on Open Source Software.

Etiel Petrinja, PhD, PEng is assistant professor at the Faculty of Computer Science of the Free University of Bolzano-Bozen, Italy. He holds a PhD in the interdisciplinary area of Information Management and Engineering received from the University of Ljubljana (Slovenia) in 2007. Previously, he worked as assistant professor at the Faculty of Civil and Geodetic Engineering of the University of Ljubljana, Slovenia. He is involved in EU funded projects related to Open Source Software in which he applies non-invasive measurement approaches. He has been reviewer and member of the program committee in international conferences. His research areas include open source development, software engineering, non-invasive measurement, software interoperability, knowledge management. He is author of more than 20 papers published in international conferences and journals.

Index